Frederick Law Olmsted

Journeys and Explorations on the Cotton Kingdom of America

Frederick Law Olmsted

Journeys and Explorations on the Cotton Kingdom of America

ISBN/EAN: 9783743400528

Manufactured in Europe, USA, Canada, Australia, Japa

Cover: Foto ©ninafisch / pixelio.de

Manufactured and distributed by brebook publishing software (www.brebook.com)

Frederick Law Olmsted

Journeys and Explorations on the Cotton Kingdom of America

JOURNEYS AND EXPLORATIONS

IN

THE COTTON KINGDOM OF AMERICA.

ADVERTISEMENT.

MR. OLMSTED'S WORKS ON THE SLAVE STATES.

SEABOARD SLAVE STATES. A Journey in the Seaboard Slave States, with Remarks on their Economy. 1 vol., 12mo. pp. 724. Price, $1.25.

TEXAS JOURNEY. A Journey through Texas: or, a Saddle Trip on the Southwestern Frontier; with a Statistical Appendix. 1 vol., 12mo. pp. 516. Price, $1.25.

JOURNEY IN THE BACK COUNTRY. A Journey in the Back Country; with a complete Index to the three volumes. 1 vol., 12mo. pp. 492. Price, $1.25.

THE COTTON KINGDOM. A Traveller's observations on Cotton and Slavery in the American Slave States. Based upon three former volumes of Journeys and Investigations by the same author. 2 vols., 12mo. pp. 384 and 408. With a Colored Statistical Map of the Cotton Kingdom and its Dependencies, mainly derived from the United States Census. Price, $2.00.

This work was, by request, prepared by its author with especial reference to English readers, and is simultaneously published in England and in this country.

DEDICATION.

TO

JOHN STUART MILL, ESQ.

SIR,

I BEG you to accept the dedication of this book as an indication of the honour in which your services in the cause of moral and political freedom are held in America, and as a grateful acknowledgment of personal obligations to them on the part of

Your obedient servant,

THE AUTHOR.

CONTENTS.

CHAPTER I.
INTRODUCTORY.—THE PRESENT CRISIS 1

CHAPTER II.
WASHINGTON 28

CHAPTER III.
VIRGINIA 88

CHAPTER IV.
THE ECONOMY OF VIRGINIA 108

CHAPTER V.
THE CAROLINAS 141

ER VI.
. 224

CHAPTER VII.
ALABAMA 272

CHAPTER VIII.
THE LOWER MISSISSIPPI 285

CHAPTER IX.
COTTON PLANTERS.—RED RIVER 342

COTTON AND SLAVERY.

CHAPTER I.

INTRODUCTORY.—THE PRESENT CRISIS.

THE mountain ranges, the valleys, and the great waters of America, all trend north and south, not east and west. An arbitrary political line may divide the north part from the south part, but there is no such line in nature: there can be none, socially. While water runs downhill, the currents and counter currents of trade, of love, of consanguinity, and fellowship, will flow north and south. The unavoidable comminglings of the people in a land like this, upon the conditions which the slavery of a portion of the population impose, make it necessary to peace that we should all live under the same laws and respect the same flag. [No government could long control its own people, no government could long exist, that would allow its citizens to be subject to such indignities under a foreign government as those to which the citizens of the United States heretofore have been required to submit under their own, for the sake of the tranquillity of the South. Nor could the South, with its present purposes, live on terms of peace with any foreign nation, between whose people and its own there was no division, except such an one as might be maintained by means of forts, frontier-guards and custom-houses, edicts, passports and spies. Scotland, Wales, and Ireland are each much better adapted for an independent government, and under an independent government would be far more likely to live at peace with England, than the South to remain peaceably separated from the North of this country.

It is said that the South can never be subjugated. It must be, or we must. It must be, or not only our American republic is a failure, but our English justice and our English law and our English freedom are failures. This Southern repudiation of obligations upon the result of an election is but a clearer warning than we have had before, that these cannot be maintained in this land any longer in such intimate association with slavery as we have hitherto tried to hope that they might. We now know that we must give them up, or give up trying to accommodate ourselves to what the South has declared, and demonstrated, to be the necessities of its state of society. Those necessities would not be less, but, on the contrary, far more imperative, were the south an independent people. If the South has reason to declare itself independent of our long-honoured constitution, and of our common court of our common laws, on account of a past want of invariable tenderness on the part of each one of our people towards its necessities, how long could we calculate to be able to preserve ourselves from occurrences which would be deemed to abrogate the obligations of a mere treaty of peace? A treaty of peace with the South as a foreign power, would be a cowardly armistice, a cruel aggravation and prolongation of war.

Subjugation! I do not choose the word, but take it, and use it in the only sense in which it can be applicable. This is a Republic, and the South must come under the yoke of freedom. not to work for us, but to work with us, on equal terms, as a free people. To work with us, for the security of a state of society, the ruling purpose and tendency of which, spite of all its bendings heretofore, to the necessities of slavery; spite of the incongruous foreign elements which it has had constantly to absorb and incorporate; spite of a strong element of excessive backwoods individualism, has, beyond all question, been favourable to sound and safe progress in knowledge, civilization, and Christianity. To this yoke the head of the South must now be lifted, or we must bend our necks to that of slavery, consenting and submitting, even more than we have been willing to do heretofore, to labour and fight, and pay for the dire needs of a small portion of our people living in an exceptional state of society, in which Cowper's poems must not be read aloud without due precautions against the listening of family servants; in which it may be treated as a crime against the public safety to teach one of the labouring classes to write; in which the names of Wilberforce and Buxton are execrated; within which the slave trade is perpetuated, and at the capital of whose rebellion, black seamen born free, taken prisoners, in merchant ships, not in arms, are even already sold into slavery with as little hesitation as ever in Barbary. One system or the other is to thrive and extend, and eventually possess and govern this whole land.

This has been long felt and acted upon at the South; and the purpose of the more prudent and conservative men, now engaged in the attempt to establish a new government in the South, was for a long time simply to obtain an advantage for what was talked of as "reconstruction;" namely, a process of change in the form and rules of our government that would disqualify us of the Free States from offering any resistance to whatever was demanded of our government, for the end in view of the extension and eternal maintenance of slavery. That men to whom the terms prudent and conservative can in any way be applied, should not have foreseen that such a scheme must be unsuccessful, only presents one more illustration of that, of which the people of England have had many in their own history, the moral myopism, to which the habit of almost constantly looking down and never up at mankind, always predisposes. That the true people of the United States could have allowed the mutiny to proceed so far, before rising in their strength to resist it, is due chiefly to the instinctive reliance which every grumbler really gets to have, under our forms of society, in the ultimate common-sense of the great body of the people, and to the incredulity with which the report has been regarded, that slavery had made such a vast difference between the character of the South and that of the country at large. Few were fully convinced that the whole proceedings of the insurgents meant anything else than a more than usually bold and scandalous way of playing the game of brag, to which we had been so long used in our politics, and of which the people of England had a little experience shortly before the passage of a certain Reform Bill. The instant effect of the first *shotted*-gun that was fired proves this. We knew then that we had to subjugate slavery, or be subjugated by it.

Peace is now not possible until the people of the South are well convinced that the form of society, to fortify which is the ostensible purpose of the war into which they have been plunged, is not worthy fighting for, or until we think the sovereignty of our convictions of Justice, Freedom, Law and the conditions of Civilization in this land to be of less worth than the lives and property of our generation.

From the St. Lawrence to the Mexican Gulf, freedom must everywhere give way to the necessities of slavery, or slavery must be accommodated to the necessary incidents of freedom.

Where the hopes and sympathies of Englishmen will be, we well know.

"The necessity to labour is incompatible with a high civilization, and with heroic spirit in those subject to it."

"The institution of African slavery is a means more effective than any other yet devised, for relieving a large body of men from the necessity of labour; consequently, states which possess it must be stronger in statesmanship and in war, than those which do not; especially must they be stronger than states in which there is absolutely no privileged class, but all men are held to be equal before the law."

"The civilized world is dependent upon the Slave States of America for a supply of cotton. The demand for this commodity has, during many years, increased faster than the supply. Sales are made of it, now, to the amount of two hundred millions of dollars in a year, yet they have a vast area of soil suitable for its production which has never been broken. With an enormous income, then, upon a steadily rising market, they hold a vast idle capital yet to be employed. Such a monopoly under such circumstances must constitute those who possess it the richest and most powerful people on the earth. The world must have cotton, and the world depends on them for it. Whatever they demand, that must be conceded them; whatever they want, they have but to stretch forth their hands and take it."

These fallacies, lodged in certain minds, generated, long ago, grand ambitions, and bold schemes of conquest and wealth. The people of the North stood in the way of these schemes. In the minds of the schemers, labour had been associated with servility, meekness, cowardice; and they were persuaded that all men not degraded by labour at the North "kept aloof from politics," or held their judgment in entire subjection to the daily wants of a working population, of no more spirit and no more patriotism than their own working men—slaves. They believed this whole people to be really in a state of dependence, and that they controlled that upon which they depended. So, to a hitherto vague and inert local partisanship, they brought a purpose of determination to overcome the North, and, as this could not be safely avowed, there was the necessity for a conspiracy, and for the cloak of a conspiracy. By means the most mendacious, the ignorant, proud, jealous, and violent free population of the cotton States and their dependencies, were persuaded that less consideration was paid to their political demands than the importance of their contentment entitled them to expect from their government, and were at length decoyed into a state of angry passion, in which they only needed leaders of sufficient audacity to bring them into open rebellion. Assured that their own power if used would be supreme, and that they had but to offer sufficient evidence of a violent and dangerous determination to overawe the sordid North, and make it submit to a "reconstruction" of the nation in a form more advantageous to themselves, they were artfully led along in a constant advance, and constant failure of attempts at intimidation, until at length they must needs take part in a desperate rebellion, or accept a position which, after the declarations they had made for the purpose of intimidation, they could not do without humiliation.

The conspirators themselves have, until recently, been able, either directly or by impositions upon patriotic, but too confiding and generous instruments, to control the treasury of the United States, its post-office, its army and navy, its arsenals, workshops, dockyards and fortresses, and, by the simple means of perjury, to either turn these agencies against the government, or at least render them ineffectual to aid it, and this at a time, when its very existence, if it were anything but a democratic republican government, and, as we think for all good purposes, by far the strongest that ever existed, would have depended on a perfect instant and unquestionable command of them. Yet I doubt not that the conspirators themselves, trust at this moment, as they ever have trusted, even less to the supposed helpless condition of the government than to the supposed advantages of the cotton monopoly to the Slave States, and to the supposed superiority of a community of privileged classes over an actual democracy.

"No! you dare not make war upon cotton; no power on earth dares to make war upon it. Cotton is king; until lately the Bank of England was king; but she tried to put her screws, as usual, the fall before the last, on the cotton crop, and was utterly vanquished. The last power has been conquered: who can doubt, that has looked at recent events, that cotton is supreme?"

These are the defiant and triumphant words of Governor Hammond, of South Carolina, addressed to the Senate of the United States, March 4th, 1858. Almost every important man of the South, has at one time or other, within a few years, been betrayed into the utterance of similar exultant anticipations; and the South would never have been led into the great and terrible mistake it has made, had it not been for this confident conviction in the minds of the men who have been passing for its statesmen. Whatever moral strength the rebellion has, abroad or at home, lies chiefly in the fact that this conviction is also held, more or less distinctly, by multitudes who know perfectly well that the commonly assigned reasons for it are based on falsehoods.

Recently, a banker, who is and always has been a loyal union man, said, commenting upon certain experiences of mine narrated in this book: "The South cannot be poor. Why their last crop alone was worth two hundred million. They must be rich:" ergo, say the conspirators, adopting the same careless conclusion, they must be powerful, and the world must feel their power, and respect them and their institutions.

My own observation of the real condition of the people of our Slave States, gave me, on the contrary, an impression that the cotton monopoly in some way did them more harm than good; and, although the written narration of what I saw was not intended to set this forth, upon reviewing it for the present publication, I find the impression has become a conviction. I propose here, therefore, to show how the main body of the observations of the book arrange themselves in my mind with reference to this question, and also to inquire how far the conclusion to which I think they tend is substantiated by the Census returns of those States.*

Coming directly from my farm in New York to Eastern Virginia, I was satisfied, after a few weeks' observation, that the most of the people lived very poorly; that the proportion of men improving their condition was much less than in any Northern community; and that the natural resources of the land were strangely unused, or were used with poor economy. It was "the hiring season," and I had daily opportunities of talking with farmers, manufacturers, miners, and labourers, with whom the value of labour and of wages was then the handiest subject of conversation. I soon perceived that labour

---

* I greatly regret, after visiting Washington for this purpose, to find that the returns of the Census of 1860, are not yet sufficiently verified and digested to be given to the public. I have therefore had to fall back upon those of 1850. The rate of increase of the slave population in the meantime is stated at 25 per cent.

was much more readily classified and measured with reference to its quality than at the North. The limit of measure I found to be the ordinary day's work of a "prime field-hand," and a prime field-hand, I found universally understood to mean, not a man who would split two cords of wood, or cradle two acres of grain in a day, but a man for whom a "trader" would give a thousand dollars, or more, to take on South, for sale to a cotton planter. I do not mean that the alternative of a sale to a trader was always had in view in determining how a man should be employed. To be just, this seldom appeared to be the case—but that, in estimating the market value of his labour, he was viewed, for the time, from the trader's point of view, or, as if the question were—What is he worth for cotton?

I soon ascertained that a much larger number of hands, at much larger aggregate wages, was commonly reckoned to be required to accomplish certain results, than would have been the case at the North. Not all results, but certain results, of a kind in which it happened that I could most readily make a confident comparison. I have been in the habit of watching men at work, and of judging of their industry, their skill, their spirit; in short, of whatever goes to make up their value to their employers, or to the community, as instruments of production; and from day to day I saw that, as a landowner, or as a citizen, in a community largely composed, or dependent upon the productive industry, of working people of such habits and disposition as I constantly saw evinced in those of Virginia, I should feel disheartened, and myself lose courage, spirit, and industry. The close proximity of the better and cheaper labour—labour seeking a field of labour—which I had left behind me, added greatly to my interest in the subject, and stimulated close inquiry. It seemed, indeed, quite incredible that there really could be such a want of better labour in this region as at first sight there appeared to be, when a supply was so near at hand. I compared notes with every Northern man I met who had been living for some time in Virginia, and some I found able to give me quite exact statements of personal experience, with which, in the cases they mentioned, it could not be doubted that labourers costing, all things considered, the same wages, had taken four times as long to accomplish certain tasks of rude work in Virginia as at the North, and that in house service, four servants accomplished less, while they required vastly more looking after, than one at the North.

I left Virginia, having remained much longer than I at first intended, in trying to satisfy myself about this matter—quite satisfied as to the general fact, not at all satisfied with any theories of demand and supply which had been offered me, or which had occurred to me, in the way of explanation of it.

My perplexity was increased by certain apparent exceptions to the general rule; but they were, all things considered, unimportant, and rather served as affording contrasts, on the ground, to satisfy me of the correctness of my general conclusion.

I subsequently returned, and spent another month in Virginia, after visiting the cotton States, and I also spent three months in Kentucky and other parts of the Slave States where the climate is unsuitable for the production of cotton, and with the information which I had in the meantime obtained, I continued to study both the question of fact, and the question of cause. The following conclusions to which my mind tended strongly in the first month, though I did not then adopt them altogether with confidence, were established at length in my convictions.

1. The cash value of a slave's labour in Virginia is, practically, the cash value of the same labour minus the

cost of its transportation, acclimatizing, and breaking in to cotton-culture in Mississippi.

2. The cost of production, or the development of natural wealth in Virginia, is regulated by the cost of slave-labour: (that is to say) the competition of white labour does not materially reduce it; though it doubtless has some effect, at least in certain districts, and with reference to certain productions or branches of industry.

3. Taking infants, aged, invalid, and vicious and knavish slaves into account, the ordinary and average cost of a certain task of labour is more than double in Virginia what it is in the Free States adjoining.

4. The use of land and nearly all other resources of wealth in Virginia is much less valuable than the use of similar property in the adjoining Free States, these resources having no real value until labour is applied to them. (The Census returns of 1850 show that the sale value of farm lands by the acre in Virginia is less than one-third the value of farm lands in the adjoining Free State of Pennsylvania, and less than one-fifth than that of the farm lands of the neighbouring Free State of New Jersey.)*

5. Beyond the bare necessities of existence, poor shelter, poor clothing, and the crudest diet, the mass of the citizen class of Virginia earn very little and are very poor—immeasurably poorer than the mass of the people of the adjoining Free States.

6. So far as this poverty is to be attributed to personal constitution, character, and choice, it is not the result of climate.

7. What is true of Virginia is measurably true of all the

* See Appendix, A 2.

border Slave States, though in special cases the resistance of slavery to a competition of free labour is more easily overcome. In proportion as this is the case, the cost of production is less, the value of production greater, the comfort of the people is greater; they are advancing in wealth as they are in intelligence, which is the best form or result of wealth.

I went on my way into the so-called cotton States, within which I travelled over, first and last, at least three thousand miles of roads, from which not a cotton plant was to be seen, and the people living by the side of which certainly had not been made rich by cotton or anything else. And for every mile of road-side upon which I saw any evidence of cotton production, I am sure that I saw a hundred of forest or waste land, with only now and then an acre or two of poor corn half smothered in weeds; for every rich man's house, I am sure that I passed a dozen shabby and half-furnished cottages, and at least a hundred cabins—mere hovels, such as none but a poor farmer would house his cattle in at the North. And I think that, for every man of refinement and education with whom I came in contact, there were a score or two superior only in the virtue of silence, and in the manner of self-complacency, to the sort of people we should expect to find paying a large price for a place from which a sight could be got at a gallows on an execution day at the North, and a much larger number of what poor men at the North would themselves describe as poor men: not that they were destitute of certain things which are cheap at the South,—fuel for instance,—but that they were almost wholly destitute of things the possession of which, at the North, would indicate that a man had begun to accumulate capital—more destitute of these, on an average, than our day-labourers. In short, except in certain limited districts, mere streaks by the side of rivers, and in a few isolated spots of especially favoured soil away from these, I found the same state of things which I had seen in Virginia, but in a more aggravated form.

At least five hundred white men told me something of their own lives and fortunes, across their own tables, and with the means of measuring the weight of their words before my eyes; and I know that while men seldom want an abundance of coarse food in the cotton States, the proportion of the free white men who live as well in any respect as our working classes at the North, on an average, is small, and the citizens of the cotton States, as a whole, are poor. They work little, and that little, badly; they earn little, they sell little; they buy little, and they have little—very little—of the common comforts and consolations of civilized life. Their destitution is not material only; it is intellectual and it is moral. I know not what virtues they have that rude men everywhere have not; but those which are commonly attributed to them, I am sure that they lack: they are not generous or hospitable; and, to be plain, I must say that their talk is not the talk of even courageous men elsewhere. They boast and lack self-restraint, yet, when not excited, are habitually reserved and guarded in expressions of opinion very much like cowardly men elsewhere.

But, much cotton is produced in the cotton States, and by the labour of somebody; much cotton is sold and somebody must be paid for it; there are rich people; there are good markets; there is hospitality, refinement, virtue, courage, and urbanity at the South. All this is proverbially true. Who produces the cotton? who is paid for it? where are, and who are, the rich and gentle people?

I can answer in part at least.

I have been on plantations on the Mississippi, the Red

River, and the Brazos bottoms, whereon I was assured that ten bales of cotton to each average prime field-hand had been raised. The soil was a perfect garden mould, well drained and guarded by levees against the floods; it was admirably tilled; I have seen but few Northern farms so well tilled: the labourers were, to a large degree, tall, slender, sinewy, young men, who worked from dawn to dusk, not with spirit, but with steadiness and constancy. They had good tools; their rations of bacon and corn were brought to them in the field, and eaten with efficient despatch between the cotton plants. They had the best sort of gins and presses, so situated that from them cotton bales could be rolled in five minutes to steam-boats, bound direct to the ports on the gulf. They were superintended by skilful and vigilant overseers. These plantations were all large, so large as to yet contain much fresh land, ready to be worked as soon as the cultivated fields gave out in fertility. If it was true that ten bales of cotton to the hand had been raised on them, then their net profit for the year had been, not less than two hundred and fifty dollars for each hand employed. Even at seven bales to the hand the profits of cotton planting are enormous. Men who have plantations producing at this rate, can well afford to buy fresh hands at fourteen hundred dollars a head. They can even afford to employ such hands for a year or two in clearing land, ditching, leveeing, fencing, and other preparatory work, buying, meantime, all the corn and bacon they need, and getting the best kind of tools and cattle, and paying fifteen per cent. per annum interest on all the capital required for this, as many of them do. All this can be well afforded to establish new plantations favourably situated, on fresh soil, if there is a reasonable probability that they can after all be made to produce half a dozen seven-bale crops. And a great many large plantations do produce seven bales to the hand for years in succession. A great many more produce seven bales occasionally. A few produce even ten bales occasionally, though by no means as often as is reported.

Now, it is not at a Roman lottery alone that one may see it, but all over the world, where a few very large prizes are promised and many very small ones, and the number of tickets is limited; these are always speculated on, and men will buy them at third and fourth hand at prices which, it is useless to demonstrate to them, must be extravagant. They go to the Jews and pledge the clothes on their back to get another biacchi to invest; they beggar themselves; they ruin their families; they risk damnation in their passionate eagerness to have a chance, when they know perfectly well that the average of chances is not worth a tithe of what they must pay for it.

The area of land on which cotton may be raised with profit is practically limitless; it is cheap; even the best land is cheap; but to the large planter it is much more valuable when held in large parcels, for obvious reasons, than when in small; consequently the best land can hardly be obtained in small tracts or without the use of a considerable capital. But there are millions of acres of land yet untouched, which if leveed and drained and fenced, and well cultivated, might be made to produce with good luck seven or more bales to the hand. It would cost comparatively little to accomplish it— one lucky crop would repay all the outlay for land and improvements—if it were not for "the hands." The supply of hands is limited. It does not increase in the ratio of the increase of the cotton demand. If cotton should double in price next year, or become worth its weight in gold, the number of negroes in the United States would not increase four per cent. unless the African slave-trade were re-established. Now step into a dealer's "jail" in Memphis, Montgomery, Vicksburg, or New Orleans, and you will hear the mezzano of the cotton lottery crying his tickets in this way: "There's a cotton nigger for you! Genuine! Look at his toes! Look at his fingers! There's a pair of legs for you! If you have got the right sile and the right sort of overseer, buy him, and put your trust in Providence! He's just as good for ten bales as I am for a julep at eleven o'clock." And this is just as true as that any named horse is sure to win the Derby. And so the price of good labourers is constantly gambled up to a point, where, if they produce ten bales to the hand, the purchaser will be as fortunate as he who draws the high prize of the lottery; where, if they produce seven bales to the hand, he will still be in luck; where, if rot, or worm, or floods, or untimely rains or frosts occur, reducing the crop to one or two bales to the hand, as is often the case, the purchaser will have drawn a blank.

That, all things considered, the value of the labour of slaves does not, on an average, by any means justify the price paid for it, is constantly asserted by the planters, and it is true. At least beyond question it is true, and I think that I have shown why, that there is no difficulty in finding purchasers for all the good slaves that can be got by traders, at prices considerably more than they are worth for the production of cotton *under ordinary circumstances*. The supply being limited, those who grow cotton on the most productive soils, and with the greatest advantages in all other respects, not only can afford to pay more than others, for all the slaves which can be brought into market, but they are driven to a ruinous competition among themselves, and slaves thus get a fictitious value like stocks "in a corner." The buyers indeed are often "cornered," and it is only the rise which almost annually has occurred in the value of cotton that has hitherto saved them from general bankruptcy. Nearly all the large planters carry a heavy load of debt from year to year, till a lucky crop coincident with a rise in the price of cotton relieves them.

The whole number of slaves engaged in cotton culture at the Census of 1850 was reckoned by De Bow to be 1,800,000,* the crops at 2,400,000 bales, which is a bale and a third to each head of slaves. This was the largest crop between 1846 and 1852. Other things being equal, for reasons already indicated, the smaller the estate of slaves, the less is their rate of production per head ; and, as a rule, the larger the slave estate the larger is the production per head. The number of slaves in cotton plantations held by owners of fifty and upwards is, as nearly as it can be fixed by the Census returns, 420,000.

If these produce on an average only two and a half bales per head (man, woman, and child), and double this is not extraordinary on the large plantations of the South-west,† it leaves an average for the smaller plantations of seven-eighths of a bale per head. These plantations are mostly in the interior, with long haulage and boatage to market. To the small planter in the interior, his cotton crop does not realize, as an average plantation price, more than seven cents a pound, or thirty dollars the bale.‡ Those who plant cotton in this small way usually raise a crop of corn, and some little else, not enough, take the country through, one year with another, to

---

* Official Census—Compend., p. 94.

† Messrs. Neill Brothers, cotton merchants of New Orleans, the most painstaking collectors of information about the cotton crop in the country, state, in a recent circular, that many of the Mississippi cotton plantations last year, after an extraordinary fertilizing flood, produced sixteen bales to the hand. The slaves on these plantations being to a large extent picked hands, as I elsewhere show, the production per head was fully eight bales.

‡ In a careful article in the *Austin State Gazette*, six and a quarter cents is given as the average net price of cotton in Texas. The small planters, having no gins or presses of their own, usually have their cotton prepared for market by large planters, for which service they of course have to pay.

supply themselves and their slaves with food; certainly not more than enough to do so, on an average. To this the Southern agricultural periodicals frequently testify. They generally raise nothing *for sale*, but cotton. And of cotton their sale, as has been shown, amounted in 1849—a favourable year—to less than the value of twenty-five dollars for each slave, young and old, which they had kept through the year.* Deducting those who hold slaves only as domestic servants from the whole number of slaveholders returned by the Census, more than half of all the slaveholders, and fully half of all the cotton-sellers, own each, not more than one family, on an average, of five slaves of all ages.† The ordinary total cash income, then, in time of peace, of fully half our cotton-planters, cannot be reckoned at more than one hundred and twenty-five dollars, or, in extraordinary years, like the last, at, say, one hundred and fifty dollars. From this they must purchase whatever clothing and other necessaries they require for the yearly supply of an average of more than ten persons (five whites and five slaves), as well as obtain tools, mechanics' work and materials, and whatever is necessary for carrying on the work of a plantation, usually of some hundred acres,‡ and must yet save enough to pay the fees of doctors, clergy, and lawyers, if they have had occasion to employ them, and their county and state taxes (we will say nothing of the education of their children, or of accumulations for the war expenses of the Confederation). My personal experience of the style of living of the greater number of cotton-planters

* There have been much larger aggregate crops since, and the price may be a cent more to the planter, but the number of slaves drawn to the larger plantations in the meantime has increased in quite equal proportion.
† Census Compend., p. 95.
‡ The average size of plantations in the South-west, including the farms and "patches" of the non-slaveholders, is 273 acres (p. 170, C. Compend.). Cotton plantations are not generally of less than 400 acres.

leads me to think this not an unfair estimate. It is mainly based upon the official returns and calculations of the United States Census of 1850, as prepared by Mr. De Bow, a leading secessionist, and it assumes nothing which is not conceded in the article on cotton in his Resources of the South. A majority of those who sell the cotton crop of the United States must be miserably poor—poorer than the majority of our day-labourers at the North.

A similar calculation will indicate that the planters who own on an average two slave families each, can sell scarcely more than three hundred dollars' worth of cotton a year, on an average; which also entirely agrees with my observations. I have seen many a workman's lodging at the North, and in England too, where there was double the amount of luxury that I ever saw in a regular cotton-planter's house on plantations of three cabins.

The next class of which the Census furnishes us means of considering separately, are planters whose slaves occupy, on an average, seven cabins, lodging five each on an average, including the house servants, aged, invalids, and children. The average income of planters of this class, I reckon from similar data, to be hardly more than that of a private of the New York Metropolitan Police Force. It is doubtless true that cotton is cultivated profitably, that is to say, so as to produce a fair rate of interest on the capital of the planter, on many plantations of this class; but this can hardly be the case on an average, all things considered.

It is not so with many plantations of the next larger class even, but it would appear to be so with these on an average. That is to say, where the quarters of a cotton plantation number half a score of cabins or more, (which method of classification I use that travellers may the more readily recall their observations of the appearance of such plantations, when

I think that their recollections will confirm these calculations) there are usually other advantages for the cultivation, cleaning, pressing, shipping, and disposing of cotton, by the aid of which the owner obtains a fair return for the capital invested, and may be supposed to live, if he knows how, in a moderately comfortable way. The whole number of slaveholders of this large class in all the Slave States is, according to De Bow's Compendium of the Census, 7,929, among which are all the great sugar, rice, and tobacco-planters. Less than seven thousand, certainly, are cotton-planters.

A large majority of these live, when they live on their plantations at all, in districts, almost the only white population of which consists of owners and overseers of the same class of plantations with their own. The nearest other whites will be some sand-hill vagabonds, generally miles away, between whom and these planters, intercourse is neither intimate nor friendly.

It is hardly worth while to build much of a bridge for the occasional use of two families, even if they are rich. It is less worth while to go to much pains in making six miles of good road for the use of these families. A school-house will hardly be built for the children of six rich men who will all live on an average six miles away from it, while private tutors or governesses can be paid by the earnings of a single field-hand. If zeal and fluency can be obtained in a preacher coming occasionally within reach, the interest on the cost of a tolerable education is not likely to be often paid by all who would live within half a day's journey of a house of worship, which can be built anywhere in the midst of a district of large plantations. It is not necessary to multiply illustrations like these. In short, then, if all the wealth produced in a certain district is concentrated in the hands of a few men living remote from each other, it may possibly bring to the district comfortable houses, good servants, fine wines, food and furniture, tutors and governesses, horses and carriages, for these few men, but it will not bring thither good roads and bridges, it will not bring thither such means of education and of civilized comfort as are to be drawn from libraries, churches, museums, gardens, theatres, and assembly rooms; it will not bring thither local newspapers, telegraphs, and so on. It will not bring thither that subtle force and discipline which comes of the myriad relations with and duties to a well-constituted community which every member of it is daily exercising, and which is the natural unseen compensation and complement of its more obvious constraints and inconveniences. There is, in fact, a vast range of advantages which our civilization has made so common to us that they are hardly thought of, of which the people of the South are destitute. They chiefly come from or connect with acts of co-operation, or exchanges of service; they are therefore possessed only in communities, and in communities where a large proportion of the people have profitable employment. They grow, in fact, out of employments in which the people of the community are associated, or which they constantly give to and receive from one another, with profit. The slaves of the South, though often living in communities upon plantations, fail to give or receive these advantages because the profits of their labour are not distributed to them; the whites, from not engaging in profitable employment. The whites are not engaged in profitable employment, because the want of the advantages of capital in the application of their labour, independently of the already rich, renders the prospective result of their labour so small that it is inoperative in most, as a motive for exerting themselves further than is necessary to procure the bare means of a rude subsistence; also because common labour is so poorly rewarded in the case of the slaves as to assume in their minds, as it must in the minds of the slaves themselves, a hateful aspect.

In the late act of treason of the usurpers of government in Louisiana, the commercial demand which induces a man to go to work is considered to be equivalent to slavery; and the fear that the election of Lincoln, by its tendency to open a way for the emancipation of the negroes, may lead on to a necessity for the whites to go to work, is gravely set forth as a justification for the surrender of the State to the conspiracy. Thus:—

".Fully convinced as we are that slavery * * * * * leaves to the *black labourer* a more considerable sum of comfort, happiness, and liberty than the inexorable labour required from the free servants of the whole universe, and that each emancipation of an African, without being of any benefit to him, would necessarily *condemn to slavery* one of our own race, etc."

To work industriously and steadily, especially under directions from another man, is, in the Southern tongue, to " work like a nigger;" and, from childhood, the one thing in their condition which has made life valuable to the mass of whites has been that the niggers are yet their inferiors. It is this habit of considering themselves of a privileged class, and of disdaining something which they think beneath them, that is deemed to be the chief blessing of slavery. It is termed "high tone," " high spirit," and is supposed to give great military advantages to those who possess it. It should give advantages of some sort, for its disadvantages are inexpressibly great.

But if the poor whites were ever so industriously disposed, the rich planter has a natural distaste to exchange absolute for partial authority over the instruments by which he achieves his purpose; and the employment of free and slave labour together, is almost as difficult as working, under the same yoke, an unbroken horse and a docile ox. Again, however repugnant it may be to the self-esteem, and contrary to the habits of the rich man to treat his labourers with respect, he has to do it when employing white men, from motives of self-interest which lie below the surface, and he consequently habitually avoids arranging his affairs in such a way as will make it necessary for him to offer them employment.

It may be said that on the more profitable cotton plantations, where little is raised except cotton, supplies for the maintenance of the slaves, and for carrying on the work of the plantation, are largely bought, which are raised elsewhere at the South; and that those who supply the commodities, thus required by the cotton-planter, draw from his profits which are thus distributed throughout the South, even to the non-cotton-producing States, the people of which are thus enriched. As far as all articles are concerned, in the production of which labour is a comparatively unimportant item of cost,—mules for instance, and in certain circumstances, within certain limits, swine,—this is true. But these are of small consequence. It is constantly assumed by nearly all writers on this subject, that the labour directed to the cultivation of Indian corn for the necessary sustenance of slaves engaged in cotton culture, must be just as profitably directed as if it were devoted to the cultivation of cotton itself. This is not true, although the Southern agricultural journals, and to a large extent our national agriculture reports, have for years been assuming it to be so. It is frequently spoken of, indeed, as a mystery, that the cotton-planters cannot be induced to raise the food required by their force. The reason of it is a very simple one; namely, that in the cultivation of corn their labour must come into competition with the free labour of the Northern States, as it does not in the production of cotton: and the corn-raisers of the Northern Slave States, without enjoying any monopoly of production, like that of the cotton-raisers, have to share with these, all the manifold inconveniences which result from the scarcity of good workmen, and the necessary concentration of all the effective working force of the country, limited as it is, upon the one purpose of getting cotton.

The interests of the owners of all soil in the Slave States which is not adapted to cotton culture, and of all capital not engaged in cotton culture, or in supplying slaves for it, are thus injured by the demand for cotton, they being, in fact, forced to be co-partners in an association in which they do not share the profits.

And as to what are commonly called the Cotton States, if we assume that cotton cultivation is profitable only where the production is equal to two bales for each slave employed, it will be seen that wherever the land will not yield as much as this, the owner of it suffers all the disadvantages of the difficulty of getting good labourers as much as the owner of the land which produces seven or ten bales to the hand, although none of the profits of supplying the cotton demand, which gives this extraordinary price to labour, come to him.

According to the Census,* the whole crop of cotton is produced on 5,000,000 acres. It could be produced, at the rate common on good South-western plantations, on less than half that area. The rest of the land of the Slave States, which amounts to over 500,000,000 acres, is condemned, so far as the tendencies I have indicated are not overweighed here and there by some special advantages, to non-cultivation, except for the hand-to-mouth supply of its people. And this is true not only of its agricultural but of all other of its resources.

That for all practical purposes this is not an exaggerated

* Compendium, p. 176.

statement is clearly enough shown by the difference in the market value of land, which as officially given by De Bow, is, notwithstanding the extraordinary demand of the world upon the cotton land, between four and five hundred per cent. higher in the Free than in the Slave States, the frontier and unsettled districts, Texas, California, and the territories not being considered.

One of the grand errors, out of which this rebellion has grown, came from supposing that whatever nourishes wealth and gives power to an ordinary civilized community, must command as much for a slave-holding community. The truth has been overlooked that the accumulation of wealth and the power of a nation are contingent not merely upon the primary value of the surplus of productions of which it has to dispose, but very largely also upon the way in which the income from its surplus is distributed and reinvested. Let a man be absent from almost any part of the North twenty years, and he is struck, on his return, by what we call the "improvements" which have been made. Better buildings, churches, school-houses, mills, railroads, etc. In New York city alone, for instance, at least two hundred millions of dollars have been reinvested merely in an improved housing of the people; in labour-saving machinery, waterworks, gasworks, etc., as much more. It is not difficult to see where the profits of our manufacturers and merchants are. Again, go into the country, and there is no end of substantial proof of twenty years' of agricultural prosperity, not alone in roads, canals, bridges, dwellings, barns and fences, but in books and furniture, and gardens, and pictures, and in the better dress and evidently higher education of the people. But where will the returning traveller see the accumulated cotton profits of twenty years in Mississippi? Ask the cotton-planter for them, and he will point in reply, not to dwellings, libraries, churches, school-houses, mills, railroads, or anything of the kind; he will point to his negroes—to almost nothing else. Negroes such as stood for five hundred dollars once, now represent a thousand dollars. We must look then in Virginia and those Northern Slave States which have the monopoly of supplying negroes, for the real wealth which the sale of cotton has brought to the South. But where is the evidence of it? where anything to compare with the evidence of accumulated profits to be seen in any Free State? If certain portions of Virginia have been a little improving, others unquestionably have been deteriorating, growing shabbier, more comfortless, less convenient. The total increase in wealth of the population during the last twenty years shows for almost nothing. One year's improvements of a Free State exceed it all.

It is obvious that to the community at large, even in Virginia, the profits of supplying negroes to meet the wants occasioned by the cotton demand, have not compensated for the bar which the high cost of all sorts of human service, which the cotton demand has also occasioned, has placed upon all other means of accumulating wealth; and this disadvantage of the cotton monopoly is fully experienced by the negro-breeders themselves, in respect to everything else they have to produce or obtain.*

I say all sorts of human service. What the South will have to pay for the service of true statesmanship, the world has now to see.

Whither the profits of cotton go, it is not my purpose, here, to undertake to show. I will barely notice the hypocritical statement made for the English market as an apology for this mad crime of the slaveholders, that they are greatly absorbed in contributions made by the planting States to our national treasury in payment of duties on importations.

* Evidence from Virginian witnesses is given in the Appendix, A.

The cotton-planters pay duties only on what they consume of foreign goods. A very large part of all our duties are collected on a class of goods for which there is almost no demand at all from the South, either directly or indirectly—woollen and fur goods, for instance: of the goods required for the South not a few have been practically free. The whole slave population of the South consumes almost nothing imported (nor would it, while slave, under any circumstances). The majority of the white population habitually makes use of no foreign production except chickory, which, ground with peas, they call coffee. I have never seen reason to believe that with absolute free trade the cotton States would take a tenth part of the value of our present importations. And as far as I can judge from observation of the comparative use of foreign goods at the South and at the North, not a tenth part of our duties have been defrayed by the South in the last twenty years. The most indefensible protective duty we have is one called for by the South, and which has been maintained solely to benefit the South. Our protective system had a Southern origin; its most powerful advocates have been Southerners; and there has not been a year in the last twenty, in which it could have been maintained but for Southern votes.

CHAPTER II.

WASHINGTON.

Washington, Dec. 10*th.*—To accomplish the purposes which brought me to Washington, it was necessary, on arriving here, to make arrangements to secure food and shelter while I remained. There are two thousand visitors now in Washington under a similar necessity. There are a dozen or more persons who, for a consideration, undertake to provide what they want. Mr. Dexter is reported to be the best of them, and really seems a very obliging and honestly-disposed person. To Mr. Dexter, therefore, I commit myself.

I commit myself by inscribing my name in a Register. Five minutes after I have done so, Clerk No. 4, whose attention I have hitherto been unable to obtain, suddenly catches the Register by the corner, swings it round with a jerk, and throws a hieroglyph at it, which strikes near my name. Henceforth, I figure as Boarder No. 201 (or whatever it may be). Clerk No. 4 pipes " Boarder away!" and throws key No. 201 upon the table. Turnkey No. 3 takes it, and me, and my travelling bag, up several flights of stairs, along corridors and galleries, and finally consigns me to this little square cell.

I have faith that there is a tight roof above the much-cracked ceiling; that the bed is clean; and that I shall, by-and-by, be summoned, along with hundreds of other boarders, to partake, in silent sobriety, of a " splendid " dinner.

Food and shelter. Therewith should a man be content. But my perverse nature will not be content: will be wishing things were otherwise. They say this uneasiness—this passion for change—is a peculiarity of our diseased Northern nature. The Southern man finds Providence in all that is : Satan in all that might be. That is good ; and, as I am going South, when I have accomplished my purposes at Washington, I will not here restrain the escape of my present discontent.

In my perversity I wish the dinner were not going to be so grand. My idea is that, if it were not, Mr. Dexter would save moneys, which I would like to have him expend in other ways. I wish he had more clerks, so that they would have time to be as polite to an unknown man as I see they are to John P. Hale ; and, at least, answer civil questions, when his boarders ask them. I don't like such a fearful rush of business as there is down stairs. I wish there were men enough to do the work quietly.

I don't like these cracked and variegated walls ; and, though the roof may be tight, I don't like this threatening aspect of the ceiling. It should be kept for boarders of Damoclesian ambition : I am humble.

I am humble, and I am short, and soon curried ; but I am not satisfied with a quarter of a yard of towelling, having an irregular vacancy in its centre, where I am liable to insert my head. I am not proud ; but I had rather have something else, or nothing, than these three yards of ragged and faded quarter-ply carpeting. I also would like a curtain to the window, and I wish the glass were not so dusty, and that the sashes did not rattle so in their casements ; though, as there is no other ventilation, I suppose I ought not to complain. Of course not ; but it is confoundedly cold, as well as noisy.

I don't like that broken latch; I don't like this broken chair; I would prefer that this table were not so greasy; I would rather the ashes and cinders, and the tobacco juice around the grate, had been removed before I was consigned to the cell.

I wish that less of my two dollars and a half a day went to pay for game at dinner, and interest on the cost of the mirrors and mahogany for the public parlours, and of marble for the halls, and more of it for providing me with a private room, which should be more than a barely habitable cell, which should also be a little bit tasteful, home-like, and comfortable.

I wish more of it could be expended in servants' wages.

Six times I rang the bell; three several times came three different Irish lads; entered, received my demand for a fire, and retired. I was writing, shiveringly, a full hour before the fire-man came. Now he has entered, bearing on his head a hod of coal and kindling wood, without knocking. An aged negro, more familiar and more indifferent to forms of subserviency than the Irish lads, very much bent, seemingly with infirmity; an expression of impotent anger in his face, and a look of weakness, like a drunkard's. He does not look at me, but mutters unintelligibly.

"What's that you say?"

"Tink I can make a hundred fires at once?"

"I don't want to sit an hour waiting for a fire, after I have ordered one, and you must not let me again."

"Nebber let de old nigger have no ress—hundred gemmen tink I kin mak dair fires all de same minit; all get mad at an ole nigger; I ain't a goin to stan it—nebber get no ress—up all night—haint got nautin to eat nor drink dis blessed mornin—hundred gemmen—"

"That's not my business; Mr. Dexter should have more servants"

"So he ort ter, master, dat he had; one ole man ain't enough for all dis house, is it, master? hundred gemmen—"

"Stop—here's a quarter for you: now I want you to look out that I have a good fire, and keep the hearth clean in my room as long as I stay here. And when I send for you I want you to come immediately. Do you understand?"

"I'le try, master—you jus look roun and fine me when you want yer fire; I'll be roun somewhere. You got a newspaper, sir, I ken take for a minit? I won't hurt it."

I gave him one; and wondered what use he could put it to, that would not hurt it. He opened it to a folio, and spread it before the grate, so the draft held it in place, and it acted as a blower. I asked if there were no blowers? "No." "But haven't you got any brush or shovel?" I inquired, seeing him get down upon his knees again and sweep the cinders and ashes he had thrown upon the floor with the sleeve of his coat, and then take them up with his hands;— No, he said, his master did not give him such things.

"Are you a slave?"

"Yes, sir."

"Do you belong to Mr. Dexter?"

"No, sir—he hires me of de man dat owns me. Don't you tink I'se too ole a man for to be knock roun at dis kind of work, massa?—hundred gemmen all want dair fires made de same minute, and caus de old nigger can't do it all de same minute, ebbery one tinks dey's boun to scold him all de time; nebber no rest for him, no time."

Washington, Dec. 14th.—I called to-day on Mr. C., whose fine farm, from its vicinity to Washington, and its excellent management, as well as from the hospitable habits of its owner, has a national reputation. It is some two thousand acres in extent, and situated just without the District, in Maryland.

The residence is in the midst of the farm, a quarter of a mile from the high road—the private approach being judiciously carried through large pastures which are divided only by slight, but close and well-secured wire fences. The kept grounds are limited, and in simple but quiet taste; being surrounded only by wires, they merge, in effect, into the pastures. There is a fountain, an ornamental dove-cote, and ice-house, and the approach road, nicely gravelled and rolled, comes up to the door with a fine sweep.

I had dismounted and was standing before the door, when I heard myself loudly hailed from a distance.

"Ef yer wants to see master, sah, he's down thar—to the new stable."

I could see no one; and when tired of holding my horse, I mounted, and rode on in search of the new stable. I found it without difficulty; and in it Mr. and Mrs. C. With them were a number of servants, one of whom now took my horse with alacrity. I was taken at once to look at a very fine herd of cows, and afterwards led upon a tramp over the farm, and did not get back to the house till dinner-time.

Mr. C. is a large hereditary owner of slaves, which, for ordinary field and stable work, constitute his labouring force. He has employed several Irishmen for ditching; and for this work, and this alone, he thought he could use them to better advantage than negroes. He would not think of using Irishmen for common farm-labour, and made light of their coming in competition with slaves. Negroes at hoeing and any steady field-work, he assured me, would " do two to their one;" but his main objection to employing Irishmen was derived from his experience of their unfaithfulness—they were dishonest, would not obey explicit directions about their work, and required more personal supervision than negroes. From what he had heard and seen of Germans, he supposed they did better than Irish. He mentioned that there were several Germans who had come here as labouring men, and worked for wages several years, who had now got possession of small farms, and were reputed to be getting rich.* He was disinclined to converse on the topic of slavery; and I therefore made no inquiries about the condition and habits of his negroes, or his management of them. They seemed to live in small and rude log-cabins, scattered in different parts of the farm. Those I saw at work appeared to me to move very slowly and awkwardly, as did also those engaged in the stable. These also were very stupid and dilatory in executing any orders given to them, so that Mr. C. would frequently take the duty off their hands into his own, rather than wait for them, or make them correct their blunders: they were much, in these respects, like what our farmers call dumb Paddies, that is, Irishmen who do not readily understand the English language, and who are still weak and stiff from the effects of the emigrating voyage. At the entrance-gate was a porter's lodge, and as I approached, I saw a black face peeping at me from it, but, both when I entered and left, I was ob' ged to dismount and open the gate myself.

Altogether it struck me—slaves coming here as they naturally did in direct comparison with free labourers, as commonly employed on my own and my neighbours' farms, in

* " There is a small settlement of Germans, about three miles from me, who, a few years since (with little or nothing beyond their physical abilities to aid them), seated themselves down in a poor, miserable, old field, and have, by their industry, and means obtained by working round among the neighbours, effected a change which is really surprising and pleasing to behold, and who will, I have no doubt, become wealthy, provided they remain prudent, as they have hitherto been industrious."—F. A. CLOPPER (Montgomery Co.), Maryland, in Patent Of. Rept., 1851

exactly similar duties—that they must be difficult to direct efficiently, and that it must be irksome and trying to one's patience to have to superintend their labour.

Washington, Dec. 16*th*.—Visiting the market-place, early on Tuesday morning, I found myself in the midst of a throng of a very different character from any I have ever seen at the North. The majority of the people were negroes; and, taken as a whole, they appeared inferior in the expression of their face and less well-clothed than any collection of negroes I had ever seen before. All the negro characteristics were more clearly marked in each than they often are in any at the North. In their dress, language, manner, motions—all were distinguishable almost as much by their colour, from the white people who were distributed among them, and engaged in the same occupations—chiefly selling poultry, vegetables, and small country produce. The white men were, generally, a mean-looking people, and but meanly dressed, but differently so from the negroes.

Most of the produce was in small, rickety carts, drawn by the smallest, ugliest, leanest lot of oxen and horses that I ever saw. There was but one pair of horses in over a hundred that were tolerably good—a remarkable proportion of them were maimed in some way. As for the oxen, I do not believe New England and New York together could produce a single yoke as poor as the best of them.

The very trifling quantity of articles brought in and exposed for sale by most of the market-people was noticeable; a peck of potatoes, three bunches of carrots, two cabbages, six eggs and a chicken, would be about the average stock in trade of all the dealers. Mr. F. said that an old negro woman once came to his door with a single large turkey, which she pressed him to buy. Struck with her fatigued appearance, he made some inquiries of her, and ascertained that she had been several days coming from home, had travelled mainly on foot, and had brought the turkey and nothing else with her. "Ole massa had to raise some money somehow, and he could not sell anyting else, so he tole me to catch the big gobbler, and tote um down to Washington and see wot um would fotch."

Land may be purchased, within twenty miles of Washington, at from ten to twenty dollars an acre. Most of it has been once in cultivation, and, having been exhausted in raising tobacco, has been, for many years, abandoned, and is now covered by a forest growth. Several New Yorkers have lately speculated in the purchase of this sort of land, and, as there is a good market for wood, and the soil, by the decay of leaves upon it, and other natural causes, has been restored to moderate fertility, have made money by clearing and improving it. By deep ploughing and liming, and the judicious use of manures, it is made quite productive; and, as equally cheap farms can hardly be found in any free State, in such proximity to as good markets for agricultural produce, there are inducements for a considerable Northern immigration hither. It may not be long before a majority of the inhabitants will be opposed to slavery, and desire its abolition within the district. Indeed, when Mr. Seward proposed in the Senate to allow them to decide that matter, the advocates of "popular sovereignty" made haste to vote down the motion.

There are, already, more Irish and German labourers and servants than *slaves;* and, as many of the objections which free labourers have to going further south, do not operate in Washington, the proportion of white labourers is every year increasing. The majority of servants, however, are now *free* negroes, which class constitutes one-fifth of the entire population. The slaves are one-fifteenth, but are mostly owned out of the district, and hired annually to those who require their services. In the assessment of taxable property, for 1853, the slaves, owned or hired in the district, were valued at three hundred thousand dollars.

The coloured population voluntarily sustain several churches, schools, and mutual assistance and improvement societies, and there are evidently persons among them of no inconsiderable cultivation of mind. Among the police reports of the City newspapers, there was lately (April, 1855), an account of the apprehension of twenty-four "genteel coloured men" (so they were described), who had been found by a watchman assembling privately in the evening, and been lodged in the watch-house. The object of their meeting appears to have been purely benevolent, and, when they were examined before a magistrate in the morning, no evidence was offered, nor does there seem to have been any suspicion that they had any criminal purpose. On searching their persons, there were found a Bible; a volume of *Seneca's Morals; Life in Earnest;* the printed constitution of a society, the object of which was said to be "*to relieve the sick and bury the dead;*" and a subscription paper *to purchase the freedom of Eliza Howard*, a young woman, whom her owner was willing to sell at $650.

I can think of nothing that would speak higher for the character of a body of poor men, servants and labourers, than to find, by chance, in their pockets, just such things as these. And I cannot value that man as a countryman, who does not feel intense humiliation and indignation, when he learns that such men may not be allowed to meet privately together, with such laudable motives, in the capital city of the United States, without being subject to disgraceful punishment. One of the prisoners, a slave named Joseph Jones, was ordered to be flogged; four others, called in the papers free men, and named John E. Bennett, Chester Taylor, George Lee, and Aquila Barton, were sent to the workhouse; and the remainder, on paying costs of court, and fines, amounting, in the aggregate, to one hundred and eleven dollars, were permitted to range loose again.

CHAPTER III.

VIRGINIA.—GLIMPSES BY RAILROAD.

Richmond, Dec. 16*th.*—From Washington to Richmond, Virginia, by the regular great southern route—steamboat on the Potomac to Acquia Creek, and thence direct by rail. The boat makes 55 miles in 3½ hours, including two stoppages (12½ miles an hour); fare $2 (3·6 cents a mile). Flat rail; distance, 75 miles; time 5½ hours (13 miles an hour); fare, $3 50 (4⅔ cents a mile).

Not more than a third of the country, visible on this route, I should say, is cleared; the rest mainly a pine forest. Of the cleared land, not more than one quarter seems to have been lately in cultivation; the rest is grown over with briars and bushes, and a long, coarse grass of no value. But two crops seem to be grown upon the cultivated land—maize and wheat. The last is frequently sown in narrow beds and carefully surface-drained, and is looking remarkably well.

A good many old plantation mansions are to be seen; generally standing in a grove of white oaks, upon some hill-top. Most of them are constructed of wood, of two stories, painted white, and have, perhaps, a dozen rude-looking little log-cabins scattered around them, for the slaves. Now and then, there is one of more pretension, with a large porch or gallery in front, like that of Mount Vernon. These are generally in a heavy, compact style; less often, perhaps, than similar establishments at the North, in markedly bad, or vulgar taste, but seem in sad need of repairs.

The more common sort of habitations of the white people are either of logs or loosely boarded frames, a brick chimney running up outside, at one end : everything very slovenly and dirty about them. Swine, hounds, and black and white children, are commonly lying very promiscuously together on the ground about the doors.

I am struck with the close cohabitation and association of black and white—negro women are carrying black and white babies together in their arms ; black and white children are playing together (not going to school together) ; black and white faces are constantly thrust together out of the doors, to see the train go by.

A fine-looking, well-dressed, and well-behaved coloured young man sat, together with a white man, on a seat in the cars. I suppose the man was his master ; but he was much the less like a gentleman of the two. The railroad company advertise to take coloured people only in second-class trains ; but servants seem to go with their masters everywhere. Once, to-day, seeing a lady entering the car at a way-station, with a family behind her, and that she was looking about to find a place where they could be seated together, I rose, and offered her my seat, which had several vacancies round it. She accepted it, without thanking me, and immediately installed in it a stout negro woman ; took the adjoining seat herself, and seated the rest of her party before her. It consisted of a white girl, probably her daughter, and a bright and very pretty mulatto girl. They all talked and laughed together ; and the girls munched confectionary out of the same paper, with a familiarity and closeness of intimacy that would have been noticed with astonishment, if not with manifest displeasure, in almost any chance company at the North

When the negro is definitely a slave, it would seem that the alleged natural antipathy of the white race to associate with him is lost.

I am surprised at the number of fine-looking mulattoes, or nearly white-coloured persons, that I see. The majority of those with whom I have come personally in contact are such. I fancy I see a peculiar expression among these—a contraction of the eyebrows and tightening of the lips—a spying, secretive, and counsel-keeping expression.

But the great mass, as they are seen at work, under overseers, in the fields, appear very dull, idiotic, and brute-like; and it requires an effort to appreciate that they are, very much more than the beasts they drive, our brethren—a part of ourselves. They are very ragged, and the women especially, who work in the field with the men, with no apparent distinction in their labour, disgustingly dirty. They seem to move very awkwardly, slowly, and undecidedly, and almost invariably stop their work while the train is passing.

One tannery and two or three saw-mills afforded the only indications I saw, in seventy-five miles of this old country—settled before any part of Massachusetts—of any industrial occupation other than corn and wheat culture, and fire-wood chopping. At Fredericksburg we passed through the streets of a rather busy, poorly-built town; but altogether, the country seen from the railroad, bore less signs of an active and prospering people than any I ever travelled through before, for an equal distance.

Richmond, at a glance from adjacent high ground, through a dull cloud of bituminous smoke, upon a lowering winter's day, has a very picturesque appearance, and I was reminded of the sensation produced by a similar *coup d'œil* of Edinburgh. It is somewhat similarly situated upon and among some considerable hills; but the moment it is examined at all in detail, there is but one spot, in the whole picture, upon which the eye is at all attracted to rest. This is the Capitol, a Grecian edifice, standing alone, and finely placed on open and elevated ground, in the centre of the town. It was built soon after the Revolution, and the model was obtained by Mr. Jefferson, then Minister to France, from the Maison Carrée.

A considerable part of the town, which contains a population of 28,000, is compactly and somewhat substantially built, but is without any pretensions to architectural merit, except in a few modern private mansions. The streets are not paved, and but few of them are provided with side walks other than of earth or gravel. The town is lighted with gas, and furnished with excellent water by an aqueduct.

On a closer view of the Capitol, a bold deviation from the Grecian model is very noticeable. The southern portico is sustained upon a very high blank wall, and is as inaccessible from the exterior as if it had been intended to fortify the edifice from all ingress other than by scaling-ladders. On coming round to the west side, however, which is without a colonnade, a grand entrance, reached by a heavy buttress of stone steps, is found. This incongruity diminishes, in some degree, the usual inconvenience of the Greek temple for modern public purposes, for it gives speedy access to a small central rotunda, out of which doors open into the legislative halls and offices.

If the walling up of the legitimate entrance has caused the impression, in a stranger, that he is being led to a prison or fortress, instead of the place for transacting the public business of a Free State by its chosen paid agents, it is not removed when on approaching this side door, he sees before it an armed sentinel—a meek-looking man in a livery of many colours, embarrassed with a bright-bayoneted firelock, which he hugs gently, as though the cold iron, this frosty day, chilled his arm.

He belongs to the Public Guard of Virginia, I am told; a

company of a hundred men (more or less), enlisted under an Act of the State, passed in 1801, after a rebellion of the coloured people, who, under one "General Gabriel," attempted to take the town, in hopes to gain the means of securing their freedom. Having been betrayed by a traitor, as insurgent slaves almost always are, they were met, on their approach, by a large body of well-armed militia, hastily called out by the Governor. For this, being armed only with scythe-blades, they were unprepared, and immediately dispersed. "General Gabriel" and the other leaders, one after another, were captured, tried, and hanged, the militia in strong force guarding them to execution. Since then, a disciplined guard, bearing the warning motto, "*Sic semper tyrannis!*" has been kept constantly under arms in the Capitol, and no man can enter the legislative temple of Virginia without being reminded that "Eternal vigilance is the price of ——."

It was not till I had passed the guard, unchallenged, and stood at the door-way, that I perceived that the imposing edifice, as I had thought it at a distance, was nothing but a cheap stuccoed building; nor would anything short of test by touch have convinced me that the great State of Virginia would have been so long content with such a parsimonious pretence of dignity as is found in imitation granite and imitation marble.

There is an instance of parsimony, without pretence, in Richmond, which Ruskin himself, if he were a traveller, could not be expected to applaud. The railroad company which brings the traveller from Washington, so far from being open to the criticism of having provided edifices of a style of architecture only fitted for palaces, instead of a hall suited to conflicts with hackney-coachmen, actually has no sort of stationary accommodations for them at all, but sets them down, rain or shine, in the middle of one of the main streets. The adjoining hucksteries, barbers' shops, and bar-rooms, are evidently all the better patronized for this fine simplicity; but I should doubt if the railroad stock advanced in value by it.

Richmond.—On a Sunday afternoon I met a negro funeral procession, and followed after it to the place of burial. There was a decent hearse, of the usual style, drawn by two horses; six hackney coaches followed it, and six well-dressed men, mounted on handsome saddle-horses, and riding them well, rode in the rear of these. Twenty or thirty men and women were also walking together with the procession, on the side walk. Among all there was not a white person.

Passing out into the country, a little beyond the principal cemetery of the city (a neat, rural ground, well filled with monuments and evergreens), the hearse halted at a desolate place, where a dozen coloured people were already engaged heaping the earth over the grave of a child, and singing a wild kind of chant. Another grave was already dug immediately adjoining that of the child, both being near the foot of a hill, in a crumbling bank—the ground below being already occupied, and the graves advancing in irregular terraces up the hill-side—an arrangement which facilitated labour.

The new comers, setting the coffin—which was neatly made of stained pine—upon the ground, joined in the labour and the singing, with the preceding party, until a small mound of earth was made over the grave of the child. When this was completed, one of those who had been handling a spade, sighed deeply and said—

"Lord Jesus, have marcy on us—now! you Jim—you! see yar! you jes lay dat yar shovel cross dat grave—so fash—dah—yes, dat's right."

A shovel and a hoe-handle having been laid across the unfilled grave, the coffin was brought and laid upon them, a on a trestle; after which, lines were passed under it, by which it was lowered to the bottom.

Most of the company were of a very poor appearance, rude and unintelligent, but there were several neatly-dressed and very good-looking men. One of these now stepped to the head of the grave, and, after a few sentences of prayer, held a handkerchief before him as if it were a book, and pronounced a short exhortation, as if he were reading from it. His manner was earnest, and the tone of his voice solemn and impressive, except that, occasionally, it would break into a shout or kind of howl at the close of a long sentence. I noticed several women near him, weeping, and one sobbing intensely. I was deeply influenced myself by the unaffected feeling, in connection with the simplicity, natural, rude truthfulness, and absence of all attempt at formal decorum in the crowd.

I never in my life, however, heard such ludicrous language as was sometimes uttered by the speaker. Frequently I could not guess the idea he was intending to express. Sometimes it was evident that he was trying to repeat phrases that he had heard used before, on similar occasions, but which he made absurd by some interpolation or distortion of a word, thus: "We do not see the end here! oh no, my friends! there will be a *putrification* of this body!" the context failing to indicate whether he meant purification or putrefaction, and leaving it doubtful if he attached any definite meaning to the word himself. He quoted from the Bible several times, several times from hymns, always introducing the latter with "In the words of the poet, my brethren;" he once used the same form, before a verse from the New Testament, and once qualified his citation by saying, "I *believe* the Bible says that."

He concluded by throwing a handful of earth on the coffin, repeating the usual words, slightly disarranged, and then took a shovel, and, with the aid of six or seven others, proceeded very rapidly to fill the grave. Another man had in the mean time, stepped into the place he had first occupied at the head of the grave; an old negro, with a very singularly distorted face, who raised a hymn, which soon became a confused chant —the leader singing a few words alone, and the company then either repeating them after him or making a response to them, in the manner of sailors heaving at the windlass. I could understand but very few of the words. The music was wild and barbarous, but not without a plaintive melody. A new leader took the place of the old man, when his breath gave out (he had sung very hard, with much bending of the body and gesticulation), and continued until the grave was filled, and a mound raised over it.

A man had, in the mean time, gone into a ravine near by, and now returned with two small branches, hung with withered leaves, that he had broken off a beech tree: these were placed upright, one at the head, the other at the foot of the grave. A few sentences of prayer were then repeated in a low voice by one of the company, and all dispersed. No one seemed to notice my presence at all. There were about fifty coloured people in the assembly, and but one other white man besides myself. This man lounged against the fence, outside the crowd, an apparently indifferent spectator, and I judged he was a police officer, or some one procured to witness the funeral, in compliance with the law which requires that a white man shall always be present at any meeting, for religious exercises, of the negroes.

The greater part of the coloured people, on Sunday, seemed to be dressed in the cast-off fine clothes of the white people, received, I suppose, as presents, or purchased of the Jews, whose shops show that there must be considerable importation of such articles, probably from the North, as there is from

England into Ireland. Indeed, the lowest class, especially among the younger, remind me much, by their dress, of the "lads" of Donnybrook; and when the funeral procession came to its destination, there was a scene precisely like that you may see every day in Sackville Street, Dublin,—a dozen boys in ragged clothes, originally made for tall men, and rather folded round their bodies than worn, striving who should hold the horses of the gentlemen when they dismounted to attend the interment of the body. Many, who had probably come in from the farms near the town, wore clothing of coarse gray "negro-cloth," that appeared as if made by contract, without regard to the size of the particular individual to whom it had been allotted, like penitentiary uniforms. A few had a better suit of coarse blue cloth, expressly made for them evidently, for " Sunday clothes."

Some were dressed with foppish extravagance, and many in the latest style of fashion. In what I suppose to be the fashionable streets, there were many more well-dressed and highly-dressed coloured people than white; and among this dark gentry the finest French cloths, embroidered waistcoats, patent-leather shoes, resplendent brooches, silk hats, kid gloves, and *eau de mille fleurs*, were quite common. Nor was the fairer, or rather the softer sex, at all left in the shade of this splendour. Many of the coloured ladies were dressed not only expensively, but with good taste and effect, after the latest Parisian mode. Some of them were very attractive in appearance, and would have produced a decided sensation in any European drawing-room. Their walk and carriage were more often stylish and graceful. Nearly a fourth part seemed to me to have lost all African peculiarity of feature, and to have acquired, in place of it, a good deal of that voluptuousness of expression which characterizes many of the women of the South of Europe.

There was no indication of their belonging to a subject race, except that they invariably gave the way to the white people they met. Once, when two of them, engaged in conversation and looking at each other, had not noticed his approach, I saw a Virginian gentleman lift his walking-stick and push a woman aside with it. In the evening I saw three rowdies, arm-in-arm, taking the whole of the sidewalk, hustle a black man off it, giving him a blow, as they passed, that sent him staggering into the middle of the street. As he recovered himself he began to call out to, and threaten them. Perhaps he saw me stop, and thought I should support him, as I was certainly inclined to: "Can't you find anything else to do than to be knockin' quiet people round! You jus' come back here, will you? Here, you! *don't care if you is white.* You jus' come back here, and I'll teach you how to behave—knockin' people round!—don't care if I does hab to go to der watch-house." They passed on without noticing him further, only laughing jeeringly—and he continued: "You come back here, and I'll make you laugh; you is jus' three white nigger cowards, dat's what *you* be."

I observe, in the newspapers, complaints of growing insolence and insubordination among the negroes, arising, it is thought, from too many privileges being permitted them by their masters, and from too merciful administration of the police laws with regard to them. Except in this instance, however, I have seen not the slightest evidence of any independent manliness on the part of the negroes towards the whites. As far as I have yet observed, they are treated very kindly and even generously as servants, but their manner to white people is invariably either sullen, jocose, or fawning.

The pronunciation and dialect of the negroes, here, is generally much more idiomatic and peculiar than with us. As I write, I hear a man shouting, slowly and deliberately, meaning to say *there*: "*Dah! dah!* DAH!"

Among the people you see in the streets, full half, I should think, are more or less of negro blood, and a very decent, civil people these seem, in general, to be; more so than the labouring class of whites, among which there are many very ruffianly-looking fellows. There is a considerable population of foreign origin, generally of the least valuable class; very dirty German Jews, especially, abound, and their characteristic shops (with their characteristic smells, quite as bad as in Cologne) are thickly set in the narrowest and meanest streets, which seem to be otherwise inhabited mainly by negroes.

Immense waggons, drawn by six mules each, the teamster always riding on the back of the near-wheeler, are a characteristic feature of the streets. On the canal, a long, narrow-canoe-like boat, perhaps fifty feet long and six wide, and drawing but a foot or two of water, is nearly as common as the ordinary large boats, such as are used on our canals. They come out of some of the small, narrow, crooked streams, connected with the canals, in which a difficult navigation is effected by poleing. They are loaded with tobacco, flour, and a great variety of raw country produce. The canal boatmen seem rude, insolent, and riotous, and every facility is evidently afforded them, at Richmond, for indulging their peculiar appetites and tastes. A great many low eating, and, I should think, drinking, shops are frequented chiefly by the negroes. Dancing and other amusements are carried on in these at night.

From reading the comments of Southern statesmen and newspapers on the crime and misery which sometimes result from the accumulation of poor and ignorant people, with no intelligent masters to take care of them, in our Northern towns, one might get the impression that Southern towns—

especially those not demoralized by foreign commerce—were comparatively free from a low and licentious population. From what I have seen, however, I am led to think that there is at least as much vice, and of what we call rowdyism, in Richmond, as in any Northern town of its size.

Richmond.—Yesterday morning, during a cold, sleety storm, against which I was struggling, with my umbrella, to the post-office, I met a comfortably-dressed negro leading three others by a rope; the first was a middle-aged man; the second a girl of, perhaps, twenty; and the last a boy, considerably younger. The arms of all three were secured before them with hand-cuffs, and the rope by which they were led passed from one to another; being made fast at each pair of hand-cuffs. They were thinly clad, the girl especially so, having only an old ragged handkerchief around her neck, over a common calico dress, and another handkerchief twisted around her head. They were dripping wet, and icicles were forming, at the time, on the awning bars.

The boy looked most dolefully, and the girl was turning around, with a very angry face, and shouting, "O pshaw! Shut up!"

"What are they?" said I, to a white man, who had also stopped, for a moment, to look at them. "What's he going to do with them?"

"Come in a canal boat, I reckon: sent down here to be sold.—That ar's a likely gal."

Our ways lay together, and I asked further explanation. He informed me that the negro-dealers had confidential servants always in attendance, on the arrival of the railroad trains and canal packets, to take any negroes that might have come consigned to them, and bring them to their marts.

Nearly opposite the post-office was another singular group

of negroes. They consisted of men and boys, and each carried a coarse, white blanket, drawn together at the corners so as to hold some articles; probably, extra clothes. They stood in a row, in lounging attitudes, and some of them, again, were quarrelling, or reproving one another. A villanous-looking white man stood in front of them. Presently, a stout, respectable man, dressed in black according to the custom, and without any overcoat or umbrella, but with a large, golden-headed walking-stick, came out of the door of an office, and, without saying a word, walked briskly up the street; the negroes immediately followed, in file; the other white man bringing up the rear. They were slaves that had been sent into the town to be hired out as servants or factory hands. The gentleman in black was, probably, the broker in the business.

Near the post-office, opposite a large livery and sale stable, I turned into a short, broad street, in which were a number of establishments, the signs on which indicated that they were occupied by "Slave Dealers," and that "Slaves, for Sale or to Hire," were to be found within them. They were much like Intelligence Offices, being large rooms partly occupied by ranges of forms, on which sat a few comfortably and neatly clad negroes, who appeared perfectly cheerful, each grinning obsequiously, but with a manifest interest or anxiety, when I fixed my eye on them for a moment.

In Chambers' Journal for October, 1853,* there is an account of the Richmond slave marts, and the manner of conducting business in them, to which I shall refer the reader, in lieu of any further narration of my own observations on this subject. (See Appendix B.) I did not myself happen

---

* William Chambers has published the article in a separate form, with some others, under the title of 'American Slavery and Colours.' Mr. Russell, of the *Times*, has given a later case at Montgomery.

to witness, during fourteen months that I spent in the Slave States, any sale of negroes by auction. This must not be taken as an indication that negro auctions are not of frequent occurrence (I did not, so far as I now recollect, witness the sale of anything else, at auction, at the South). I saw negroes advertised to be sold at auction, very frequently.

The hotel at which I am staying, "The American," Milberger Smith, from New York, proprietor, is an excellent one. I have never, this side the Atlantic, had my comforts provided for better, in my private room, with so little annoyance from the servants. The chamber-servants are negroes, and are accomplished in their business; (the dining-room servants are Irish). A man and a woman attend together upon a few assigned rooms, in the hall adjoining which they are constantly in waiting; your bell is answered immediately, your orders are quickly and quietly followed, and your particular personal wants anticipated as much as possible, and provided for, as well as the usual offices performed, when you are out. The man becomes your servant while you are in your room; he asks, at night, when he comes to request your boots, at what time he shall come in the morning, and then, without being very exactly punctual, he comes quietly in, makes your fire, sets the boots before it, brushes and arranges your clothes, lays out your linen, arranges your dressing gear, asks if you want anything else of him before breakfast, opens the shutters, and goes off to the next room. I took occasion to speak well of him to my neighbour one day, that I might judge whether I was particularly favoured.

"Oh, yes," he said, "Henry was a very good boy, very— valuable servant—quite so—would be worth two thousand dollars, if he was a little younger—easy."

At dinner, a venerable looking man asked another—
" Niggers are going high now, aint they ?"

"Yes, sir."

"What would you consider a fair price for a woman thirty years old, with a young-one two years old?"

"Depends altogether on her physical condition, you know.—Has she any other children?"

"*Yes; four.*"

"——Well—I reckon about seven to eight hundred."

"I bought one yesterday—gave six hundred and fifty."

"Well, sir, if she's tolerable likely, you did well."

This morning I visited a farm, situated on the bank of James River, near Richmond.

The labour upon it was entirely performed by slaves. I did not inquire their number, but I judged there were from twenty to forty. Their "quarters" lined the approach-road to the mansion, and were well-made and comfortable log cabins, about thirty feet long by twenty wide, and eight feet wall, with a high loft and shingle roof. Each divided in the middle, and having a brick chimney outside the wall at either end, was intended to be occupied by two families. There were square windows, closed by wooden ports, having a single pane of glass in the centre. The house-servants were neatly dressed, but the field-hands wore very coarse and ragged garments.

During the three hours, or more, in which I was in company with the proprietor, I do not think ten consecutive minutes passed uninterrupted by some of the slaves requiring his personal direction or assistance. He was even obliged, three times, to leave the dinner-table.

"You see," said he, smiling, as he came in the last time, "a farmer's life, in this country, is no sinecure." Then turning the conversation to slavery, he observed. in answer to a remark of mine, "I only wish your philanthropists would contrive some satisfactory plan to relieve us of it ; the trouble and the responsibility of properly taking care of our negroes, you may judge, from what you see yourself here, is anything bu enviable. But what can we do that is better ? Our free negroes—and I believe it is the same at the North as it is here—are a miserable set of vagabonds, drunken, vicious, worse off, it is my honest opinion, than those who are retained in slavery. I am satisfied, too, that our slaves are better off, as they are, than the majority of your free labouring classes at the North."

I expressed my doubts.

" Well, they certainly are better off than the English agricultural labourers, or, I believe, those of any other Christian country. Free labour might be more profitable to us: I am inclined to think it would be. The slaves are excessively careless and wasteful, and, in various ways—which, without you lived among them, you could hardly be made to understand —subject us to very annoying losses.

" To make anything by farming, here, a man has got to live a hard life. You see how constantly I am called upon—and, often, it is about as bad at night as by day. Last night I did not sleep a wink till near morning ; I am quite worn out with it, and my wife's health is failing. But I cannot rid myself of it."

I asked why he did not employ an overseer.

" Because I do not think it right to trust to such men as we have to use, if we use any, for overseers."

" Is the general character of overseers bad ?"

" They are the curse of this country, sir; the worst men in the community. * * * * But lately, I had another sort of fellow offer—a fellow like a dancing-master, with kid gloves, and wrist-bands turned up over his coat-sleeves, and all so nice, that I was almost ashamed to talk to him in my old coat and slouched hat. Half a bushel of recommendations he had with him, too. Well, he was not the man for me—not half the gentleman, with all his airs, that Ned here is"—(a black servant, who was bursting with suppressed laughter, behind his chair).

"Oh, they are interesting creatures, sir," he continued, "and, with all their faults, have many beautiful traits. I can't help being attached to them, and I am sure they love us." In his own case, at least, I did not doubt; his manner towards them was paternal—familiar and kind; and they came to him like children who have been given some task, and constantly are wanting to be encouraged and guided, simply and confidently. At dinner, he frequently addressed the servant familiarly, and drew him into our conversation as if he were a family friend, better informed, on some local and domestic points, than himself.

I have been visiting a coal-pit: the majority of the mining labourers are slaves, and uncommonly athletic and fine-looking negroes; but a considerable number of white hands are also employed, and they occupy all the responsible posts. The slaves are, some of them, owned by the mining company; but the most are hired of their owners, at from $120 to $200 a year, the company boarding and clothing them. (I understood that it was customary to give them a certain allowance of money and let them find their own board.)

The white hands are mostly English or Welsh. One of them, with whom I conversed, told me that he had been here several years; he had previously lived some years at the North. He got better wages here than he earned at the North, but he was not contented, and did not intend to remain. On pressing him for the reason of his discontent, he said, after some hesitation, he would rather live where he could be more free; a man had to be too "discreet" here: if one happened to say anything that gave offence, they thought no more of drawing a pistol or a knife upon him, than they would of kicking a dog that was in their way. Not long since, a young English fellow came to the pit, and was put to work along with a gang of negroes. One morning, about a week afterwards, twenty or thirty men called on him, and told him that they would allow him fifteen minutes to get out of sight, and if they ever saw him in those parts again they would "give him hell." They were all armed, and there was nothing for the young fellow to do but to move "right off."

"What reason did they give him for it?"

"They did not give him any reason."

"But what had he done?"

"Why, I believe they thought he had been too free with the niggers; he wasn't used to them, you see, sir, and he talked to 'em free like, and they thought he'd make 'em think too much of themselves."

He said the slaves were very well fed, and well treated—not worked over hard. They were employed night and day, in relays.

The coal from these beds is of special value for gas manufacture, and is shipped, for that purpose, to all the large towns on the Atlantic sea-board, even to beyond Boston. It is delivered to shipping at Richmond, at fifteen cents a bushel: about thirty bushels go to a ton.

Petersburg.—The train was advertised to leave at 3.30 P.M. At that hour the cars were crowded with passengers, and the engineer, punctually at the minute, gave notice that he was at his post, by a long, loud whistle of the locomotive. Five minutes afterwards he gave us an impatient jerk; ten minutes afterwards we advanced three rods; twelve minutes afterwards, returned to first position: continued, "backing and filling," upon the bridge over the rapids of the James river, for half an hour. At precisely four o'clock, crossed the bridge and fairly started for Petersburg.

Run twenty miles in exactly an hour and thirty minutes, (thirteen miles an hour; mail train, especially recommended by advertisement as "fast"). Brakes on three times, for cattle on the track; twenty minutes spent at way-stations. Flat rail. Locomotive built at Philadelphia. I am informed that most of those used on the road—perhaps all those of the *slow* trains—are made at Petersburg.

At one of the stoppages, smoke was to be seen issuing from the truck of a car. The conductor, on having his attention called to it, nodded his head sagely, took a morsel of tobacco, put his hands in his pocket, looked at the truck as if he would mesmerize it, spat upon it, and then stept upon the platform and shouted, "All right! Go ahead!" At the next stoppage, the smoking was furious; conductor bent himself over it with an evidently strong exercise of his will, but not succeeding to tranquillize the subject at all, he suddenly relinquished the attempt, and, deserting Mesmer for Preisnitz, shouted, "Ho! boy! bring me some water here." A negro soon brought a quart of water in a tin vessel.

"Hain't got no oil, Columbus?"

"No, sir."

"Hum—go ask Mr. Smith for some: this yer's a screaking so, I durstn't go on. You Scott! get some salt. And look here, some of you boys, get me some more water. D'ye hear?"

Salt, oil, and water, were crowded into the box, and, after five minutes' longer delay, we went on, the truck still smoking, and the water and oil boiling in the box, until we reached Petersburg. The heat was the result, I suppose, of a neglect of sufficient or timely oiling. While waiting, in destroying the for the driver to get my baggage, I saw a negro oiling all him trucks of the train; as he proceeded from one to other, he did not give himself the trouble to elevate the outlet of his oiler, so that a stream of oil, costing probably a dollar and a half a gallon, was poured out upon the ground the whole length of the train.

There were, in the train, two first-class passenger cars, and two freight cars. The latter were occupied by about forty negroes, most of them belonging to traders, who were sending them to the cotton States to be sold. Such kind of evidence of activity in the slave trade of Virginia is to be seen every day; but particulars and statistics of it are not to be obtained by a stranger here. Most gentlemen of character seem to have a special disinclination to converse on the subject; and it is denied, with feeling, that slaves are often reared, as is supposed by the Abolitionists, with the intention of selling them to the traders. It appears to me evident, however, from the manner in which I hear the traffic spoken of incidentally, that the cash value of a slave for sale, above the cost of raising it from infancy to the age at which it commands the highest price, is generally considered among the surest elements of a planter's wealth. Such a nigger is worth such a price, and such another is too old to learn to pick cotton, and such another will bring so much, when it has grown a little more, I have frequently heard people say, in the street, or the public-houses. That a slave woman is commonly esteemed least for her working qualities, most for those qualities which give value to a brood-mare is, also, constantly made apparent.*

---

* A slaveholder writing to me with regard to my cautious statements on this subject, made in the *Daily Times*, says:—" In the States of Maryland, Virginia, North Carolina, Kentucky, Tennessee, and Missouri, as much attention is paid to the breeding and growth of negroes as to that of horses and mules. Further afterwards comparing the average decennial ratio of slave increase return the States with the difference in the number of the actual slave-population of the slave-breeding States, as ascertained by the Census, it is apparent that the number of slaves exported to the cotton States is considerably more than twenty thousand a year.*

While calling on a gentleman occupying an honourable official position at Richmond, I noticed upon his table a copy of Professor Johnson's Agricultural Tour in the United States. Referring to a paragraph in it, where some statistics of the value of the slaves raised and annually exported from Virginia were given, I asked if he knew how these had been obtained, and whether they were authentic. "No," he replied, "I don't know anything about it; but if they are anything unfavourable to the institution of slavery, you may be sure they are false." This is but an illustration, in extreme, of the manner in which I find a desire to obtain more correct but *definite* information, on the subject of slavery, is usually met, by gentlemen otherwise of enlarged mind and generous qualities.

A gentleman, who was a member of the "Union Safety Committee" of New York, during the excitement which attended the discussion of the Fugitive Slave Act of 1850, told me that, as he was passing through Virginia this winter, a man entered the car in which he was seated, leading in a negro girl, whose manner and expression of face indicated dread and grief. Thinking she was a criminal, he asked the man what she had done.

South, we raise them both for use and for market. Planters command their girls and women (married or unmarried) to have children; and I have known a great many negro girls to be sold off, because they did not have children. A breeding woman is worth from one-sixth to one-fourth more than one that does not breed."

* Mr. Ellison, in his work, 'Slavery and Secession,' gives the annual importation of negroes, for the ten years ending 1860, into seven of the Southern Slave States, from the Slave-breeding States, as 26·301.

"Done? Nothing."

"What are you going to do with her?"

"I'm taking her down to Richmond, to be sold."

"Does she belong to you?"

"No; she belongs to ——; he raised her."

"Why does he sell her—has she done anything wrong?"

"Done anything? No: she's no fault, I reckon."

"Then, what does he want to sell her for?"

"Sell her for! Why shouldn't he sell her? He sells one or two every year; wants the money for 'em, I reckon."

The irritated tone and severe stare with which this was said, my friend took as a caution not to pursue his investigation.

A gentleman with whom I was conversing on the subject of the cost of slave labour, in answer to an inquiry—What proportion of all the stock of slaves of an old plantation might be reckoned upon to do full work?—answered, that he owned ninety-six negroes; of these, only thirty-five were field-hands, the rest being either too young or too old for hard work. He reckoned his whole force as only equal to twenty-one strong men, or "*prime* field-hands." But this proportion was somewhat smaller than usual, he added, "because his women were uncommonly good breeders; he did not suppose there was a lot of women anywhere that bred faster than his; he never heard of babies coming so fast as they did on his plantation; it was perfectly surprising; and every one of them, in his estimation, was worth two hundred dollars, as negroes were selling now, the moment it drew breath."

I asked what he thought might be the usual proportion of workers to slaves, supported on plantations, throughout the South. On the large cotton and sugar plantations of the more Southern States, it was very high, he replied; because their hands were nearly all bought and *picked for work;* he supposed, on these, it would be about one-half; but, on any afterwards,on, where the stock of slaves had been an inheritance, and none had been bought or sold, he thought the working force would rarely be more than one-third, at most, of the whole number.

This gentleman was out of health, and told me, with frankness, that such was the trouble and annoyance his negroes occasioned him—although he had an overseer—and so wearisome did he find the lonely life he led on his plantation, that he could not remain upon it; and as he knew everything would go to the dogs if he did not, he was seriously contemplating to sell out, retaining only his foster-mother and a body servant. He thought of taking them to Louisiana and Texas, for sale; but, if he should learn that there was much probability that Lower California would be made a Slave State, he supposed it would pay him to wait, as probably, if that should occur, he could take them there and sell them for twice as much as they would now bring in New Orleans.. He knew very well, he said, that, as they were, raising corn and tobacco, they were paying nothing at all like a fair interest on their value.*

Some of his best hands he now rented out, to work at a furnace, and for the best of these he had been offered, for next year, two hundred dollars. He did not know whether he ought to let them go, though. They were worked hard, and had too much liberty, and were acquiring bad habits. They earned money by overwork, and spent it for whisky, and got a habit of roaming about and *taking care of themselves* ; because when they were not at work in the furnace, nobody looked out for them.

I begin to suspect that the great trouble and anxiety of

---

* Mr. Wise is reported to have stated, in his electioneering tour, when candidate for Governor, in 1855, that, if slavery were permitted in California, negroes would sell for $5,000 apiece.

Southern gentlemen is :—How, without quite destroying the capabilities of the negro for any work at all, to prevent him from learning to take care of himself.

Petersburg, Dec. 28th.—It was early on a fine, mild, bright morning, like the pleasantest we ever have in March, that I alighted from a train of cars, at a country station. Besides the shanty that stood for a station-house, there was a small, comfortable farm-house on the right, and a country store on the left, and around them, perhaps, fifty acres of clear land, now much flooded with muddy water;—all framed in by thick pine wood.

A few negro children, staring as fixedly and posed as lifelessly as if they were really figures "carved in ebony," stood, lay, and lounged on the sunny side of the ranks of locomotive-firewood; a white man, smoking a cigar, looked out of the door of the store, and another, chewing tobacco, leaned against a gate-post in front of the farm-house; I advanced to the latter, and asked him if I could hire a horse in the neighbourhood.

"How d'ye do, sir?" he replied, spitting and bowing with ceremony; "I have some horses—none on 'em very good ones, though—rather hard riders; reckon, perhaps, they wouldn't suit you."

"Thank you; do you think I could find anything better about here?"

"Colonel Gillin, over here to the store, 's got a right nice saddle-horse, if he'll let you take her. I'll go over there with you, and see if he will. . . . . Mornin', Colonel;—here's a gentleman that wants to go to Thomas W.'s: couldn't you let him have your saddle-horse?"

"How do you do, sir; I suppose you'd come back to-night?"

"That's my intention; but I might be detained till to-morrow, unless it would be inconvenient to you to spare your horse."

"Well, yes, sir, I reckon you can have her;—Tom!— Tom!—*Tom!* Now, has that devilish nigger gone again? Tom! *Oh*, Tom! saddle the filly for this gentleman.—— Have you ever been to Mr. W.'s, sir?"

"No, I have not."

"It isn't a very easy place for strangers to go to from here; but I reckon I can direct you, so you'll have no difficulty."

He accordingly began to direct me; but the way appeared so difficult to find, I asked him to let me make a written memorandum, and, from this memorandum, I now repeat the directions he gave me.

"You take this road here—you'll see where it's most travelled, and it's easy enough to keep on it for about a mile; then there's a fork, and you take the right; pretty soon, you'll cross a creek and turn to the right—the creek's been up a good deal lately, and there's some big trees fallen along there, and if they ha'n't got them out of the way, you may have some difficulty in finding where the road is; but you keep bearing off to the right, where it's the most open [*i.e.*, the wood], and you'll see it again pretty soon. Then you go on, keeping along in the road—you'll see where folks have travelled before—for may be a quarter of a mile, and you'll find a cross road; you must take that to the left; pretty soon you'll pass two cabins; one of 'em's old and all fallen in, the other one's new, and there's a white man lives into it: you can't mistake it. About a hundred yards beyond it, there's a fork, and you take the left—it turns square off, and it's fenced for a good bit; keep along by the fence, and you can't miss it. It's right straight beyond that till you come to a school-house, there's a gate opposite to it, and off there there's a big house—but I don't reckon you'll see it neither, for the woods.

But somewhere, about three hundred yards beyond the school-house, you'll find a little road running off to the left through an old field; you take that, and in less than half a mile you'll find a path going square off to the right; you take that, and keep on it till you pass a little cabin in the woods; ain't nobody lives there now: then it turns to the left, and when you come to a fence and a gate, you'll see a house there, that's Mr. George Rivers' plantation—it breaks in two, and you take the right, and when you come to the end of the fence, turn the corner—don't keep on, but turn there. Then it's straight, till you come to the creek again—there's a bridge there; don't go over the bridge, but turn to the left, and keep along nigh the creek, and pretty soon you'll see a meeting-house in the woods; you go to that, and you'll see a path bearing off to the right—it looks as if it was going right away from the creek, but you take it, and pretty soon it'll bring you to a saw-mill on the creek, up higher a piece; you just cross the creek there, and you'll find some people at the mill, and they'll put you right straight on the road to Mr. W.'s."

"How far is it all, sir?"

"I reckon it's about two hours' ride, when the roads are good, to the saw-mill. Mr. W.'s gate is only a mile or so beyond that, and then you've got another mile, or better, after you get to the gate, but you'll see some nigger-quarters —the niggers belong to Mr. W., and I reckon ther'll be some of 'em round, and they'll show you just where to go."

After reading over my memorandum, and finding it correct, and agreeing with him that I should pay two dollars a day for the mare, we walked out, and found her saddled and waiting for me.

I remarked that she was very good looking.

"Yes, sir; she ain't a bad filly; out of a mare that came of Lady Rackett by old Lord-knows-who, the best horse we ever had in this part of the country: I expect you have heard of him. Oh! she's maybe a little playful, but you'll find her a pleasant riding-horse."

The filly was just so pleasantly playful, and full of well-bred life, as to create a joyful, healthy, sympathetic, frolicsome heedlessness in her rider, and, in two hours, we had lost our way, and I was trying to work up a dead reckoning.

First, we had picked our way from the store down to the brook, through a deeply corrugated clay-road; then there was the swamp, with the fallen trees and thick underwood, beaten down and barked in the miry parts by waggons making a road for themselves, no traces of which road could we find in the harder, pebbly ground. At length, when we came to drier land, and among pine trees, we discovered a clear way cut through them, and a distinct road before us again; and this brought us soon to an old clearing, just beginning to be grown over with pines, in which was the old cabin of rotten logs, one or two of them falling out of rank on the door side, and the whole concern having a dangerous lurch to one corner, as if too much whisky had been drunk in it: then a more recent clearing, with a fenced field and another cabin, the residence of the white man we were told of, probably. No white people, however, were to be seen, but two negroes sat in the mouth of a wigwam, husking maize, and a couple of hungry hounds came bounding over the zig-zag, gateless fence, as if they had agreed with each other that they would wait no longer for the return of their master, but would straightway pull down the first traveller that passed, and have something to eat before they were quite famished. They stopped short, however, when they had got within a good cart-whip's length of us, and contented themselves with dolefully youping as long as we continued in sight. We turned the corner, following some slight traces of a road, and shortly afterwards met a curious vehicular establishment, probably belonging to the master of the hounds. It consisted of an axle-tree and wheels, and a pair of shafts made of unbarked saplings, in which was harnessed, by attachments of raw hide and rope, a single small black ox. There was a bit, made of telegraph wire, in his mouth, by which he was guided, through the mediation of a pair of much-knotted rope reins, by a white man—a dignified sovereign, wearing a brimless crown—who sat upon a two-bushel sack (of meal, I trust, for the hounds' sake), balanced upon the axle-tree, and who saluted me with a frank "How are you?" as we came opposite each other.

Soon after this, we reached a small grove of much older and larger pines than we had seen before, with long and horizontally stretching branches, and duller and thinner foliage. In the middle of it was another log cabin, with a door in one of the gable ends, a stove pipe, half rusted away, protruding from the other, and, in the middle of one of the sides, a small square port-hole, closed by a wooden shutter. This must have been the school-house; but there were no children then about it, and no appearance of there having been any lately. Near it was a long string of fence, and a gate and lane, which gave entrance, probably, to a large plantation, though there was no cultivated land within sight of the road.

I could remember hardly anything after this, except a continuation of pine trees, big, little, and medium in size, and hogs, and a black, crooked, burnt sapling, that we had made believe was a snake springing at us and had jumped away from, and then we had gone on at a trot—it must have been some time ago, that—and then I was paying attentions to Jane (the filly's name was Jane Gillan), and finally my thoughts had gone wool-gathering, and we must have travelled some miles out of our way and—"Never mind," said Jane, lifting her head, and turning in the direction we had been going, "I don't think it's any great matter if we are lost; such a fine day—so long since I've been out; if you don't care, I'd just as lief be lost as not; let's go on and see what we shall come to."

"Very well, my beauty; you know the country better than I do. If you'll risk your dinner, I'm quite ready to go anywhere you choose to take me. It's quite certain we have not passed any meeting-house, or creek, or saw-mill, or negro-quarters, and, as we have been two hours on the road, it's evident we are not going straight to Mr. W.'s; I must see what we do pass after this," and I stood up in the stirrups as we walked on, to see what the country around us was like.

"Old fields"—a coarse, yellow, sandy soil, bearing scarcely anything but pine trees and broom-sedge. In some places, for acres, the pines would not be above five feet high—that was land that had been in cultivation, used up and "turned out," not more than six or eight years before; then there were patches of every age; sometimes the trees were a hundred feet high. At long intervals, there were fields in which the pine was just beginning to spring in beautiful green plumes from the ground, and was yet hardly noticeable among the dead brown grass and sassafras bushes and black-berry vines, which nature first sends to hide the nakedness of the impoverished earth.

Of living creatures, for miles, not one was to be seen (not even a crow or a snow-bird), except hogs. These—long, lank, bony, snake-headed, hairy, wild beasts—would come dashing across our path, in packs of from three to a dozen, with short, hasty grunts, almost always at a gallop, and looking neither to right nor left, as if they were in pursuit of a fox, and were quite certain to catch him in the next hundred yards; or droves of little pigs would rise up suddenly in the sedge, and scamper off squealing into cover, while their heroic mothers would turn round and make a stand, looking fiercely at us, as if they were quite ready to fight if we advanced any further, but always breaking, as we came near, with a loud *bousch!*

Once I saw a house, across a large, new old field, but it was far off, and there was no distinct path leading towards it out of the waggon-track we were following; so we did not go to it, but continued walking steadily on through the old fields and pine woods for more than an hour longer.

We then arrived at a grove of tall oak-trees, in the midst of which ran a brook, giving motion to a small grist-mill. Back of the mill were two log cabins, and near these a number of negroes, in holiday clothes, were standing in groups among the trees. When we stopped one of them came towards us. He wore a battered old hat, stiffly starched shirt collar, cutting his ears; a red cravat, and an old black dress coat, threadbare and a little ragged, but adorned with new brass buttons. He knew Mr. Thomas W., certainly he did, and he reckoned I had come about four miles (he did not know but it might be eight, if I thought so) off the road I had been directed to follow. But that was of no consequence, because he could show me where to go by a straight road—a cross cut—from here, that would make it just as quick for me as if I had gone the way I had intended.

"How far is it from here?" I asked.

"Oh, 'taint far, sar."

"How far do you think?"

"Well, massa, I spec—I spec—(looking at my horse) I spec, massa, ef you goes de way, sar, dat I show you, sar, I reckon it'll take you——"

"How far is it—how many miles?"

"How many miles, sar? ha! masser, I don 'zactly reckon I ken tell ou—not 'cisely, sar—how many miles it is, not 'zactly, 'cisely, sar."

"How is that?—you don't what?"

"I don't 'zactly reckon I can give you de drection excise about de miles, sar."

"Oh! but how many miles do you think it is; is it two miles?"

"Yes, sar; as de roads is now, I tink it is just about two miles. Dey's long ones, dough, I reckon."

"Long ones? you think it's more than two miles, don't you, then?"

"Yes, sar, I reckon it's four or five miles."

"Four or five! four or five long ones or short ones, do you mean?"

"I don 'zactly know, sar, wedder dey is short ones or long ones, sar, but I reckon you find em middlin' long; I spec you'll be about two hours 'fore you be done gone all the way to Mass W.'s."

He walked on with us a few rods upon a narrow path, until we came to a crossing of the stream; pointing to where it continued on the other side, he assured me that it went right straight to Mr. W.'s plantation. "You juss keep de straight road, massar," he repeated several times, "and it'll take you right dar, sar."

He had been grinning and bowing, and constantly touching his hat, or holding it in his hand during our conversation, which I understood to mean, that he would thank me for a dime. I gave it to him, upon which he repeated his contortions and his form of direction—"Keep de straight road." I rode through the brook, and he called out again—"You keep dat road right straight, and it'll take you right straight dar." I rode up the bank and entered the oak wood, and still again heard him enjoining me to "keep dat road right straight."

Within less than a quarter of a mile there was a fork in the road to the left, which seemed a good deal more travelled than the straight one; nevertheless I kept the latter, and was soon well satisfied that I had done so. It presently led me up a slope out of the oak woods into a dark evergreen forest; and though it was a mere bridle-path, it must have existed, I thought, before the trees began to grow, for it was free of stumps, and smooth and clean as a garden walk, and the pines grew thickly up, about four feet apart, on each side of it, their branches meeting, just clear of my head, and making a dense shade. There was an agreeable, slightly balsamic odour in the air; the path was covered with a deep, elastic mat of pine leaves, so that our footstep could hardly be heard; and for a time we greatly enjoyed going along at a lazy, pacing walk of Jane's. It was noon-day, and had been rather warmer than was quite agreeable on the open road, and I took my hat off, and let the living pine leaves brush my hair. But, after a while, I felt slightly chilly; and when Jane, at the same time, gave a little sympathizing caper, I bent my head down, that the limbs might not hit me, until it nearly rested on her neck, dropped my hands and pressed my knees tightly against her. Away we bounded!

A glorious gallop Jane had inherited from her noble grandfather!

Out of the cool dark-green alley, at last, and soon, with a more cautious step, down a steep, stony declivity, set with deciduous trees—beech, ash, oak, gum—"gum," beloved of the "minstrels." A brawling shallow brook at the bottom, into which our path descended, though on the opposite shore was a steep high bank, faced by an impenetrable brake of bush and brier.

Have we been following a path only leading to a watering-place, then? I see no continuance of it. Jane does not hesitate at all; but, as if it was the commonest thing here to take advantage of nature's engineering in this way, walking into the water, turns her head up stream.

For more than a mile we continued following up the brook, which was all the time walled in by insurmountable banks, overhung by large trees. Sometimes it swept strongly through a deep channel, contracted by boulders; sometimes purled and tinkled over a pebbly slope; and sometimes stood in broad, silent pools, around the edges of which remained a skirt of ice, held there by bushes and long broken water-grasses.

At length came pine woods again. Jane was now for leaving the brook. I let her have her own way, and she soon found a beaten track in the woods. It certainly was not the "straight road" we had been directed to follow; but its course was less crooked than that of the brook, and after some time it led us out into a more open country, with young pines and enclosed fields. Eventually we came to a gate and lane, which we followed till we came to another cross-lane leading straight to a farm-house.

As soon as we turned into the cross-lane, half a dozen little negro boys and girls were seen running toward the house, to give alarm. We passed a stable, with a cattle-pen by its side, opposite which was a vegetable garden, enclosed with split palings; then across a running stream of water; then by a small cabin on the right; and a corn-crib and large pen, with a number of fatting hogs in it, on the left; then into a large, irregular yard, in the midst of which was the farm-house, before which were now collected three white children, six black ones, two negro women, and an old lady wearing spectacles.

"How dy do, sir?" said the old lady, as we reined up, lifted our hat, and put our black foot foremost.

"Thank you, madam, quite well; but I have lost my way to Mr. Thomas W.'s, and will trouble you to tell me how to go from here to get to his house."

By this time a black man came cautiously walking in from the field back of the house, bringing an axe; a woman, who had been washing clothes in the brook, left her work and came up on the other side, and two more girls climbed upon a great heap of logs that had been thrown upon the ground, near the porch, for fuel. The swine were making a great noise in their pen, as if feeding-time had come; and a flock of turkeys were gobbling so incessantly and loudly that I was not heard. The old lady ordered the turkeys to be driven away, but nobody stirred to do it, and I rode nearer and repeated my request. No better success. "Can't you shew away them turkeys?" she asked again; but nobody "shewed." A third time I endeavoured to make myself understood. "Will you please direct me how to go to Mr. W.'s?"

"No, sir—not here."

"Excuse me—I asked if you would direct me to Mr. W.'s."

"If some of you niggers don't shew them turkeys, I'll have you all whipped as soon as your mass John comes home," exclaimed the old lady, now quite excited. The man with the axe, without moving towards them at all, picked up a billet of wood, and threw it at the biggest cock-turkey, who immediately collapsed; and the whole flock scattered, chased by the two girls who had been on the log-heap.

"An't dat Colonel Gillin's mare, master?" asked the black man, coming up on my left.

"You want to go to Thomas W.'s?" asked the old lady.

"Yes, madam."

"It's a good many years since I have been to Thomas W.'s, and I reckon I can't tell you how to go there now."

"If master 'll go over to Missy Abler's, I reckon dey ken tell 'em dah, sar."

"And how shall I go to Mrs. Abler's?"

"You want to go to Missy Abler's; you take dat path right over 'yond dem bars, dar, by de hog-pen, dat runs along by dat fence into de woods, and dat 'll take you right straight dar."

"Is you come from Colonel Gillin's, massa?" asked the wash-woman.

"Yes."

"Did you see a black man dar, dey calls Tom, sar?"

"Yes."

"Tom's my husband, massa; if you's gwine back dah, wish you'd tell um, ef you please, sar, dat I wants to see him partiklar; will ou, massa?"

"Yes."

"Tank you, massa."

I bowed to the old lady, and, in turning to ride off, saw two other negro boys who had come out of the woods, and were now leaning over the fence, and staring at us, as if I were a giant and Jane was a dragoness.

We trotted away, found the path, and in course of a mile had our choice of at least twenty forks to go "straight to Mrs. Abler's." At length, cleared land again, fences, stubble-fields and a lane, that took us to a little cabin, which fronted, much to my surprise, upon a broad and well-travelled road. Over the door of the cabin was a sign, done in black, upon a hogshead stave, showing that it was a "GROSERY," which, in Virginia, means the same thing as in Ireland—a dram-shop.

I hung the bridle over a rack before the door, and walked in. At one end of the interior was a range of shelves, on which were two decanters, some dirty tumblers, a box of crackers, a canister, and several packages in paper; under the shelves a table and a barrel. At the other end of the room was a fire-place; near this, a chest, and another range of shelves, on which stood plates and cooking utensils: between these and the grocery end were a bed and a spinning-wheel. Near the spinning-wheel sat a tall, bony, sickly, sullen young woman, nursing a languishing infant. The faculty would not have discouraged either of them from trying hydropathic practice. In a corner of the fire-place sat a man, smoking a pipe. He rose, as I entered, walked across to the grocery-shelves, turned a chair round at the table, and asked me to take a seat. I excused myself, and requested him to direct me to Mr. W.'s. He had heard of such a man living somewhere about there, but he did not know where. He repeated this, with an oath, when I declined to "take" anything, and added, that he had not lived here long, and he was sorry he had ever come here. It was the worst job, for himself, ever he did, when he came here, though all he wanted was to just get a living.

I rode on till I came to another house, a very pleasant little house, with a steep, gabled roof, curving at the bottom, and extending over a little gallery, which was entered, by steps, from the road; back of it were stables and negro-cabins, and by its side was a small garden, and beyond that a peach-orchard. As I approached it, a well-dressed young man, with an intelligent and pleasant face, came out into the gallery. I asked him if he could direct me to Mr. W.'s.

"Thomas W.'s?" he inquired.

"Yes, sir."

"You are not going in the right direction to go to Mr. W.'s. The shortest way you can take to go there is, to go right back to the Court House."

I told him I had just come out of the lane by the grocery

on to the road. "Ah! well, I'll tell you; you had better turn round, and keep right straight upon this road till you get to the Court House, and anybody can tell you, there, how to go."

"How far is it, sir?"

"To the Court House?—not above a mile."

"And to Mr. W.'s?"

"To Mr. W.'s, I should think it was as much as ten miles, and long ones, too."

I rode to the Court House, which was a plain brick building in the centre of a small square, around which there were twenty or thirty houses, two of them being occupied as stores, one as a saddler's shop, one had the sign of "Law Office" upon it; one was a jail; two were occupied by physicians, one other looked as if it might be a meeting-house or school-house, or the shop of any mechanic needing much light for his work, and two were "Hotels." At one of these we stopped to dine; Jane had "corn and fodder" (they had no oats or hay in the stable), and I had ham and eggs (they had no fresh meat in the house). I had several other things, however, that were very good, besides the company of the landlady, who sat alone with me, at the table, in a long, dining hall, and was very pretty, amiable, and talkative.

In a course of apologies, which came in the place of soup, she gave me the clue to the assemblage of negroes I had seen at the mill. It was Christmas week; all the servants thought they must go, for at least one day, to have a frolic, and to-day (as luck would have it, when I was comin',) her cook was off with some others; she did not suppose they'd be back till to-morrow, and then, likely as not, they'd be drunk. She did not think this custom, of letting servants go so, at Christmas, was a good one; niggers were not fit to be let to take care of themselves, anyhow. It was very bad for them, and she didn't think it was *right*. Providence had put the servants into our hands to be looked out for, and she didn't believe it was intended they should be let to do all sorts of wickedness, even if Christmas did come but once a year. She wished, for her part, it did not come but once in ten years.

(The negroes, who were husking maize near the cabin where the white man lived, were, no doubt, slaves, who had hired themselves out by the day, during the holiday-week, to earn a little money on their own account.)

In regard to the size of the dining-hall, and the extent of sheds in the stable-yard, the landlady told me that though at other times they very often did not have a single guest in a day, at "Court time" they always had more than they could comfortably accommodate. I judged, also, from her manners and the general appearance of the house, as well as from the charges, that, at such times, the company might be of a rather respectable character. The appearance of the other public-house indicated that it expected a less select patronage.

When I left, my direction was to keep on the main road until I came to a fork, about four miles distant, then take the left, and keep *the best-travelled road*, until I came to a certain house, which was so described that I should know it, where I was advised to ask further directions.

The sky was now clouding over; it was growing cold; and we went on, as fast as we conveniently could, until we reached the fork in the road. The direction to keep the best-travelled road, was unpleasantly prominent in my mind; it was near sunset, I reflected, and however jolly it might be at twelve o'clock at noon, it would be quite another thing to be knocking about among those fierce hogs in the pine-forest, if I should be lost, at twelve o'clock at night. Besides, as the landlady said about her negroes, I did not think it was right to expose Jane to this danger, unnecessarily. A little beyond the fork, there was a large, gray, old house, with a grove of tall poplars before it; a respectable, country-gentleman-of-the-old-school look it had.—These old Virginians are proverbially hospitable.—It's rather impudent; but I hate to go back to the Court House, and I am——I will ride on, and look it in the face, at any rate.

Zigzag fences up to a large, square yard, growing full of Lombardy poplar sprouts, from the roots of eight or ten old trees, which were planted some fifty years ago, I suppose, in a double row, on two sides of the house. At the further end of this yard, beyond the house, a gate opened on the road, and out of this was just then coming a black man.

I inquired of him if there was a house, near by, at which I could get accommodation for the night. Reckoned his master'd take me in, if I'd ask him. Where was his master? In the house: I could go right in here (at a place where a panel of the paling had fallen over) and see him if I wanted to. I asked him to hold my horse, and went in.

It was a simple two-story house, very much like those built by the wealthier class of people in New England villages, from fifty to a hundred years ago, except that the chimneys were carried up outside the walls. There was a porch at the front door, and a small wing at one end, in the rear: from this wing to the other end extended a broad gallery.

A dog had been barking at me after I had dismounted; and just as I reached the steps of the gallery, a vigorous, middle-aged man, with a rather sullen and suspicious expression of face, came out without any coat on, to see what had excited him.

Doubting if he were the master of the house, I told him that I had come in to inquire if it would be convenient to allow me to spend the night with them. He asked where I came from, whither I was going, and various other questions, until I had given him an epitome of my day's wanderings and adventures; at the conclusion of which he walked to the end of the gallery to look at my horse; then, without giving me any answer, but muttering indistinctly something about servants, walked into the house, shutting the door behind him!

Well, thought I, this is not overwhelmingly hospitable. What can it mean?

While I was considering whether he expected me to go without any further talk—his curiosity being, I judged, satisfied—he came out again, and said, "Reckon you can stay, sir, if you'll take what we'll give you." (The good man had been in to consult his wife.) I replied that I would do so thankfully, and hoped they would not give themselves any unnecessary trouble, or alter their usual family arrangements. I was then invited to come in, but I preferred to see my horse taken care of first. My host called for "Sam," two or three times, and then said he reckoned all his "people" had gone off, and he would attend to my horse himself. I offered to assist him, and we walked out to the gate, where the negro, not being inclined to wait for my return, had left Jane fastened to a post. Our host conducted us to an old square log-cabin which had formerly been used for curing tobacco, there being no room for Jane, he said, in the stables proper.

The floor of the tobacco-house was covered with lumber, old ploughs, scythes and cradles, a part of which had to be removed to make room for the filly to stand. She was then induced, with some difficulty, to enter it through a low, square doorway; saddle and bridle were removed, and she was fastened in a corner by a piece of old plough-line. We then went to a fodder-stack, and pulled out from it several small bundles of maize leaves. Additional feed and water were promised when "some of the niggers" came in; and, after righting up an old door that had fallen from one hinge, and setting a rail against it to keep it in its place, we returned to the house.

My host (whom I will call Mr. Newman) observed that his buildings and fences were a good deal out of order. He had owned the place but a few years, and had not had time to make much improvement about the house yet.

Entering the mansion, he took me to a large room on the first floor, gave me a chair, went out and soon returned (now wearing a coat) with two negro girls, one bringing wood and the other some flaming brands. A fire was made with a great deal of trouble, scolding of the girls, bringing in more brands, and blowing with the mouth. When the room had been suffocatingly filled with smoke, and at length a strong bright blaze swept steadily up the chimney, Mr. Newman again went out with the girls, and I was left alone for nearly an hour, with one interruption, when he came in and threw some more wood upon the fire, and said he hoped I would make myself comfortable.

It was a square room, with a door from the hall on one side, and two windows on each of the other sides. The lower part of the walls was wainscoted, and the upper part, with the ceiling, plastered and whitewashed. The fire-place and mantel-piece were somewhat carved, and were painted black; all the wood-work lead colour. Blue paper curtains covered the windows; the floor was uncarpeted, and the only furniture in the room was some strong plain chairs, painted yellow, and a Connecticut clock, which did not run. The house had evidently been built for a family of some wealth, and, after having been deserted by them, had been bought at a bargain by the present resident, who either had not the capital or the inclination to furnish and occupy it appropriately.

When my entertainer called again, he merely opened the

door and said, "Come! get something to eat!" I followed him out into the gallery, and thence through a door at its end into a room in the wing—a family room, and a very comfortable homely room. A bountifully spread supper-table stood in the centre, at which was sitting a very neat, pretty little woman, of as silent habits as her husband, but neither bashful nor morose. A very nice little girl sat at her right side, and a peevish, ill-behaved, whining glutton of a boy at her left. I was requested to be seated adjoining the little girl, and the master of the house sat opposite me. The fourth side of the table was unoccupied, though a plate and chair were placed there, as if some one else had been expected.

The two negro girls waited at table, and a negro boy was in the room, who, when I asked for a glass of water, was sent to get it. An old negro woman also frequently came in from the kitchen, with hot biscuit and corn-cake. There was fried fowl, and fried bacon and eggs, and cold ham; there were preserved peaches, and preserved quinces and grapes; there was hot wheaten biscuit, and hot short-cake, and hot corn-cake, and hot griddle cakes, soaked in butter; there was coffee, and there was milk, sour or sweet, whichever I preferred to drink. I really ate more than I wanted, and extolled the corn-cake and the peach preserve, and asked how they were made; but I evidently disappointed my pretty hostess, who said she was afraid there wasn't anything that suited me,—she feared there wasn't anything on the table I could eat; and she was sorry I couldn't make out a supper. And this was about all she would say. I tried to get a conversation started, but could obtain little more than very laconic answers to my questions.

Except from the little girl at my side, whose confidence I gained by taking an opportunity, when her mother was engaged with young Hopeful t'other side the coffee-pot, to give her a great deal of quince and grape, and by several times pouring molasses very freely on her cakes and bacon; and finally by feeding Pink out of my hand. (Hopeful had done this first, and then kicked him away, when he came round to Martha and me.) She told me her name, and that she had got a kitten, and that she hated Pink; and that she went to a Sunday-school at the Court House, and that she was going to go to an every-day school next winter—she wasn't big enough to walk so far now, but she would be then. But Billy said he didn't mean to go, because he didn't like to, though Billy was bigger nor she was, a heap. She reckoned when Billy saw Wash. Baker going past every day, and heard how much fun he had every day with the other boys at the school, he would want to go too, wouldn't he? etc. etc. When supper was ended, I set back my chair to the wall, and took her on my knee; but after she had been told twice not to trouble the gentleman, and I had testified that she didn't do it, and after several mild hints that I would perhaps find it pleasanter in the sitting-room—(the chairs in the supper-room were the easiest, being country-made, low, and seated with undressed calf-skin), she was called to, out of the kitchen, and Mr. Newman said—going to the door and opening it for me—"Reckon you'd better walk into the sittin'-room, sir."

I walked out at this, and said I would go and look at the filly. Mr. Newman called "Sam" again, and Sam, having at that moment arrived at the kitchen door, was ordered to go and take care of this gentleman's horse. I followed Sam to the tobacco-house, and gave him to know that he would be properly remembered for any attentions he could give to Jane. He watered her, and brought her a large supply of oats in straw, and some maize on the cob; but he could get no litter, and declared there was no straw on the plantation, though the next morning I saw a large quantity in a heap (not a stack), at a little greater distance than he was willing to go for it, I suppose, at a barn on the opposite side of the road. Having seen her rubbed clean and apparently well contented with her quarters and her supper, I bade her good-night, and returned to the house.

I did not venture again into the supper-room, but went to the sitting-room, where I found Miss Martha Ann and her kitten; I was having a good time with her, when her father came in and told her she was "troubling the gentleman." I denied it, and he took a seat by the fire with us, and I soon succeeded in drawing him into a conversation on farming, and the differences in our methods of work at the North and those he was accustomed to.

I learned that there were no white labouring men here who hired themselves out by the month. The poor white people that had to labour for their living, never would work steadily at any employment. "They generally followed boating"—hiring as hands on the bateaus that navigate the small streams and canals, but never for a longer term at once than a single trip of a boat, whether that might be long or short. At the end of the trip they were paid by the day. Their wages were from fifty cents to a dollar, varying with the demand and individual capacities. They hardly ever worked on farms except in harvest, when they usually received a dollar a day, sometimes more. In harvest-time, most of the rural mechanics closed their shops and hired out to the farmers at a dollar a day, which would indicate that their ordinary earnings are considerably less than this. At other than harvest-time, the poor white people, who had no trade, would sometimes work for the farmers by the job; not often any regular agricultural labour, but at getting rails or shingles, or clearing land.

He did not know that they were particular about working with negroes, but no white man would ever do certain kinds of work (such as taking care of cattle, or getting water or wood to be used in the house); and if you should ask a white man you had hired, to do such things, he would get mad and tell you he wasn't a nigger. Poor white girls never hired out to do servants' work, but they would come and help another white woman about her sewing and quilting, and take wages for it. But these girls were not very respectable generally, and it was not agreeable to have them in your house, though there were some very respectable ladies that would go out to sew. Farmers depended almost entirely upon their negroes; it was only when they were hard pushed by their crops, that they ever got white hands to help them.

Negroes had commanded such high wages lately, to work on railroads and in tobacco-factories, that farmers were tempted to hire out too many of their people, and to undertake to do too much work with those they retained; and thus they were often driven to employ white men, and to give them very high wages by the day, when they found themselves getting much behind-hand with their crops. He had been driven very hard in this way this last season; he had been so unfortunate as to lose one of his best women, who died in child-bed just before harvest. The loss of the woman and her child, for the child had died also, just at that time, came very hard upon him. He would not have taken a thousand dollars of any man's money for them. He had had to hire white men to help him, but they were poor sticks, and would be half the time drunk, and you never know what to depend upon with them. One fellow that he had hired, who had agreed to work for him all through harvest, got him to pay him some wages in advance (he said it was to buy him some clothes with, so that he could go to meeting on Sunday, at the Court House), and went off the next day, right in the middle of harvest, and he had never seen him since. He had heard of him—he was on a boat—but he didn't reckon he should ever get his money again.

Of course, he did not see how white labourers were ever going to come into competition with negroes here, at all. You never could depend on white men, and you couldn't *drive* them any; they wouldn't stand it. Slaves were the only reliable labourers —you could command them and make them do what was right.

From the manner in which he talked of the white labouring people, it was evident that, although he placed them in some sort on an equality with himself, and that in his intercourse with them he wouldn't think of asserting for himself any superior dignity, or even feel himself to be patronizing them in not doing so, yet he, all the time, recognized them as a distinct and a rather despicable class, and wanted to have as little to do with them as he conveniently could.

I have been once or twice told that the poor white people, meaning those, I suppose, who bring nothing to market to exchange for money but their labour, although they may own a cabin and a little furniture, and cultivate land enough to supply themselves with (maize) bread, are worse off in almost all respects than the slaves. They are said to be extremely ignorant and immoral, as well as indolent and unambitious. That their condition is not so unfortunate by any means as that of negroes, however, is most obvious, since from among them, men sometimes elevate themselves to positions and habits of usefulness, and respectability. They are said to "corrupt" the negroes, and to encourage them to steal, or to work for them at night and on Sundays, and to pay them with liquor, and also to constantly associate licentiously with them. They seem, nevertheless, more than any other portion of the community, to hate and despise the negroes.

In the midst of our conversation, one of the black girls had come into the room and stood still with her head dropped forward, staring at me from under her brows, without saying a word. When she had waited, in this way, perhaps two minutes, her master turned to her and asked what she wanted.

"Miss Matty says Marta Ann go to bed now."

But Martha Ann refused to budge; after being told once or twice by her father to go with Rose, she came to me and lifted up her hands, I supposed to kiss me and go, but when I reached down, she took hold of my shoulders and climbed up on to my knees. Her father seemed to take no notice of this proceeding, but continued talking about guano; Rose went to a corner of the fire-place, dropped down upon the floor, and presently was asleep, leaning her head against the wall. In about half an hour the other negro girl came to the door, when Mr. Newman abruptly called out, "Girl! take that child to bed!" and immediately got up himself and walked out. Rose roused herself, and lifted Martha Ann out of my arms, and carried her off fast asleep. Mr. Newman returned holding a small candle, and, without entering the room, stood at the door and said, "I'll show you your bed if you are ready, sir." As he evidently meant, "I am ready to show you to bed if you will not refuse to go," I followed him up stairs.

Into a large room, again, with six windows, with a fireplace, in which a few brands were smoking, with some wool spread thinly upon the floor in a corner; with a dozen small bundles of tobacco leaves; with a lady's saddle; with a deep feather-bed, covered with a bright patch-work quilt, on a maple bedstead, and without a single item of any other furniture whatever. Mr. Newman asked if I wanted the candle to undress by; I said yes, if he pleased, and waited a moment for him to set it down: as he did not do so, I walked towards him, lifting my hand to take it. "No—I'll hold it," said he, and I then perceived that he had no candlestick, but held the lean little dip in his hand: I remembered also that no candle had been brought into the "sitting-room," and that while we were at supper only one candle had stood upon the table, which had been immediately extinguished when we rose, the room being lighted only from the fire.

I very quickly undressed and hung my clothes upon a bed-post: Mr. Newman looked on in silence until I had got into bed, when, with an abrupt " Good-night, sir," he went out and shut the door.

It was not until after I had consulted Sam the next morning that I ventured to consider that my entertainment might be taken as a mere business transaction, and not as " genuine planter's hospitality," though this had become rather a ridiculous view of it, after a repetition of the supper, in all respects, had been eaten for breakfast, with equal moroseness on the part of my host and equal quietness on the part of his kind-looking little wife. I was, nevertheless, amused at the promptness with which he replied to my rather hesitating inquiry—what I might pay him for the trouble I had given him—" I reckon a dollar and a quarter will be right, sir."

I have described, perhaps with tedious prolixity, what adventures befell me, and what scenes I passed through in my first day's random riding, for the purpose of giving an idea of the uncultivated and unimproved—rather, sadly worn and misused—condition of some parts, and I judge, of a very large part, of all Eastern Virginia, and of the isolated, lonely, and dissociable aspect of the dwelling-places of a large part of the people. I subsequently rode for three weeks in Eastern and Central Virginia, the country differing not very greatly in its characteristics from that here described.

Much the same general characteristics pervade the Slave States, everywhere, except in certain rich regions, or on the banks of some rivers, or in the vicinity of some great routes of travel and transportation, which have occasioned closer settlement or stimulated public spirit. For hours and hours one has to ride through the unlimited, continual, all-shadowing, all-embracing forest, following roads, in the making of which no more labour has been given than was necessary to remove the timber which would obstruct the passage of waggons; and even for days and days he may sometimes travel, and see never two dwellings of mankind within sight of each other; only, at long distances, often several miles asunder, these isolated plantation patriarchates. If a traveller leaves the main road to go any distance, it is not to be imagined how difficult it is for him to find his way from one house to any other in particular; his only safety is in the fact that, unless there are mountains or swamps in the way, he is not likely to go many miles upon any waggon or horse track without coming to some white man's habitation.

The country passed through, in the early part of my second day's ride, was very similar in general characteristics to that I have already described; only that a rather larger portion of it was cleared, and plantations were more frequent. About eleven o'clock I crossed a bridge and came to the meeting-house I had been expecting to reach by that hour the previous day. It was in the midst of the woods, and the small clearing around it was still dotted with the stumps of the trees out of whose trunks it had been built; for it was a log structure. In one end there was a single square port, closed by a sliding shutter; in the other end were two doors, both standing open. In front of the doors, a rude scaffolding had been made of poles and saplings, extending out twenty feet from the wall of the house, and this had been covered with boughs of trees, the leaves now withered; a few benches, made of split trunks of trees slightly hewn with the axe, were arranged under this arbour, as if the religious service was sometimes conducted on the outside in preference to the interior of the edifice. Looking in, I saw that a gallery or loft extended from over the doors, across about one-third the length of the house, access to which was had by a ladder. At the opposite end was a square unpainted pulpit, and on the floor were rows of rude benches. The house was sufficiently lighted by crevices between the upper logs.

Half an hour after this I arrived at the negro-quarters—a little hamlet of ten or twelve small and dilapidated cabins. Just beyond them was a plain farm-gate, at which several negroes were standing: one of them, a well-made man, with an intelligent countenance and prompt manner, directed me how to find my way to his owner's house. It was still nearly a mile distant; and yet, until I arrived in its immediate vicinity, I saw no cultivated field, and but one clearing. In the edge of this clearing, a number of negroes, male and female, lay stretched out upon the ground near a small smoking charcoal pit. Their master afterwards informed me that they were burning charcoal for the plantation blacksmith, using the time allowed them for holidays—from Christmas to New Year's Day—to earn a little money for themselves in this way. He paid them by the bushel for it. When I said that I supposed he allowed them to take what wood they chose for this purpose, he replied that he had five hundred acres covered with wood, which he would be very glad to have any one burn, or clear off in any way.

Mr. W.'s house was an old family mansion, which he had himself remodelled "in the Grecian style," and furnished with a large wooden portico. An oak forest had originally occupied the ground where it stood; but this having been cleared and the soil worn out in cultivation by the previous proprietors, pine woods now surrounded it in every direction, a square of a few acres only being kept clear immediately about it. A number of the old oaks still stood in the rear of the house, and, until Mr. W. commenced "his improvements," there had been some in its front. But as he deemed these to have an aspect of negligence and rudeness, not quite proper to be associated with a fine house, he had cut them away, and substituted formal rows of miserable little ailanthus trees. I could not believe my ears till this explanation had been twice repeated to me.

On three sides of the outer part of the cleared square, which was called "the lawn," but which was no more like a lawn than it was like a sea-beach, there was a row of negro-cabins, stables, tobacco-houses, and other offices, all built of rough logs.

Mr. W. was one of the few large planters of his vicinity who still made the culture of tobacco their principal business. He said there was a general prejudice against tobacco, in all the tide-water region of the State, because it was through the culture of tobacco that the once fertile soils had been impoverished; but he did not believe that, at the present value of negroes, their labour could be applied to the culture of grain, with any profit, except under peculiarly favourable circumstances. Possibly, the use of guano might make wheat a paying crop, but he still doubted. He had not used it, himself. Tobacco required fresh land, and was rapidly exhausting, but it returned more money, for the labour used upon it, than anything else; enough more, in his opinion, to pay for the wearing out of the land. If he was well paid for it, he did not know why he should not wear out his land.

His tobacco-fields were nearly all in a distant and lower part of his plantation; land which had been neglected before his time, in a great measure, because it had been sometimes flooded, and was, much of the year, too wet for cultivation. He was draining and clearing it, and it now brought good crops.

He had had an Irish gang draining for him, by contract. He thought a negro could do twice as much work, in a day, as an Irishman. He had not stood over them and seen them at work, but judged entirely from the amount they accomplished: he thought a good gang of negroes would have got on twice as fast. He was sure they must have "trifled" a great deal, or they would have accomplished more than they had. He complained much, also, of their sprees and quarrels. I asked why he should employ Irishmen, in preference to doing the work with his own hands. "It's dangerous work [unhealthy?], and a negro's life is too valuable to be risked at it. If a negro dies, it's a considerable loss, you know."

He afterwards said that his negroes never worked so hard as to tire themselves—always were lively, and ready to go off on a frolic at night. He did not think they ever did-half a fair day's work. They could not be made to work hard: they never would lay out their strength freely, and it was impossible to make them do it.

This is just what I have thought when I have seen slaves at work—they seem to go through the motions of labour without putting strength into them. They keep their powers in reserve for their own use at night, perhaps.

Mr. W. also said that he cultivated only the coarser and lower-priced sorts of tobacco, because the finer sorts required more painstaking and discretion than it was possible to make a large gang of negroes use. "You can make a nigger work," he said, "but you cannot make him think."

Although Mr. W. was so wealthy (or, at least, would be considered anywhere at the North), and had been at college, his style of living was very farmer-like, and thoroughly Southern. On their plantations, generally, the Virginia gentlemen seem to drop their full dress and constrained town habits, and to live a free, rustic, shooting-jacket life. We dined in a room that extended out, rearwardly, from the house, and which, in a Northern establishment, would have been the kitchen. The cooking was done in a detached log-cabin, and the dishes brought some distance, through the open air, by the servants. The outer door was left constantly open, though there was a fire in an enormous old fire-place, large enough, if it could have been distributed sufficiently, to have lasted a New York seamstress the best part of the winter. By the door there was indiscriminate admittance to negro children and fox-hounds, and, on an average, there were four of these, grinning or licking their chops, on either side of my chair, all the time I was at the table. A stout woman acted as head waitress, employing two handsome little mulatto boys as her aids in communicating with the kitchen, from which relays of hot corn-bread, of an excellence quite new to me, were brought at frequent intervals. There was no other bread, and but one vegetable served—sweet potato, roasted in ashes, and this, I thought, was the best sweet potato, also, that I ever had eaten; but there were four preparations of swine's flesh, besides fried fowls, fried eggs, cold roast turkey, and opossum, cooked, I know not how, but it somewhat resembled baked sucking-pig. The only beverages on the table were milk and whisky.

I was pressed to stay several days with Mr. W., and should have been glad to do so, had not another engagement prevented. When I was about to leave, an old servant was directed to get a horse, and go with me, as guide, to the railroad station at Col. Gillin's. He followed behind me, and I had great difficulty in inducing him to ride near enough to converse with me. I wished to ascertain from him how old the different stages of the old-field forest-growth, by the side of our road, might be; but for a long time, he was, or pretended to be, unable to comprehend my questions. When he did so, the most accurate information he could give me was, that he reckoned such a field (in which the pines were now some sixty feet high) had been planted with tobacco the year his old master bought him. He thought he was about twenty years old then, and that now he was forty. He had every appearance of being seventy.

He frequently told me there was no need for him to go any further, and that it was a dead straight road to the station, without any forks. As he appeared very eager to return, I was at length foolish enough to allow myself to be prevailed upon to dispense with his guidance; gave him a quarter of a dollar for his time that I had employed, and went on alone. The road, which for a short distance further was plain enough, soon began to ramify, and, in half an hour, we were stumbling along a dark wood-path, looking eagerly for a house. At length, seeing one across a large clearing, we went through a long lane, opening gates and letting down bars, until we met two negroes, riding a mule, who were going to the plantation near the school-house which we had seen the day before. Following them thither, we knew the rest of the way (Jane gave a bound and neighed, when we struck the old road, showing that she had been lost, as well as I, up to the moment).

It was twenty minutes after the hour given in the time-table for the passage of the train, when I reached the station, but it had not arrived; nor did it make its appearance for a quarter of an hour longer; so I had plenty of time to deliver Tom's wife's message and take leave of Jane. I am sorry to say she appeared very indifferent, and seemed to think a good deal more of Tom than of me. Mr. W. had told me that the train would, probably, be half an hour behind its advertised time, and that I had no need to ride with haste, to reach it. I asked Col. Gillin if it would be safe to always calculate on the train being half an hour late: he said it would not; for, although usually that much behind the time-table, it was sometimes half an hour ahead of it. So those, who would be safe, had commonly to wait an hour. People, therefore, who wished to go not more than twenty miles from home, would find it more convenient, and equally expeditious, taking all things into account, to go in their own conveyances—there being but few who lived so near the station that they would not have to employ a horse and servant to get to it.

——————. ——. I have been visiting a farm, cultivated entirely by free labour. The proprietor told me that he was first led to disuse slave-labour, not from any economical considerations, but because he had become convinced that there was an essential wrong in holding men in forced servitude with any other purpose than to benefit them alone, and because he was not willing to allow his own children to be educated as slave-masters. His father had been a large slaveholder, and he felt very strongly the bad influence it had had on his own character. He wished me to be satisfied that Jefferson uttered a great truth when he asserted that slavery was more pernicious to the white race than the black. Although, therefore, a chief part of his inheritance had been in slaves, he had liberated them all.

Most of them had, by his advice, gone to Africa. These he had frequently heard from. Except a child that had been drowned, they were, at his last account, all alive, in general good health, and satisfactorily prospering. He had lately received a letter from one of them, who told him that he was "*trying* to preach the Gospel," and who had evidently greatly improved, both intellectually and morally, since he left here. With regard to those going North, and the common opinion that they encountered much misery, and would be much better off here, he said that it entirely depended on the general character and habits of the individual: it was true of those who were badly brought up, and who had acquired indolent and vicious habits, especially if they were drunkards, but, if of some intelligence and well trained, they generally represented themselves to be successful and contented.

He mentioned two remarkable cases, that had come under his own observation, of this kind. One was that of a man who had been free, but, by some fraud and informality of his papers, was re-enslaved. He ran away, and afterwards negotiated, by correspondence, with his master, and purchased his freedom. This man he had accidentally met, fifteen years afterwards, in a Northern city; he was engaged in profitable and increasing business, and showed him, by his books, that he was possessed of property to the amount of ten thousand dollars. He was living a great deal more comfortably and wisely than ever his old master had done. The other case was that of a coloured woman, who had obtained her freedom, and who became apprehensive that she also was about to be fraudulently made a slave again. She fled to Philadelphia, where she was nearly starved, at first. A little girl, who heard her begging in the streets to be allowed to work for bread, told her that her mother was wanting some washing done, and she followed her home. The mother, not knowing her, was afraid to trust her with the articles to be washed. She prayed so earnestly for the job, however—suggesting that she might be locked into a room until she had completed it—that it was given her.

So she commenced life in Philadelphia. Ten years afterwards he had accidentally met her there; she recognized him immediately, recalled herself to his recollection, manifested the greatest joy at seeing him, and asked him to come to her house, which he found a handsome three-story building, furnished really with elegance; and she pointed out to him, from the window, three houses in the vicinity that she owned and rented. She showed great anxiety to have her children well educated, and was employing the best instructors for them which she could procure in Philadelphia.

He considered the condition of slaves to have much improved since the Revolution, and very perceptibly during the last twenty years. The original stock of slaves, the imported Africans, he observed, probably required to be governed with much greater severity, and very little humanity was exercised or thought of with regard to them. The slaves of the present day are of a higher character; in fact, he did not think more than half of them were full-blooded Africans. Public sentiment condemned the man who treated his slaves with cruelty. The owners were mainly men of some cultivation, and felt a family attachment to their slaves, many of whom had been the playmates of their boyhood. Nevertheless, they were frequently punished severely, under the impulse of temporary passion, often without deliberation, and on unfounded suspicion. This was especially the case where they were left to overseers, who, though sometimes men of intelligence and piety, were more often coarse, brutal, and licentious; drinking men, wholly unfitted for the responsibility imposed on them.

With regard to the value of slave-labour, this gentleman is confident that, at present, he has the advantage in employing free men instead of it. It has not been so until of late, the price of slaves having much advanced within ten years, while immigration has made free white labourers more easy to be procured.

He has heretofore had some difficulty in obtaining hands

when he needed them, and has suffered a good deal from the demoralizing influence of adjacent slave-labour, the men, after a few months' residence, inclining to follow the customs of the slaves with regard to the amount of work they should do in a day, or their careless mode of operation. He has had white and black Virginians, sometimes Germans, and latterly Irish. Of all these, he has found the Irish on the whole the best. The poorest have been the native white Virginians; next, the free blacks: and though there have been exceptions, he has not generally paid these as high as one hundred dollars a year, and has thought them less worth their wages than any he has had. At present, he has two white natives and two free coloured men, but both the latter were brought up in his family, and are worth twenty dollars a year more than the average. The free black, he thinks, is generally worse than the slave, and so is the poor white man. He also employs, at present, four Irish hands, and is expecting two more to arrive, who have been recommended to him, and sent for by those he has. He pays the Irishmen $120 a year, and boards them. He has had them for $100; but these are all excellent men, and well worth their price. They are less given to drinking than any men he has ever had; and one of them first suggested improvements to him in his farm, that he is now carrying out with prospects of considerable advantage. Housemaids, Irish girls, he pays $3 and $6 a month.

He does not apprehend that in future he shall have any difficulty in obtaining steady men, who will accomplish much more work than any slaves. There are some operations, such as carting and spreading dung, and all work with the fork, spade, or shovel, at which his Irishmen will do, he thinks, over fifty per cent. more in a day than any negroes he has ever known. On the whole, he is satisfied that at present free-labour is more profitable than slave-labour, though his success is not so evident that he would be willing to have attention particularly called to it. His farm, moreover, is now in a transition state from one system of husbandry to another, and appearances are temporarily more unfavourable on that account.

The wages paid for slaves, when they are hired for agricultural labour, do not differ at present, he says, from those which he pays for his free labourers. In both cases the hiring party boards the labourer, but, in addition to money and board, the slave-employer has to furnish clothing, and is subject, without redress, to any losses which may result from the carelessness or malevolence of the slave. He also has to lose his time if he is unwell, or when from any cause he is absent or unable to work.

The slave, if he is indisposed to work, and especially if he is not treated well, or does not like the master who has hired him, will sham sickness—even make himself sick or lame—that he need not work. But a more serious loss frequently arises, when the slave, thinking he is worked too hard, or being angered by punishment or unkind treatment, "getting the sulks," takes to "the swamp," and comes back when he has a mind to. Often this will not be till the year is up for which he is engaged, when he will return to his owner, who, glad to find his property safe, and that it has not died in the swamp, or gone to Canada, forgets to punish him, and immediately sends him for another year to a new master.

"But, meanwhile, how does the negro support life in the swamp?" I asked.

"Oh, he gets sheep and pigs and calves, and fowls and turkeys; sometimes they will kill a small cow. We have often seen the fires, where they were cooking them, through the woods, in the swamp yonder. If it is cold, he will crawl under a fodder-stack, or go into the cabins with some of the other negroes, and in the same way, you see, he can get all the corn, or almost anything else he wants.

"He steals them from his master?"

"From any one; frequently from me. I have had many a sheep taken by them."

"It is a common thing, then?"

"Certainly, it is, very common, and the loss is sometimes exceedingly provoking. One of my neighbours here was going to build, and hired two mechanics for a year. Just as he was ready to put his house up, the two men, taking offence at something, both ran away, and did not come back at all till their year was out, and then their owner immediately hired them out again to another man."

These negroes "in the swamp," he said, were often hunted after, but it was very difficult to find them, and, if caught, they would run again, and the other negroes would hide and assist them. Dogs to track them he had never known to be used in Virginia.

Saturday, Dec. 25th.—From Christmas to New-Year's Day, most of the slaves, except house servants, enjoy a freedom from labour; and Christmas is especially holiday, or Saturnalia, with them. The young ones began last night firing crackers, and I do not observe that they are engaged in any other amusement to-day; the older ones are generally getting drunk, and making business for the police. I have seen large gangs coming in from the country, and these contrast much in their general appearance with the town negroes. The latter are dressed expensively, and frequently more elegantly than the whites. They seem to be spending money freely, and I observe that they, and even the slaves that wait upon me at the hotel, often have watches, and other articles of value.

The slaves have a good many ways of obtaining "spending money," which though in law belonging to their owner, as the property of a son under age does to his father, they are never dispossessed of, and use for their own gratification, with even less restraint than a wholesome regard for their health and moral condition may be thought to require. A Richmond paper, complaining of the liberty allowed to slaves in this respect, as calculated to foster an insubordinate spirit, speaks of their "champagne suppers." The police broke into a gambling cellar a few nights since, and found about twenty negroes at "high play," with all the usual accessories of a first-class "Hell." It is mentioned that, among the number taken to the watch-house, and treated with lashes the next morning, there were some who had previously enjoyed a high reputation for piety, and others of a very elegant or foppish appearance.

Passing two negroes in the street, I heard the following:

"———Workin' in a tobacco factory all de year roun', an' come Christmas only twenty dollars! Workin' mighty hard, too—up to twelve o'clock o' night very often—an' then to hab a nigger oberseah!"

"A nigger!"

"Yes—dat's it, yer see. Wouldn't care if 'twarn't for dat. Nothin' but a dirty nigger! orderin' 'round, jes' as if he was a wite man!"

It is the custom of tobacco manufacturers to hire slaves and free negroes at a certain rate of wages per year. A task of 45 lbs. per day is given them to work up, and all that they choose to do more than this they are paid for—payment being made once a fortnight; and invariably this over-wages is used by the slave for himself, and is usually spent in drinking, licentiousness, and gambling. The man was grumbling that he had saved but $20 to spend at the holidays.

Sitting with a company of smokers last night, one of them, to show me the manner in which a slave of any ingenuity or cunning would manage to avoid working for his master's profit, narrated the following anecdote. He was executor of an estate in which, among other negroes, there was one very smart man, who, he knew perfectly well, ought to be earning for the estate $150 a year, and who could do it if he chose, yet whose wages for a year, being let out by the day or job, had amounted to but $18, while he had paid for medical attendance upon him 45. Having failed in every other way to make him earn anything, he proposed to him that he should purchase his freedom and go to Philadelphia, where he had a brother. He told him that if he would earn a certain sum ($400 I believe), and pay it over to the estate for himself, he would give him his free papers. The man agreed to the arrangement, and by his overwork in a tobacco factory, and some assistance from his free brother, soon paid the sum agreed upon, and was sent to Philadelphia. A few weeks afterwards he met him in the street, and asked him why he had returned. "Oh, I don't like dat Philadelphy, massa; an't no chance for coloured folks dere; spec' if I'd been a runaway, de wite folks dere take care o' me; but I couldn't git anythin' to do, so I jis borrow ten dollar of my broder, and cum back to old Virginny."

"But you know the law forbids your return. I wonder that you are not afraid to be seen here; I should think Mr. —— [an officer of police] would take you up."

"Oh! I look out for dat, massa; I juss hire myself out to Mr.—— himself, ha! ha! He tink I your boy."

And so it proved; the officer, thinking that he was permitted to hire himself out, and tempted by the low wages at which he offered himself, had neglected to ask for his written permission, and had engaged him for a year. He still lived with the officer, and was an active, healthy, good servant to him.

A well-informed capitalist and slave-holder remarked, that negroes could not be employed in cotton factories. I said that I understood they were so in Charleston, and some other places at the South.

"It may be so, yet," he answered, "but they will have to give it up."

The reason was, he said, that the negro could never be trained to exercise judgment; he cannot be made to use his mind; he always depends on machinery doing its own work, and cannot be made to watch it. He neglects it until something is broken or there is great waste. "We have tried rewards and punishments, but it makes no difference. It's his nature and you cannot change it. All men are indolent and have a disinclination to labour, but this is a great deal stronger in the African race than in any other. In working niggers, we must always calculate that they will not labour at all except to avoid punishment, and they will never do more than just enough to save themselves from being punished, and no amount of punishment will prevent their working carelessly and indifferently. It always seems on the plantation as if they took pains to break all the tools and spoil all the cattle that they possibly can, even when they know they'll be directly punished for it."

As to rewards, he said, "They only want to support life: they will not work for anything more; and in this country it would be hard to prevent their getting that." I thought this opinion of the power of rewards was not exactly confirmed by the narrative we had just heard, but I said nothing. "If you could move," he continued, "all the white people from the whole seaboard district of Virginia and give it up to the negroes that are on it now; just leave them to themselves, in ten years' time there would not be an acre of land cultivated, and nothing would be produced, except what grew spontaneously.

[The Hon. Willoughby Newton, by the way, seems to think that if it had not been for the introduction of guano, a similar desolation would have soon occurred without the Africanization of the country. He is reported to have said:—

["I look upon the introduction of guano, and the success attending its application to our barren lands, in the light of a special interposition of Divine Providence, to save the northern neck of Virginia from reverting entirely into its former state of wilderness and utter desolation. Until the discovery of guano—more valuable to us than the mines of California—I looked upon the possibility of renovating our soil, of ever bringing it to a point capable of producing remunerating crops, as utterly hopeless. Our up-lands were all worn out, and our bottom-lands fast failing, and if it had not been for guano, to revive our last hope, a few years more and the whole country must have been deserted by all who desired to increase their own wealth, or advance the cause of civilization by a proper cultivation of the earth."]

I said I supposed that they were much better off, more improved intellectually, and more kindly treated in Virginia than further South. He said I was mistaken in both respects —that in Louisiana, especially, they were more intelligent, because the amalgamation of the races was much greater, and they were treated with more familiarity by the whites; besides which, the laws of Louisiana were much more favourable to them. For instance, they required the planter to give slaves 200 pounds of pork a year: and he gave a very apt anecdote, showing the effect of this law, but which, at the same time, made it evident that a Virginian may be accustomed to neglect providing sufficient food for his force, and that they sometimes suffer greatly for want of it. I was assured, however, that this was very rare—that, generally, the slaves were well provided for—always allowed a sufficient quantity of meal, and, generally, of pork—were permitted to raise pigs and poultry, and in summer could always grow as many vegetables as they wanted. It was observed, however, that they frequently neglect to provide for themselves in this way, and live mainly on meal and bacon. If a man does not provide well for his slaves, it soon becomes known; he gets the name of a "nigger killer," and loses the respect of the community.

The general allowance of food was thought to be a peck and a half of meal, and three pounds of bacon a week. This, it was observed, is as much meal as they can eat, but they would be glad to have more bacon; sometimes they receive four pounds, but it is oftener that they get less than three. It is distributed to them on Saturday nights; or, on the better managed plantations, sometimes on Wednesday, to prevent their using it extravagantly, or selling it for whisky on Sunday. This distribution is called the "drawing," and is made by the overseer to all the heads of families or single negroes. Except on the smallest plantations, where the cooking is done in the house of the proprietor, there is a cook-house, furnished with a large copper for boiling, and an oven. Every night the negroes take their "mess," for the next day's breakfast and dinner, to the cook, to be prepared for the next day. Custom varies as to the time it is served out to them; sometimes at morning and noon, at other times at noon and night. Each negro marks his meat by cuts, so that he shall know it from the rest, and they observe each other's rights with regard to this, punctiliously.

After breakfast has been eaten early in the cabins, at sunrise, or a little before in winter, and perhaps a little later in summer, they go to the field. At noon dinner is brought to them, and, unless the work presses, they are allowed two hours' rest. Very punctually at sunset they stop work and are at liberty, except that a squad is detached once a week for shelling corn, to go to the mill for the next week's drawing of meal. Thus they work in the field about eleven hours a day, on an average. Returning to the cabins, wood "ought to have been" carted for them; but if it has not been, they then go the woods and "tote" it home for themselves. They then make a fire—a big, blazing fire at this season, for the supply of fuel is unlimited—and cook their own supper, which will be a bit of bacon fried, often with eggs, corn-bread baked in the spider after the bacon, to absorb the fat, and perhaps some sweet potatoes roasted in the ashes. Immediately after supper they go to sleep, often lying on the floor or a bench in preference to a bed. About two o'clock they very generally rouse up and cook and eat, or eat cold, what they call their "mornin' bit;" then sleep again till breakfast. They generally save from their ration of meal: commonly as much as five bushels of meal was sent to town by my informant's hands every week, to be sold for them. Upon inquiry, he almost always found that it belonged to only two or three individuals, who had traded for it with the rest; he added, that too often the exchange was for whisky, which, against his rules, they obtained of some rascally white people in the neighbourhood, and kept concealed. They were very fond of whisky, and sometimes much injured themselves with it.

To show me how well they were supplied with eggs, he said that once a vessel came to anchor, becalmed, off his place, and the captain came to him and asked leave to purchase some eggs of his people. He gave him permission, and called the cook to collect them for him. The cook asked how many she should bring. "Oh, all you can get," he answered—and she returned after a time, with several boys assisting her, bringing nearly two bushels, all the property of the slaves, and which they were willing to sell at four cents a dozen.

One of the smokers explained to me that it is bad economy, not to allow an abundant supply of food to "a man's force." If not well provided for, the negroes will find a way to provide for themselves. It is, also, but simple policy to have them well lodged and clothed. If they do not have comfortable cabins and sufficient clothing, they will take cold, and be laid up. He lost a valuable negro, once, from having neglected to provide him with shoes.

The houses of the slaves are usually log-cabins, of various degrees of comfort and commodiousness. At one end there is a great open fire-place, which is exterior to the wall of the house, being made of clay in an inclosure, about eight feet square and high, of logs. The chimney is sometimes of brick, but more commonly of lath or split sticks, laid up like log work and plastered with mud. They enjoy great roaring fires, and, as the common fuel is pine, the cabin, at night when the door is open, seen from a distance, appears like a fierce furnace. The chimneys often catch fire, and the cabin is destroyed. Very little precaution can be taken against this danger.* Several cabins are placed near together, and they are called "the quarters." On a plantation of moderate size there will be but one "quarters." The situation chosen

* "AN INGENIOUS NEGRO.—In Lafayette, Miss., a few days ago, a negro, who, with his wife and three children, occupied a hut upon the plantation of Col. Peques, was very much annoyed by fleas. Believing that they congregated in great numbers beneath the house, he resolved to destroy them by fire; and accordingly, one night when his family were asleep, he raised a plank in the floor of the cabin, and, procuring an armful of shucks, scattered them on the ground beneath, and lighted them. The consequence was, that the cabin was consumed, and the whole family, with the exception of the man who lighted the fire, was burned to death."—*Journal of Commerce.*

for it has reference to convenience of obtaining water from springs and fuel from the woods.

As to the clothing of the slaves on the plantations, they are said to be usually furnished by their owners or masters, every year, each with a coat and trousers, of a coarse woollen or woollen and cotton stuff (mostly made, especially for this purpose, in Providence, R. I.) for winter, trousers of cotton osnaburghs for summer, sometimes with a jacket also of the same ; two pairs of strong shoes, or one pair of strong boots and one of lighter shoes for harvest ; three shirts, one blanket, and one felt hat.

The women have two dresses of striped cotton, three shifts, two pairs of shoes, etc. The women lying-in are kept at knitting short sacks, from cotton, which, in Southern Virginia, is usually raised for this purpose on the farm, and these are also given to the negroes. They also purchase clothing for themselves, and, I notice especially, are well supplied with handkerchiefs, which the men frequently, and the women nearly always, wear on their heads. On Sundays and holidays they usually look very smart, but when at work, very ragged and slovenly.

At the conclusion of our bar-room session, some time after midnight, as we were retiring to our rooms, our progress up stairs and along the corridors was several times impeded, by negroes lying fast asleep, in their usual clothes only, upon the floor. I asked why they were not abed, and was answered by a gentleman, that negroes never wanted to go to bed ; they always preferred to sleep on the floor.

That "slaves are liars," or, as they say here, "niggers will lie," always has been proverbial. "They will lie in their very prayers to God," said one, and I find illustrations of the trouble that the vice occasions on every hand here. I just heard this, from a lady. A housemaid, who had the reputation of being especially devout, was suspected by her mistress of having stolen from her bureau several trinkets. She was charged with the theft, and vociferously denied it. She was watched, and the articles discovered openly displayed on her person as she went to church. She still, on her return, denied having them—was searched, and they were found in her pockets. When reproached by her mistress, and lectured on the wickedness of lying and stealing, she replied with the confident air of knowing the ground she stood upon, " Law,.mam, don't say I's wicked; ole Aunt Ann says it allers right for us poor coloured people to 'popiate whatever of de wite folk's blessins de Lord puts in our way ;" old Aunt Ann being a sort of mother in the coloured Israel of the town.

It is told me as a singular fact, that everywhere on the plantations, the agrarian notion has become a fixed point of the negro system of ethics : that the result of labour belongs of right to the labourer, and on this ground, even the religious feel justified in using "massa's" property for their own temporal benefit. This they term " taking," and it is never admitted to be a reproach to a man among them that he is charged with it, though " stealing," or taking from another than their master, and particularly from one another, is so. They almost universally pilfer from the household stores when they have a safe opportunity.

Jefferson says of the slaves :

"Whether further observation will or will not verify the conjecture, that nature has been less bountiful to them in the endowments of the head, I believe that in those of the heart she will have done them justice. That disposition to theft, with which they have been branded, must be ascribed to their situation, and not to any depravity of the moral sense. The man in whose favour no laws of property exist, probably feels himself less bound to respect those made in favour of others. When arguing for ourselves, we lay it down as fundamental, that laws, to be just, must give a reciprocation of right; that without this, they are mere arbitrary rules, founded in force, and not in conscience; and it is a problem which I give to the master to solve, whether the religious precepts against the violation of property were not framed for him as well as his slave? and whether the slave may not as justifiably take a little from one who has taken all from him, as he may slay one who would slay him? That a change of the relations in which a man is placed should change his ideas of moral right and wrong, is neither new, nor peculiar to the colour of the blacks. Homer tells us it was so, 2,600 years ago:

" ' Jove fixed it certain, that whatever day
Makes man a slave, takes half his worth away.' "

CHAPTER IV.

THE ECONOMY OF VIRGINIA.

An Englishman will cross three thousand miles of sea, and, landing in our Free States, find, under a different sky and climate, a people speaking the same language, influenced by the same literature, giving allegiance to the same common law, and with not very dissimilar tastes, manners, or opinions, on the whole, to those of his own people. What most strikes him is an apparent indifference to conditions of living which he would at home call shabby. He will find men, however, at whose homes he will hardly see anything, either of substance, custom, or manner, by which he would know that he was out of England, and if he asks how these manage to get waiters who do not smell of the stable; and grooms who keep stirrups bright; roofs which do not leak; lawns which are better than stubble fields; walks which are not grassy; fences which do not need shoreing up; staunch dogs; clean guns; strong boots and clothes that will go whole through a thicket; the true answer will be, by taking double the pains and paying double as much as would be necessary to secure the same results in England, and that few men are willing or able to do this.

I make half a day's journey southward here, and I find, with an equal resemblance between the people and those I left, an indifference to conditions of living, which Mrs. Stowe's Ophelia describes as "shiftless," and which makes the same sort of impression on my mind, as the state of things at the North does upon an Englishman's. But, in this case, there has been no change in the skies; I wear the same clothing, or if I come from the low sea-board and, going in-land, gain elevation, I need some better protection against cold. I also find exceptions; how are they to be accounted for? The first step does not seem difficult. In this well-provided, hospitable, and most agreeable household, for instance, there are four times as many servants as in one which would otherwise be as similar as possible to it at the North; to say nothing of the governess, or of the New York plumber, who has been at work here for a month; or of the doctor, who, having come fifteen miles to lance the baby's gums, stays of course to dine with us; or of the German, who I am told—such is the value of railroads even at a distance—left Richmond only at nine o'clock last night, and having tuned the piano, will return in time for his classes there to-morrow; or of the patent chain-pump pedlar, whose horses have been knocked up in crossing the swamp; or of the weekly mail-carrier, who cannot go on till the logs which have floated off the bridge are restored. Mr. T. means soon, he tells me, to build a substantial bridge there, because his nearest respectable neighbours are in that direction. His nearest neighbours on this side of the creek, by the way, he seems to regard with suspicion. They live in solitary cabins, and he don't think they do a day's work in a year; but they somehow manage to always have corn enough to keep themselves from starving, and as they certainly don't raise half enough for this, the supposition is that his negroes steal it and supply it in exchange for whisky. Clearly the negroes do get whisky, somewhere; for even their preacher, who has been a capital blacksmith, and but for this vice would be worth $2500, was taken with delirium tremens last Sunday night, and set one of the outhouses on fire, so that the energetic Mr. T., who will have things right about his "place," has determined to get rid of him, and will have him sold for what he will fetch at the sheriff's sale at the County House to-morrow; ard Prior, the overseer, must go to Richmond immediately, to see about a new blacksmith, for the plumber says that until one is got he must stand idle, and the ploughs are all needing repair. A less energetic man would keep old Joe, in spite of his vice, on account of his old wife and many children, and out of regard to the spiritual interests of his flock, for when not very drunk, old Joe is reckoned the best preacher in five counties. But Mr. T. is determined to live like a gentleman; he is not going to have the hoofs of his thorough-breds spoiled; and he will have hot and cold water laid on; and he tells Prior that if he can find a first-rate shoer, young, healthy, active, and strong, and handy at anything in the way of his trade, not to lose him, if he has to go as high as $250, for the year; or, if necessary, he will buy such an one outright, at any fair price, if he can have him on trial for a month. If there is none in market, he must try to induce that Scotchman who hung the bells to come up again for a few days. "Treat him like a gentleman," he says, "and tell him he will be paid whatever he asks, and make as if it were a frolic."

$250 a year, and a man's board and clothing, with iron, coal, and, possibly, doctor's bills to be added, is certainly a high price to pay for the blacksmith's work of a single farm. This exceptional condition, then, it is obvious on the face of things, is maintained at an enormous expense, not only of money, but of nerve, time, temper, if not of humanity, or the world's judgment of humanity. There is much inherited wealth, a cotton plantation or two in Mississippi and a few slips of paper in a broker's office in Wall Street, that account for the comfort of this Virginia farmer, as, with something of the pride which apes humility, he likes to style himself. And after all he has no road on which he can drive his fine horses; his physician supposes the use of chloric ether, as an anasthetic agent, to be a novel and interesting subject of after-dinner eloquence; he has no church within twenty miles, but one of logs, attendance on which is sure to bring on an attack of neuralgia with his wife, and where only an ignorant ranter of a different faith from his own preaches at irregular intervals; there is no school which he is willing that his children should attend; his daily papers come weekly, and he sees no books except such as he has especially ordered from Norton or Stevens.

This being the exception, how is it with the community as a whole?

As a whole, the community makes shift to live, some part tolerably, the most part wretchedly enough, with arrangements such as one might expect to find in a country in stress of war. Nothing which can be postponed or overlooked, without immediate serious inconvenience, gets attended to. One soon neglects to inquire why this is not done or that; the answer is so certain to be that there is no proper person to be got to do it without more trouble (or expense) than it is thought to be worth. Evidently habit reconciles the people to do without much, the permament want of which would seem likely to be intolerable to those who had it in possession. Nevertheless, they complain a good deal, showing that the evil is an increasing one. Verbal statements to the same effect as the following, written by a Virginian to the 'Journal of Commerce,' are often heard.

"Hundreds of farmers and planters, mill owners, tobacconists, cotton factories, iron works, steam-boat owners, master builders, contractors, carpenters, stage proprietors, canal boat owners, railroad companies, and others, are, and have been short of hands these five years past, in Maryland, Virginia, and the Carolinas. They pay $150 or $200 a year each hand, and his board, and stealing, and if that hand be present or absent, sick or well, it is all the same. His clothes cost say $30 more, and in many cases the hirer has to pay his policy of life insurance.'

For all that, labourers are being constantly sent away. I have not been on or seen a railroad train, departing southward, that it did not convey a considerable number of the best class of negro labourers, in charge of a trader who was intending to sell them to cotton-planters. Thus it is evident that, great as is the need for more labourers here, there is a still greater demand for them to raise cotton; and in order to supply this demand, the Virginians suffer the most extreme inconvenience. The wonder is, that their own demand for labour is not supplied by free labourers. But it appears that where negro slavery has long existed, certain occupations are, by custom, assigned to the slaves, and a white man is not only reluctant to engage himself in those occupations, but is greatly disinclined to employ other whites in them. I have often asked: "Why do you not employ white men?" (for this or that purpose for which slaves could not be procured;) and, almost always, the reply has been given in a tone which indicated a little feeling, which, if I do not misapprehend it, means that the employment of whites in duties upon which slaves are ordinarily employed is felt to be not only humiliating to the whites employed, but also to the employer.

Nor is this difficulty merely a matter of sentiment. I have been answered: "Our poor white men will not do such work if they can very well help it, and they will do no more of it than they are obliged to. They will do a few days' work when it is necessary to provide themselves with the necessaries of life, but they are not used to steady labour; they work reluctantly, and will not bear driving; they cannot be worked to advantage with slaves, and it is inconvenient to look after them, if you work them separately." And then, when I push the inquiries by asking, why not send North and get some of our labourers? "Well—the truth is, I have been used to driving niggers, and I don't think I could drive white men. I should not know how to manage them." So far as I understand the matter, then, Virginia is in this position: there are slaves enough in most of the country to mainly exclude white labourers from labouring men's occupations and to make the white people dependent on slave-labour for certain things; but the slaves being drawn off almost as fast as they grow up to grow cotton in the more Southern States, and those which remain being managed with almost as much regard for this demand as for the local demand for labour, this local demand is not systematically provided for; and even if there were the intention to provide for it, there are no sufficient means to do so, as the white population increases in number much more rapidly than the slave.* I do not mean that no whites are employed in the ordinary occupations of slaves in Virginia. In some parts there are few or no slaves, and the white people who live in these parts, of course do not live without having work done; but even in these districts it is hardly possible to find men or women, who are willing and able to serve others well and faithfully, on wages. In some parts white working men also drift in slowly from the Free States, but they are too few and scattered to perceptibly affect the habits of the people and customs of the country,

* From 1850 to 1860, the rate of increase of the free population has been 16·44 per cent.; of the slave, 3·88. (From a recent official statement of the Census Office.) A somewhat parallel case to that of the Virginia slaveholder is that of a breeder of blooded stock. A Flying Dutchman is used upon occasion as a charger, but under no pressure of the harvest will you find him put before the cart. I have more than once heard the phrase used, "Niggers are worth too much" to be used in such and such work. Instances of this are given hereafter.

while they rapidly adapt themselves to these habits and customs. Thus it is questionable if as yet they do not add more to the general demand for labour than they supply to reduce it.

Still, it is where slaves remain in the greatest numbers, proportionately to the whites, that the scarcity of labourers, or what is practically the same thing, the cost of getting desirable work done, is most obvious. Schools, churches, roads, bridges, fences, houses, stables, are all more frequent, and in better repair, where the proportion of whites to slaves is large, than in the "negro counties," as some are popularly designated, from the preponderance of the slave population in them. I find this observation confirmed by an examination of the Census returns and other documents.

In the North-western counties, Cabell, Mason, Brooke, and Tyler, in or adjoining which there are no large towns, but a free labouring population, with slaves in ratio to the freemen as one to fifteen only, the value of land is over seven dollars and three quarters an acre.

In Southampton, Surrey, James Town and New Kent, in which the slave population is as 1 to 2·2, the value of land is but little more than half as much— $4.50 an acre.

The value of land of course rises with its availability to contribute to the wants of men, and it can only be made available as labour can be applied to it.

In Surrey, Prince George, Charles City, and James, adjoining counties on James River, and originally having some of the most productive soil in the State, and now supplied with the public conveniences which have accrued in two hundred years of occupation by a civilized and Christian community, the number of slaves being at present, to that of whites as 1 to 1·9, the value of land is but $6 an acre.

In Fairfax, another of the first settled counties, and in

which, twenty-years ago, land was even less in value than in the James River counties, it is now become worth twice as much.

The slave population, once greater than that of whites, has been reduced by emigration and sale, till there are now less than half as many slaves as whites. In the place of slaves has come another sort of people. The change which has taken place, and the cause of it, is thus simply described in the Agricultural Report of the County to the Commissioner of Patents.*

"In appearance, the county is so changed in many parts, that a traveller who passed over it ten years ago would not now recognize it. Thousands and thousands of acres had been cultivated in tobacco by the former proprietors, would not pay the cost, and were abandoned as worthless, and became covered with a wilderness of pines. These lands have been purchased by Northern emigrants; the large tracts divided and subdivided and cleared of pines; and neat farm-houses and barns, with smiling fields of grain and grass in the season, salute the delighted gaze of the beholder. Ten years ago it was a mooted question whether Fairfax lands could be made productive; and if so, would they pay the cost? This problem has been satisfactorily solved by many, and in consequence of the above altered state of things school-houses and churches have doubled in number."

The following substantiates what I have said of the inavailability of the native whites for supplying the place of the negroes exported to the cotton plantations.

From the Patent Office Report for 1847.

" As to the price of labour, our mechanics charge from one to two dollars a day. As to agricultural labour, we have none. Our poor are poor because *they will not work,* therefore are seldom employed.

"CHAS. YANCEY,
"*Buckingham Co., Virginia.*"

The sentence, " As to agricultural labour, we have none," must mean no free labour, the number of slaves in this county being according to the Census 8,161, or nearly 3,000 more

* See ' Patent Office Report, 1852.'

than the whole white population. There are also 250 free negroes in the county.

From a Correspondent of the 'American Agriculturist,' Feb. 14, 1855.
"As to labourers, we work chiefly slaves, not because they are cheaper, but rather because they are the only *reliable* labour we can get. The whites here engage to work for *less price than the blacks* can be got for; yet they will not work well, and *rarely work out the time specified.* If any of your friends come here and wish to work whites, I would advise them by all means to bring them with them; for our white labourers are far inferior to our blacks, and our black labour is far inferior to what we read and hear of your labourers. "C. G. G.
"*Albemarle Co., Virginia.*"

In Albemarle there are over thirteen thousand slaves to less than twelve thousand whites.

Among the native Virginians I find most intelligent men, very ready to assert that slavery is no disadvantage to Virginia, and, as necessary to the maintenance of this assertion, that slave-labour is no dearer than free-labour, that is, than free-labour would be, if slavery did not exist. It is even said— and, as I have shown, it is practically true, at least wherever slavery has not in a great measure withdrawn from the field— that white labour cannot live in competition with slave-labour. In other words, the holder of slave-labour controls the local market for labour, and the cost of slave-labour fixes the cost of everything which is produced by slave-labour. But it is a mistake which the Virginians generally make, when they jump from this to the conclusion that slave-labour is therefore cheaper under all circumstances than free-labour. It is evident that slaves are valuable for another purpose than to supply the local demand for their labour, namely, to supply the demand of the cotton planter; consequently those slaves which are employed to supply the local demand, must be employed either at a loss, or at what they are worth to the cotton planter. Whether this is more or less than free-labour would cost if the field were open, can only be ascertained by comparing the cost of slave-labour in Virginia with the cost of free-labour in the Free States.

An exact comparison on a large scale I cannot find the means of making, but I have taken a great many notes which lead me with confidence to a few important general conclusions.

Wages.—Many thousand slaves have been hired in Eastern Virginia during the time of my visit. The wages paid for able working men—sound, healthy, in good condition, and with no especial vices, from twenty to thirty years old—are from $110 to $140; the average, as nearly as I can ascertain, from very extended inquiry, being $120 per year, with board and lodging, and certain other expenses. These wages must represent exactly the cost of slave-labour, because any considerations which would prevent the owner of a slave disposing of his labour for those wages, when the labour for his own purposes would not be worth as much, are so many hindrances upon the free disposal of his property, and thereby deduct from its actual value, as measured with money.

As the large majority of slaves are employed in agricultural labour, and many of those, hired at the prices I have mentioned, are taken directly from the labour of the farm, and are skilled in no other, these wages represent the cost of agricultural labour in Eastern Virginia.

In New York, the usual wages for similar men, if Americans, white or black, are exactly the same in the money part; for Irish or German labourers the most common wages are 10 per month, for summer, and $8 per month, for winter, or from $96 to $120 a year, the average being about $108.

The hirer has, in addition to paying wages for the slave, to feed and to clothe him; the free labourer requires also to be boarded, but not to be clothed by his employer. The opinion is universal in Virginia, that the slaves are better fed than the Northern labourers. This is, however, a mistake, and we must consider that the board of the Northern labourer would cost at least as much more as the additional cost of clothing to the slave. Comparing man with man, with reference simply to equality of muscular power and endurance, my final judgment is, that the wages for common labourers are twenty-five per cent. higher in Virginia than in New York.

Loss from disability of the labourer.—This to the employer of free labourers need be nothing. To the slave-master it is of varying consequence: sometimes small, often excessively embarrassing, and always a subject of anxiety and suspicion. I have not yet made the inquiry on any plantation where as many as twenty negroes are employed together, that I have not found one or more of the field-hands not at work, on account of some illness, strain, bruise, or wound, of which he or she was complaining; and in such cases the proprietor or overseer has, I think, never failed to express his suspicion that the invalid was really as well able to work as anyone else on the plantation. It is said to be nearly as difficult to form a satisfactory diagnosis of negroes' disorders as it is of infants', because their imagination of symptoms is so vivid, and because not the smallest reliance is to be placed on their accounts of what they have felt or done. If a man is really ill, he fears lest he should be thought to be simulating, and therefore exaggerates all his pains, and locates them in whatever he supposes to be the most vital parts of his system.

Frequently the invalid slaves neglect or refuse to use the remedies prescribed for their recovery. They conceal pills, for instance, under their tongue, and declare that they have swallowed them, when, from their producing no effect, it will be afterwards evident that they have not. This general custom I heard ascribed to habit, acquired when they were not very ill, and were loth to be made quite well enough to have to go to work again.

Amusing incidents, illustrating this difficulty, I have heard narrated, showing that the slave rather enjoys getting a severe wound that lays him up:—he has his hand crushed by the fall of a piece of timber, and after the pain is alleviated, is heard to exclaim, "Bress der Lord—der haan b'long to masser—don't reckon dis chile got no more corn to hoe dis yaar, no how."

Mr. H., of North Carolina, observed to me, in relation to this difficulty, that a man who had had much experience with negroes could generally tell, with a good deal of certainty, by their tongue, and their pulse, and their general aspect, whether they were really ill or not.

"Last year," said he, "I hired out one of my negroes to a railroad contractor. I suppose that he found he had to work harder than he would on the plantation, and became discontented, and one night he left the camp without asking leave. The next day he stopped at a public-house, and told the people he had fallen sick working on the railroad, and was going home to his master. They suspected he had run away, and, as he had no pass, they arrested him and sent him to the jail. In the night the sheriff sent me word that there was a boy, who said he belonged to me, in the jail, and he was very sick indeed, and I had better come and take care of him. I suspected how it was, and, as I was particularly engaged, I did not go near him till towards night, the next day. When I came to look at him, and heard his story, I felt quite sure that he was not sick; but, as he pretended to be suffering very much, I told the sheriff to give him plenty of salts and senna, and to be careful that he did not get much of anything to eat. The next day I got a letter from the contractor, telling me that my nigger had run away, without any cause. So I rode over to the jail again, and told them to continue the same treatment until the boy got a good deal worse or a good deal better. Well, the rascal kept it up for a week, all the time groaning so, you'd think he couldn't live many hours longer; but, after he had been in seven days, he all of a sudden said he'd got well, and wanted something to eat. As soon as I heard of it, I sent them word to give him a good paddling,* and handcuff him, and send him back to the railroad. I had to pay them for taking up a runaway, besides the sheriff's fees, and a week's board of the boy to the county."

But the same gentleman admitted that he had sometimes been mistaken, and had made men go to work when they afterwards proved to be really ill; therefore, when one of his people told him he was not able to work, he usually thought, " Very likely he'll be all the better for a day's rest, whether he's really ill or not," and would let him off without being particular in his examination. Lately he had been getting a new overseer, and when he was engaging him, he told him that this was his way. The overseer replied, " It's my way, too, now; it didn't use to be, but I had a lesson. There was a nigger one day at Mr. ——'s who was sulky and complaining; he said he couldn't work. I looked at his tongue, and it was right clean, and I thought it was nothing but damned sulkiness, so I paddled him, and made him go to work; but, two days after, he was under ground. He was a good eight hundred dollar nigger, and it was a lesson to me about taming possums, that I ain't agoing to forget in a hurry."

The liability of women, especially, to disorders and irregularities which cannot be detected by exterior symptoms, but

* Not something to eat, but punishment with an instrument like a ferule.

which may be easily aggravated into serious complaints, renders many of them nearly valueless for work, because of the ease with which they can impose upon their owners. "The women on a plantation," said one extensive Virginian slave-owner to me, " will hardly earn their salt, after they come to the breeding age: they don't come to the field, and you go to the quarters, and ask the old nurse what's the matter, and she says, 'Oh, she's not well, master; she not fit to work, sir;' and what can you do? You have to take her word for it that something or other is the matter with her, and you dare not set her to work; and so she lay up till she feels like taking the air again, and plays the lady at your expense."

I was on a plantation where a woman had been excused from any sort of labour for more than two years, on the supposition that she was dying of phthisis. At last the overseer discovered that she was employed as a milliner and dress-maker by all the other coloured ladies of the vicinity; and upon taking her to the house, it was found that she had acquired a remarkable skill in these vocations. She was hired out the next year to a fashionable dress-maker in town, at handsome wages; and as, after that, she did not again " raise blood," it was supposed that when she had done so before, it had been by artificial means. Such tricks every army and navy surgeon is familiar with.

The interruption and disarrangement of operations of labour, occasioned by slaves " running away," frequently causes great inconvenience and loss to those who employ them. It is said to often occur when no immediate motive can be guessed at for it—when the slave has been well treated, well fed, and not over-worked; and when he will be sure to suffer hardship from it, and be subject to severe punishment on his return, or if he is caught.

This is often mentioned to illustrate the ingratitude and

especial depravity of the African race. I should suspect it to be, if it cannot be otherwise accounted for, the natural instinct of freedom in a man, working out capriciously, as the wild instincts of domesticated beasts and birds sometimes do.

But the learned Dr. Cartwright, of the University of Louisiana, believes that slaves are subject to a peculiar form of mental disease, termed by him *Drapetomania*, which, like a malady that cats are liable to, manifests itself by an irrestrainable propensity to *run away;* and in a work on the diseases of negroes, highly esteemed at the South for its patriotism and erudition, he advises planters of the proper preventive and curative measures to be taken for it.

He asserts that, "with the advantage of proper medical advice, strictly followed, this troublesome practice of running away, that many negroes have, can be almost entirely prevented." Its symptoms and the usual empirical practice on the plantations are described: "Before negroes run away, unless they are frightened or panic-struck, they become sulky and dissatisfied. The cause of this sulkiness and dissatisfaction should be inquired into and removed, or they are apt to run away or fall into the negro consumption." When sulky or dissatisfied without cause, the experience of those having most practice with *drapetomania*, the Doctor thinks, has been in favour of "whipping them *out of it.*" It is vulgarly called, "whipping the devil *out of them*," he afterwards informs us.

Another droll sort of "indisposition," thought to be peculiar to the slaves, and which must greatly affect their value, as compared with free labourers, is described by Dr. Cartwright, as follows:—

"DYSÆSTHESIA ÆTHIOPICA, or Hebetude of Mind and Obtuse Sensibility of Body. * * * From the careless movements of the individuals affected with this complaint, they are apt to do much mischief, which appears as if ntentional, but is mostly owing to the stupidness of mind and insensibility of the nerves induced by the disease. Thus they break, waste, any destroy everything they handle—abuse horses and cattle—tear, burn, or rend their own clothing, and, paying no attention to the rights of property, steal others to replace what they have destroyed. They wander about at night, and keep in a half-nodding state by day. They slight their work—cut up corn, cane, cotton, and tobacco, when hoeing it, as if for pure mischief. They raise disturbances with their overseers, and among their fellow-servants, without cause or motive, and seem to be insensible to pain when subjected to punishment. * * *

"When left to himself, the negro indulges in his natural disposition to idleness and sloth, and does not take exercise enough to expand his lungs and vitalize his blood, but dozes out a miserable existence in the midst of filth and uncleanliness, being too indolent, and having too little energy of mind, to provide for himself proper food and comfortable clothing and lodging. The consequence is, that the blood becomes so highly carbonized and deprived of oxygen that it not only becomes unfit to stimulate the brain to energy, but unfit to stimulate the nerves of sensation distributed to the body. * * *

"This is the disease called *Dysæsthesia* (a Greek term expressing the dull or obtuse sensation that always attends the complaint). When roused from sloth by the stimulus of hunger, he takes anything he can lay his hands on, and tramples on the rights as well as on the property of others, with perfect indifference. When driven to labour by the compulsive power of the white man, he performs the task assigned to him in a headlong, careless manner, treading down with his feet or cutting with his hoe the plants he is put to cultivate—breaking the tools he works with, and spoiling everything he touches that can be injured by careless handling. Hence the overseers call it 'rascality,' supposing that the mischief is intentionally done. * * *

"The term, 'rascality,' given to this disease by overseers, is founded on an erroneous hypothesis, and leads to an incorrect empirical treatment, which seldom or never cures it."

There are many complaints described in Dr. Cartwright's treatise, to which the negroes, in slavery, seem to be peculiarly subject.

"More fatal than any other is congestion of the lungs, *peripneumonia notha*, often called cold plague, etc. * * *

"The *Frambæsia*, Piam, or Yaws, is a *contagious* disease, communicable by contact among those who greatly neglect cleanliness. It is supposed to be communicable, in a modified form, to the white race, among whom it resembles pseudo syphilis, or some disease of the nose, throat, or larynx. * * *

"Negro-consumption, a disease almost unknown to medical men of the

Northern States and of Europe, is also sometimes fearfully prevalent among the slaves. 'It is of importance,' says the Doctor, 'to know the pathognomic signs in its early stages, not only in regard to its treatment, but to detect impositions, as negroes afflicted with this complaint are often for sale; the acceleration of the pulse, on exercise, incapacitates them for labour, as they quickly give out, and have to leave their work. This induces their owners to sell them, although they may not know the cause of their inability to labour. Many of the negroes brought South, for sale, are in the incipient stages of this disease; they are found to be inefficient labourers, and are sold in consequence thereof. The effect of superstition—a firm belief that he is poisoned or conjured—upon the patient's mind, already in a morbid state (dysæsthesia), and his health affected from hard usage, over-tasking or exposure, want of wholesome food, good clothing, warm, comfortable lodging, with the distressing idea (sometimes) that he is an object of hatred or dislike, both to his master or fellow-servants, and has no one to befriend him, tends directly to generate that erythism of mind which is the essential cause of negro-consumption.' * * * 'Remedies should be assisted by removing the *original cause* of the dissatisfaction or trouble of mind, and by using every means to make the patient comfortable, satisfied, and happy.'"

Longing for home generates a distinct malady, known to physicians as *Nostalgia*, and there is a suggestive analogy between the treatment commonly employed to cure it and that recommended in this last advice of Dr. Cartwright.

Discipline.—Under the slave system of labour, discipline must always be maintained by physical power. A lady of New York, spending a winter in a Southern city, had a hired slave-servant, who, one day, refused outright to perform some ordinary light domestic duty required of her. On the lady's gently remonstrating with her, she immediately replied: "You can't make me do it, and I won't do it: I aint afeard of you whippin' me." The servant was right; the lady could not whip her, and was too tender-hearted to call in a man, or to send her to the guard-house to be whipped, as is the custom with Southern ladies, when their patience is exhausted, under such circumstances. She endeavoured, by kindness and by appeals to the girl's good sense, to obtain a moral control over her; but, after suffering continual annoyance and inconvenience, and after an intense trial of her feelings, for some time, she was at length obliged to go to her owner, and beg him to come and take her away from the house, on any terms. It was no better than having a lunatic or a mischievous and pilfering monomaniac quartered on her.*

But often when courage and physical power, with the strength of the militia force and the army of the United States, if required, at the back of the master, are not wanting, there are a great variety of circumstances that make a resort to punishment inconvenient, if not impossible.

Really well-trained, accomplished, and docile house-servants are seldom to be purchased or hired at the South, though they are found in old wealthy families rather oftener than first-rate English or French servants are at the North. It is, doubtless, a convenience to have even moderately good servants who cannot, at any time of their improved value or your necessity, demand to have their pay increased, or who cannot be drawn away from you by prospect of smaller demands and kinder treatment at your neighbour's; but I believe few of those who are incessantly murmuring against this healthy operation of God's good law of supply and demand would be willing to purchase exemption from it, at the price with which the masters and mistresses of the South do. They would pay, to get a certain amount of work done, three or four times as much, to the owner of the best sort of hired slaves, as they do to the commonest, stupidest Irish domestic drudges at the North, though the nominal wages by the week or year, in Virginia, are but little more than in New York.

* The *Richmond American* has a letter from Raleigh, N.C., dated Sept. 18, which says: "On yesterday morning, a beautiful young lady, Miss Virginia Frost, daughter of Austin Frost, an engineer on the Petersburg and Weldon Railroad, and residing in this city, was shot by a negro girl, and killed instantly. Cause—reproving her for insolent language."

The number of servants usually found in a Southern family, of any pretension, always amazes a Northern lady. In one that I have visited, there are exactly three negroes to each white, the negroes being employed solely in the house.

(A Southern lady, of an old and wealthy family, who had been for some time visiting a friend of mine in New York, said to her, as she was preparing to return home: "I cannot tell you how much, after being in your house so long, I dread to go home, and to have to take care of our servants again. We have a much smaller family of whites than you, but we have twelve servants, and your two accomplish a great deal more, and do their work a great deal better than our twelve. You think your girls are very stupid, and that they give you much trouble: but it is as nothing. There is hardly one of our servants that can be trusted to do the simplest work without being stood over. If I order a room to be cleaned, or a fire to be made in a distant chamber, I never can be sure I am obeyed unless I go there and see for myself. If I send a girl out to get anything I want for preparing the dinner, she is as likely as not to forget what is wanted, and not to come back till after the time at which dinner should be ready. A hand-organ in the street will draw all my girls out of the house; and while it remains near us I have no more command over them than over so many monkeys. The parade of a military company has sometimes entirely prevented me from having any dinner cooked; and when the servants, standing in the square looking at the soldiers, see my husband coming after them, they only laugh, and run away to the other side, like playful children.* And, when I reprimand them, they only say they don't mean to do anything wrong,

* In the city of Columbia, S.C., the police are required to prevent the negroes from running in this way after the military. Any negro neglecting to leave the vicinity of a parade, when ordered by a policeman or any military officer, is required, by the ordinance, to be whipped at the guard-house.

or they won't do it again, all the time laughing as though it was all a joke. They don't mind it at all. They are just as playful and careless as any wilful child; and they never will do any work if you don't compel them.")

The slave employer, if he finds he has been so unfortunate as to hire a sulky servant, who cannot be made to work to his advantage, has no remedy but to solicit from his owner a deduction from the price he has agreed to pay for his labour, on the same ground that one would from a livery-stable keeper, if he had engaged a horse to go a journey, but found that he was not strong or skilful enough to keep him upon the road. But, if the slave is the property of his employer, and becomes "rascally," the usual remedy is that which the veterinary surgeon recommended when he was called upon for advice how to cure a jibing horse: "*Sell* him, my lord." "Rascals" are "sent South" from Virginia, for the cure or alleviation of their complaint, in much greater numbers than consumptives are from the more Northern States.

"How do you manage, then, when a man misbehaves, or is sick?" I have been often asked by Southerners, in discussing this question.

If he is sick, I simply charge against him every half day of the time he is off work, and deduct it from his wages. If he is careless, or refuses to do what in reason I demand of him, I discharge him, paying him wages to the time he leaves. With new men in whom I have not confidence, I make a written agreement, before witnesses, on engaging them, that will permit me to do this. As for "rascality," I never had but one case of anything approaching to what you call so. A man insolently contradicted me in the field: I told him to leave his job and go to the house, took hold and finished it myself, then went to the house, made out a written statement of account, counted out the balance in money due to him, gave him the statement and the money, and told him he must go. He knew that he had failed of his duty, and that the law would sustain me, and we parted in a friendly manner, he expressing regret that his temper had driven him from a situation which had been agreeable and satisfactory to him. The probability is, that this single experience educated him so far that his next employer would have no occasion to complain of his "rascality;" and I very much doubt if any amount of corporeal punishment would have improved his temper in the least.

"*Sogering.*"—That slaves have to be "humoured" a great deal, and that they very frequently cannot be made to do their master's will, I have seen much evidence. Not that they often directly refuse to obey an order, but when they are directed to do anything for which they have a disinclination, they undertake it in such a way that the desired result is sure not to be accomplished. They cannot be driven by fear of punishment to do that which the labourers in free communities do cheerfully from their sense of duty, self-respect, or regard for their reputation and standing with their employer. A gentleman who had some free men in his employment in Virginia, that he had procured in New York, told me that he had been astonished, when a dam that he had been building began to give way in a freshet, to see how much more readily than negroes they would obey his orders, and do their best without orders, running into the water waist-deep, in mid-winter, without any hesitation or grumbling.

The manager of a large candle-factory in London, in which the labourers are treated with an unusual degree of confidence and generosity, writes thus in a report to his directors:—

"The present year promises to be a very good one as regards profit, in consequence of the enormous increase in the demand for candles. No mere driving of the men and boys, by ourselves and those in authority under us, would have produced the sudden and very great increase of manufacture, necessary for keeping pace with this demand. It has been effected only by the hearty good-will with which the factory has worked, the men and boys making the great extra exertion, which they saw to be necessary to prevent our getting hopelessly in arrears with the orders, as heartily as if the question had been, how to avert some difficulty threatening themselves personally. One of the foremen remarked with truth, a few days back: 'To look on them, one would think each was engaged in a little business of his own, so as to have only himself affected by the results of his work.'"

A farmer in Lincolnshire, England, told me that once, during an extraordinary harvest season, he had a number of labourers at work without leaving the field or taking any repose for sixty hours—he himself working with them, and eating and drinking only with them during all the time. Such services men may give voluntarily, from their own regard to the value of property to be saved by it, or for the purpose of establishing their credit as worth good wages; but to require it of slaves would be intensely cruel, if not actually impossible. A man can work excessively on his own impulse as much easier than he can be driven to by another, as a horse travels easier in going towards his accustomed stable than in going from it. I mean—and every man who has ever served as a sailor or a soldier will know that it is no imaginary effect—that the actual fatigue, the waste of bodily energy, the expenditure of the physical capacity, is greater in one case than the other.

Sailors and soldiers both, are led by certain inducements to place themselves within certain limits, and for a certain time, both defined by contract, in a condition resembling, in many particulars, that of slaves; and, although they are bound by their voluntary contract and by legal and moral considerations to obey orders, the fact that force is also used to secure their obedience to their officers, scarcely ever fails to produce in them the identical vices which are complained of in slaves. They obey the letter, but defeat the intention of orders that do not please them; they are improvident, wasteful, reckless: they sham illness, and as Dr. Cartwright gives specific medical appellations to discontent, laziness, and rascality, so among sailors and soldiers, when men suddenly find themselves ill and unable to do their duty in times of peculiar danger, or when unusual labour is required, they are humorously said to be suffering under an attack of the powder-fever, the cape-fever, the ice-fever, the coast-fever, or the reefing-fever. The counteracting influences to these vices, which it is the first effort of every good officer to foster, are, first, regard to duty; second, patriotism; third, *esprit du corps*, or professional pride; fourth, self-respect, or personal pride; fifth, self-interest, hope of promotion, or of bounty, or of privileges in mitigation of their hard service, as reward for excellence. Things are never quickly done at sea, unless they are done with a will, or "cheerly," as the sailor's word is—that is, cheerfully. An army is never effective in the field when depressed in its *morale*.

None of these promptings to excellence can be operative, except in a very low degree, to counteract the indolent and vicious tendencies of the Slavery, much more pure than the slavery of the army or the ship, by which the exertions of the Virginia labourer are obtained for his employer.

Incidents, trifling in themselves, constantly betray to a stranger what must be the necessary consequences. The catastrophe of one such occurred since I began to write this letter. I requested a fire to be made in my room, as I was going out this morning. On my return, I found a grand fire—the room door having been closed upon it, and, by the way, I had to obtain assistance to open it, the lock being "out of order." Just now, while I was writing, down tumbled upon the floor, and rolled away close to the valance of the bed, half a hodfull of ignited coal, which had been so piled up on the grate, and left without a fender or any guard, that this result was almost inevitable. And such carelessness of servants you have momentarily to notice.

But the constantly-occurring delays, and the waste of time and labour that you encounter everywhere, are most annoying and provoking to a stranger. At an hotel, for instance, you go to your room and find no conveniences for washing; ring and ring again, and hear the office-keeper ring again and again. At length two servants appear together at your door, get orders, and go away. A quarter of an hour afterwards, perhaps, one returns with a pitcher of water, but no towels; and so on. Yet as the servants seem anxious to please, it can only result from want of system and order.

Until the negro is big enough for his labour to be plainly profitable to his master, he has no training to application or method, but only to idleness and carelessness. Before the children arrive at a working age, they hardly come under the notice of their owner. An inventory of them is taken on the plantation at Christmas; and a planter told me that sometimes they escaped the attention of the overseer and were not returned at all, till twelve or thirteen years old. The only whipping of slaves I have seen in Virginia, has been of these wild, lazy children, as they are being broke in to work. They cannot be depended upon a minute, out of sight.

You will see how difficult it would be, if it were attempted, to eradicate the indolent, careless, incogitant habits so formed in youth. But it is not systematically attempted, and the influences that continue to act upon a slave in the same direction, cultivating every quality at variance with industry, precision, forethought, and providence, are innumerable.

It is not wonderful that the habits of the whole community

should be influenced by, and be made to accommodate to these habits of its labourers. It irresistibly affects the whole industrial character of the people. You may see it in the habits and manners of the free white mechanics and tradespeople. All of these must have dealings or be in competition with slaves, and so have their standard of excellence made low, and become accustomed to, until they are content with slight; false, unsound workmanship. You notice in all classes, vagueness in ideas of cost and value, and injudicious and unnecessary expenditure of labour by a thoughtless manner of setting about work.* For instance, I noticed a rivet loose in my umbrella, as I was going out from my hotel during a shower, and stepped into an adjoining shop to have it repaired.

"I can't do it in less than half an hour, sir, and it will be worth a quarter," said the locksmith, replying to inquiries.

"I shouldn't think it need take you so long—it is merely a rivet to be tightened."

"I shall have to take it all to pieces, and it will take me all of half an hour."

"I don't think you need take it to pieces."

"Yes, I shall—there's no other way to do it."

"Then, as I can't well wait so long, I will not trouble you with it;" and I went back to the hotel, and with the fire-poker did the work myself, in less than a minute, as well as he could have done it in a week, and went on my way, saving half an hour and quarter of a dollar, like a "Yankee."

Virginians laugh at us for such things: but it is because they are indifferent to these fractions, or, as they say, above regarding them, that they cannot do their own business with the rest of the world; and all their commerce, as they are

* A ship's officer told me that he had noticed that it took just about three times as long to have the same repairs made in Norfolk that it did in New York.

absurdly complaining, only goes to enrich Northern men. A man forced to labour under their system is morally driven to indolence, carelessness, indifference to the results of skill, heedlessness, inconstancy of purpose, improvidence, and extravagance. Precisely the opposite qualities are those which are encouraged, and inevitably developed in a man who has to make his living, and earn all his comfort by his voluntarily-directed labour.

"It is with dogs," says an authority on the subject, "as it is with horses; no work is so well done as that which is done cheerfully." And it is with men, both black and white, as it is with horses and with dogs; it is even more so, because the strength and cunning of a man is less adapted to being "broken" to the will of another than that of either dogs or horses.

Work accomplished in a given time.—Mr. T. R. Griscom, of Petersburg, Virginia, stated to me, that he once took accurate account of the labour expended in harvesting a large field of wheat; and the result was that one quarter of an acre a day was secured for each able hand engaged in cradling, raking, and binding. The crop was light, yielding not over six bushels to the acre. In New York a gang of fair cradlers and binders would be expected, under ordinary circumstances, to secure a crop of wheat, yielding from twenty to thirty bushels to the acre, at the rate of about two acres a day for each man.

Mr. Griscom formerly resided in New Jersey; and since living in Virginia has had the superintendence of very large agricultural operations, conducted with slave-labour. After I had, in a letter, intended for publication, made use of this testimony, I called upon him to ask if he would object to my giving his name with it. He was so good as to permit me to do so, and said that I might add that the ordinary waste in harvesting wheat in Virginia, through the carelessness of the negroes, beyond that which occurs in the hands of ordinary Northern labourers, is equal in value to what a Northern farmer would often consider a satisfactory profit on his crop. He also wished me to say that it was his deliberate opinion, formed not without much and accurate observation, that four Virginia slaves do not, when engaged in ordinary agricultural operations, accomplish as much, on an average, as one ordinary free farm labourer in New Jersey.

Mr. Griscom is well known at Petersburg as a man remarkable for accuracy and preciseness; and no man's judgment on this subject could be entitled to more respect.

Another man, who had superintended labour of the same character at the North and in Virginia, whom I questioned closely, agreed entirely with Mr. Griscom, believing that four negroes had to be supported on every farm in the State to accomplish the same work which was ordinarily done by one free labourer in New York.

A clergyman from Connecticut, who had resided for many years in Virginia, told me that what a slave expected to spend a day upon, a Northern labourer would, he was confident, usually accomplish by eleven o'clock in the morning.

In a letter on this subject, most of the facts given in which have been already narrated in this volume, written from Virginia to the *New York Times*, I expressed the conviction that, at the most, not more than one-half as much labour was ordinarily accomplished in Virginia by a certain number of slaves, in a given time, as by an equal number of free labourers in New York. The publication of this letter induced a number of persons to make public the conclusions of their own experience or observations on this subject. So far as I know, these, in every case, sustained my conclusions, or, if any doubt was expressed, it was that I had under-estimated the superior economy of free-labour. As affording evidence more valuable than my own on this important point, from the better opportunities of forming sound judgment, which a residence at different times, in both Virginia and a Free State had given the writers, I have reprinted, in an Appendix, two of these letters, together with a quantity of other testimony from Southern witnesses on this subject, which I beg the reader, who has any doubt of the correctness of my information, not to neglect.

"*Driving.*"—On mentioning to a gentleman in Virginia (who believed that slave-labour was better and cheaper than free-labour), Mr. Griscom's observation, he replied: that without doubting the correctness of the statement of that particular instance, he was sure that if four men did not harvest more than an acre of wheat a day, they could not have been well "driven." He knew that, if properly driven, threatened with punishment, and punished if necessary, negroes would do as much work as it was possible for any white man to do. The same gentleman, however, at another time, told me that negroes were seldom punished ; not oftener, he presumed, than apprentices were, at the North ; that the driving of them was generally left to overseers, who were the laziest and most worthless dogs in the world, frequently not demanding higher wages for their services than one of the negroes whom they were given to manage might be hired for. Another gentleman told me that he would rather, if the law would permit it, have some of his negroes for overseers, than any white man he had ever been able to obtain in that capacity.

Another planter, whom I requested to examine a letter on the subject, that I had prepared for the *Times*, that he might, if he could, refute my calculations, or give me any facts of an opposite character, after reading it said : " The truth is, that, in general, a slave does not do half the work he easily might; and which, by being harsh enough with him, he can be made to do. When I came into possession of my plantation, I soon found the overseer then upon it was good for nothing, and told him I had no further occasion for his services: I then went to driving the negroes myself. In the morning, when I went out, one of them came up to me and asked what work he should go about. I told him to go into the swamp and cut some wood. 'Well, massa,' said he, 's'pose you wants me to do kordins we's been use to doin'; ebery nigger cut a cord a day.' 'A cord! that's what you have been used to doing, is it?' said I. 'Yes, massa, dat's wot dey always makes a nigger do roun' heah—a cord a day, dat's allers de task.' 'Well, now, old man,'* said I, 'you go and cut me two cords to-day.' 'Oh, massa! two cords! Nobody couldn' do dat. Oh! massa, dat's too hard! Nebber heard o' nobody's cuttin' more'n a cord o' wood in a day, roun' heah. No nigger couldn' do it.' 'Well, old man, you have two cords of wood cut to-night, or to-morrow morning you will have two hundred lashes—that's all there is about it. So, look sharp!' Of course, he did it, and no negro has ever cut less than two cords a day for me since, though my neighbours still get but one cord. It was just so with a great many other things—mauling rails: I always have two hundred rails mauled in a day; just twice what it is the custom, in our country, to expect of a negro, and just twice as many as my negroes had been made to do before I managed them myself.

This only makes it more probable that the amount of labour ordinarily and generally performed by slaves in Virginia is

* "Old Man" is a common title of address to any middle-aged negro in Virginia whose name is not known. "Boy" and "Old Man" may be applied to the same person. Of course, in this case, the slave is not to be supposed to be beyond his prime of strength.

very small, compared with that done by the labourers of the Free States.

Of course, it does not follow that all articles produced by such labour cost four times as much as in New York. There are other elements of cost besides labour, as land and fuel. I could not have a bushel of lime or salt or coal dug for me on my farm at Staten Island at any price. There are farms in Virginia where either could be obtained by an hour's labour.

Yet now, as I think of all the homes of which I have had a glimpse, it does not seem to me that men who are reputed to be worth $400,000 have equal advantages of wealth here with those whose property is valued at a quarter that, in the Eastern Free States; men with $40,000 live not as well here, all things considered, as men worth $10,000 at the North; and the farmer who owns half a dozen negroes, and who I suppose must be called worth $4000, does not approach in his possession of civilized comfort, the well-to-do working man with us, who rents a small house, and whose property consists in its furniture, his tools, skill, and strength, and who has a few hundred dollars laid up in the Savings-Bank, against a rainy day. I do not need to ask a farmer, then, any longer why he lifts his stable door into its place, and fastens it by leaning a log against it, as he evidently has been doing for years. He cannot afford to buy or hire a blacksmith for his little farm, and what with going and coming, and paying in corn which must be carried a number of miles over scarcely passable roads, our thriftiest farmers would wait for better times, perhaps, before they would take half the trouble or give a third as much corn as the blacksmith will want for the job, to save a minute's time whenever they needed to enter and leave their stable. And so with everything. Any substantial work costs so much, not alone in money or corn directly, but in the time and trouble of effecting the exchange, that the people make shift and do without it. And this is evidently the case not only with the people as individuals and families, but in their community. It is more obvious, if possible, in the condition of the houses of worship, the schools, the roads, the public conveyances; finally, it accounts for what at first sight appears the marvellous neglect or waste of the natural resources of the country, and it no longer surprises me that a farmer points out a coal bed, which has never been worked, in the bank of a stream which has never been dammed, in the midst of a forest of fine timber trees, with clay and lime and sand convenient, and who yet lives in a miserable smoky cabin of logs on a diet almost exclusively formed of pounded maize and bacon. Nor, when I ask, if a little painstaking here and there would not save much waste of fertility, that he should reply, that inasmuch as land enough, equally good, can be bought for six dollars an acre, the whole fertile matter can be better lost than a week's labour be spent to save all that will not go into this year's crop.

To this general rule of make shift, there is but rare exception; to the general rule of the difficulty or expense of accomplishing any ordinary aim of civilized, in distinction from savage society, I am inclined to think that there is none in Virginia. There are, however, individuals and localities and communities and enterprises, upon which the forces of wealth—including both capital and talent, or energy—seem to have concentrated, just as we sometimes observe to be the case at the North. It is true also, as Virginians are fond of asserting, that absolute destitution of the means of preserving life is more rare than at the North, but then life is barely preserved with little labour by a naked savage in the wilderness; and it must be said that a great number, I almost think a majority, of the

Eastern Virginians live but one step removed from what we should deem great destitution at the North. I am sure, upon consideration, that this phrase would convey no unjust idea of the life of the majority of the Virginians, whom I have seen, to the people of a New England manufacturing town.

I have said that there are points where the forces of wealth seem to have concentrated. As a rule the farm-labour of a slave accomplishes not half as much in a day, as at the North; that of a white man, probably, not a third; that of most mechanics, because of their carelessness and unfaithfulness, much less than of most at the North, although they are paid more than there. But it is true, there are apparent exceptions, and I have been at times a good deal puzzled by them. Generally a patient study discovers a concealed force. Most commonly, I think, the explanation is given in the converse of the maxim that "high wages are the cheapest." The workman who commands much more than the ruling rate of wages is hard to be got, and proverbially accomplishes much more for his employer than the excess of his wages indicates. The man who cannot command the current rates is the first to be dropped off on a reduction, the last to be taken on at an increase of force. As prime field-hand slaves furnish the standard of labour in Virginia, and the vast majority of labourers are far below that standard in quality, their labour is paid much less, and it is of less value relative to its cost. Most of the labouring class of Virginia are of a quality which our farmers would call "dear at any price." If, then, by unusually skilful and energetic management, under favourable circumstances, the labour of slaves, in certain instances, seems to accomplish as much for its course as that of free labourers at the North, it does not follow that results of labour of all kinds in Virginia do not cost ordinarily, and on average, twice or thrice as much as in the adjoining Free States.

Whenever I have found unusual efficiency apparent in any enterprise in Virginia—as sometimes in railroad *construction*, milling, and mining—I have thus far invariably found the negroes employed to be picked men, and, when my inquiries have been frankly answered, that they were working under some unusual stimulus. For instance, a tobacco manufacturer pays the owner of a valuable negro $140 a year for his services, undertaking also to feed and clothe him and otherwise care for his permanent value. He then offers to pay the negro a certain rate per pound for all the tobacco he works up beyond a certain quantity. One of the largest manufacturers informed me that he paid seldom less than $60 a year, and sometimes over $300, to each slave he used, in addition to the rent paid their masters, which was from $100 to $150 a year. I did not learn the averages, but suppose that, while the nominal wages for the labour of these slaves was but little more than the ruling market-rate of $120 a year, their labour really cost the manufacturer at least double that. Hardly any of the white labour employed in enterprises which are pursued with energy and efficiency is native, nor does it ever, so far as I have seen, seem to be established and at home.

CHAPTER V.

THE CAROLINAS.

Norfolk.—In order to be in time for the train of cars in which I was to leave Petersburg for Norfolk, I was called up at an unusual hour in the morning and provided with an apology for breakfast, on the ground that there had not been time to prepare anything better (though I was charged full time on the bill), advised by the landlord to hurry when I seated myself at the table, and two minutes afterwards informed that, if I remained longer, I should be too late.

Thanks to these kind precautions, I reached the station twenty minutes before the train left, and was afterwards carried, with about fifty other people, at the rate of ten miles an hour, to City-point, where all were discharged under a dirty shed, from which a wharf projected into James River.

The train was advertised to connect here with a steamboat for Norfolk. Finding no steamboat at the wharf, I feared, at first, that the delay in leaving Petersburg and the slow speed upon the road had detained us so long that the boat had departed without us. But observing no disappointment or concern expressed by the other passengers, I concluded the boat was to call for us, and had yet to arrive. An hour passed, during which I tried to keep warm by walking up and down the wharf; rain then commenced falling, and I returned to the crowded shed and asked a young man, who was engaged in cutting the letters G. W. B., with a dirk-knife, upon the head of a tobacco-cask, what was supposed to have detained the steamboat.

"Detained her? there aint no detention to her, as I know on; 'taint hardly time for her to be along yet."

Another half-hour, in fact, passed, before the steamboat arrived, nor was any impatience manifested by the passengers. All seemed to take this hurrying and waiting process as the regular thing. The women sat sullenly upon trunks and packing-cases, and watched their baggage and restrained their children; the men chewed tobacco and read newspapers; lounged first on one side and then on the other; some smoked, some walked away to a distant tavern; some reclined on the heaps of freight and went to sleep, and a few conversed quietly and intermittently with one another.

The shores of the James River are low and level—the scenery uninteresting; but frequent planters' mansions, often of considerable size and of some elegance, stand upon the bank, and sometimes these have very pretty and well-kept grounds about them, and the plantations surrounding them are cultivated with neatness and skill. Many men distinguished in law and politics here have their homes.

I was pleased to see the appearance of enthusiasm with which some passengers, who were landed from our boat at one of these places, were received by two or three well-dressed negro servants, who had come from the house to the wharf to meet them. Black and white met with kisses; and the effort of a long-haired sophomore to maintain his dignity, was quite ineffectual to kill the kindness of a fat mulatto woman, who joyfully and pathetically shouted, as she caught him off the gang-plank, "Oh Massa George, is you come back!" Field negroes, standing by, looked on with their usual besotted expression, and neither offered nor received greetings.

Jan. 10*th.*—Norfolk is a dirty, low, ill-arranged town, nearly divided by a morass. It has a single creditable public building, a number of fine private residences, and the polite society is reputed to be agreeable, refined, and cultivated, receiving a character from the families of the resident naval officers. It has all the immoral and disagreeable characteristics of a large seaport, with very few of the advantages that we should expect to find as relief to them. No lyceum or public libraries, no public gardens, no galleries of art, and though there are two "Bethels," no "home" for its seamen; no public resorts of healthful amusement; no place better than a filthy, tobacco-impregnated bar-room or a licentious dance-cellar, so far as I have been able to learn, for the stranger of high or low degree to pass the hours unoccupied by business.

Lieut. Maury has lately very well shown what advantages were originally possessed for profitable commerce at this point, in a report, the intention of which is to advocate the establishment of a line of steamers hence to Para, the port of the mouth of the Amazon. He says—

"Norfolk is in a position to have commanded the business of the Atlantic sea-board: it is midway the coast. It has a back country of great facility and resources; and, as to approaches to the ocean, there is no harbour from the St. John's to the Rio Grande that has the same facilities of ingress and egress at all times and in all weathers. * * The back country of Norfolk is all that which is drained by the Chesapeake Bay—embracing a line drawn along the ridge between the Delaware and the Chesapeake, thence northerly, including all of Pennsylvania that is in the valley of the Susquehanna, all of Maryland this side of the mountains, the valleys of the Potomac, Rappahannock, York, and James Rivers, with the Valley of the Roanoke, and a great part of the State of North Carolina, whose only outlet to the sea is by the way of Norfolk."

In a letter to the *National Intelligencer*, Oct. 31, 1854, after describing similar advantages which the town possesses, to those enumerated above, Lieut. Maury, who is a Virginian, again says—

"Its climate is delightful. It is of exactly that happy temperature where the frosts of the North bite not, and the pestilence of the South walks not. Its harbour is commodious and safe as safe can be. It is never blocked up by ice. It has the double advantage of an inner and an outer harbour. The inner harbour is as smooth as any mill-pond. In it vessels lie with perfect security, where every imaginable facility is offered for loading and unloading." * * * "The back country, which without portage is *naturally* tributary to Norfolk, not only surpasses that which is tributary to New York in mildness of climate, in fertility of soil, and variety of production, but in geographical extent by many square miles. The proportion being as *three to one* in favour of the Virginia port." * * * "The *natural* advantages, then, in relation to the sea or the back country, are superior, *beyond comparison*, to those of New York."

There is little, if any exaggeration in this estimate; yet, if a deadly, enervating pestilence had always raged here, this Norfolk could not be a more miserable, sorry little seaport town than it is. It was not possible to prevent the existence of some agency here for the transhipment of goods, and for supplying the needs of vessels, compelled by exterior circumstances to take refuge in the harbour. Beyond this bare supply of a necessitous demand, and what results from the adjoining naval rendezvous of the nation, there is nothing.

Jan. 18*th.*—The "Great Dismal Swamp," together with the smaller "Dismals" (for so the term is used here), of the same character, along the North Carolina coast, have hitherto been of considerable commercial importance as furnishing a large amount of lumber, and especially of shingles for our Northern use, as well as for exportation. The district from which this commerce proceeds is all a vast quagmire, the soil being entirely composed of decayed vegetable fibre, saturated and surcharged with water; yielding or *quaking* on the surface to the tread of a man, and a large part of it, during most of the year, half inundated with standing pools. It is divided by creeks and water-veins, and in the centre is a pond six miles long and three broad, the shores of which, strange to say, are at a higher elevation above the sea, than any other part of the swamp, and yet are of the same miry consistency. The Great Dismal is about thirty miles long and ten miles wide, on an average; its area about 200,000 acres. And the little Dismal, Aligator, Catfish, Green, and other smaller swamps, on the shores of Albemarle and Pamlico, contain over 2,000,000 acres.

The swamp belongs to a great many proprietors. Most of them own only a few acres, but some possess large tracts and use a heavy capital in the business. One, whose acquaintance I made, employed more than a hundred hands in getting out shingles alone. The value of the swamp land varies with the wood upon it, and the facility with which it can be got off, from 12½ cents to $10 an acre. It is made passable in any desired direction in which trees grow, by laying logs, cut in lengths of eight or ten feet, parallel and against each other on the surface of the soil, or "sponge," as it is called. Mules and oxen are used to some extent upon these roads, but transportation is mainly by hand to the creeks, or to ditches communicating with them or the canal.

Except by those log-roads, the swamp is scarcely passable in many parts, owing not only to the softness of the sponge, but to the obstruction caused by innumerable shrubs, vines, creepers, and briars, which often take entire possession of the surface, forming a dense brake or jungle. This, however, is sometimes removed by fires, which of late years have been frequent and very destructive to the standing timber. The most common shrubs are various smooth-leafed evergreens, and their dense, bright, glossy foliage was exceedingly beautiful in the wintry season of my visit. There is a good deal of game in the swamp—bears and wild cats are sometimes shot, raccoons and opossums are plentiful, and deer are found in the drier parts and on the outskirts. The fishing, in the interior waters, is also said to be excellent.

Nearly all the valuable trees have now been cut off from the swamp. The whole ground has been frequently gone over, the best timber selected and removed at each time, leaving the remainder standing thinly, so that the wind has more effect upon it; and much of it, from the yielding of the soft soil, is uprooted or broken off. The fires have also greatly injured it. The principal stock, now worked into shingles, is obtained *from beneath the surface*—old trunks that have been preserved by the wetness of the soil, and that are found by "sounding" with poles, and raised with hooks or pikes by the negroes.

The quarry is giving out, however; and except that lumber, and especially shingles, have been in great demand at high prices of late, the business would be almost at an end. As it is, the principal men engaged in it are turning their attention to other and more distant supplies. A very large purchase had been made by one company in the Florida everglades, and a schooner, with a gang of hands trained in the "Dismals," was about to sail from Deep Creek, for this new field of operations.

The labour in the swamp is almost entirely done by slaves; and the way in which they are managed is interesting and instructive. They are mostly hired by their employers at a rent, perhaps of one hundred dollars a year for each, paid to their owners. They spend one or two months of the winter —when it is too wet to work in the swamp—at the residence of their master. At this period little or no work is required of them; their time is their own, and if they can get any employment, they will generally keep for themselves what they are paid for it. When it is sufficiently dry—usually early in February—they go into the swamp in gangs, each gang under a white overseer. Before leaving, they are all examined and registered at the Court House; and "passes," good for a year, are given them, in which their features and the marks upon their persons are minutely described. Each man is furnished with a quantity of provisions and clothing, of which, as well as of all that he afterwards draws from the stock in the hands of the overseer, an exact account is kept.

Arrived at their destination, a rude camp is made; huts of logs, poles, shingles, and boughs being built, usually, upon some places where shingles have been worked before, and in which the shavings have accumulated in small hillocks upon the soft surface of the ground.

The slave lumberman then lives measurably as a free man; hunts, fishes, eats, drinks, smokes and sleeps, plays and works, each when and as much as he pleases. It is only required of him that he shall have made, after half a year has passed, such a quantity of shingles as shall be worth to his master so much money as is paid to his owner for his services, and shall refund the value of the clothing and provisions he has required.

No "driving" at his work is attempted or needed. No force is used to overcome the indolence peculiar to the negro. The overseer merely takes a daily account of the number of shingles each man adds to the general stock, and employs another set of hands, with mules, to draw them to a point from which they can be shipped, and where they are, from time to time, called for by a schooner.

At the end of five months the gang returns to dry land, and a statement of account from the overseer's book is drawn up, something like the following:—

Sam Bo to John Doe, Dr.

Feb. 1. To clothing (outfit)	$5 00
Mar. 10. To clothing, as per overseer's account	2 25
Feb. 1. To bacon and meal (outfit)	19 00
July 1. To stores drawn in swamp, as per overseer's account	4 75
July 1. To half-yearly hire, paid his owner .	50 00
	$81 00

Per Contra, Cr.

July 1. By 10,000 shingles, as per overseer's account, 10c.	100 00	
Balance due Sambo		$19 00

which is immediately paid him, and of which, together with the proceeds of sale of peltry which he has got while in the swamp, he is always allowed to make use as his own. No liquor is sold or served to the negroes in the swamp, and, as their first want when they come out of it is an excitement, most of their money goes to the grog-shops.

After a short vacation, the whole gang is taken in the schooner to spend another five months in the swamp as before. If they are good hands and work steadily, they will commonly be hired again, and so continuing, will spend most of their lives at it. They almost invariably have excellent health, as have also the white men engaged in the business. They all consider the water of the "Dismals" to have a medicinal virtue, and quite probably it is a mild tonic. It is greenish in colour, and I thought I detected a slightly resinous taste upon first drinking it. Upon entering the swamp also, an agreeable resinous odour, resembling that of a hemlock forest, was perceptible.

The negroes working in the swamp were more sprightly and straightforward in their manner and conversation than any field-hand plantation negroes that I saw at the South; two or three of their employers with whom I conversed spoke well of them, as compared with other slaves, and made no complaints of "rascality" or laziness.

One of those gentlemen told me of a remarkable case of providence and good sense in a negro that he had employed in the swamp for many years. He was so trustworthy, that he had once let him go to New York as cook of a lumber schooner, when he could, if he had chosen to remain there, have easily escaped from slavery.

Knowing that he must have accumulated considerable money, his employer suggested to him that he might *buy* his freedom, and he immediately determined to do so. But when, on applying to his owner, he was asked $500 for himself, a price which, considering he was an elderly man, he thought too much, he declined the bargain; shortly afterwards, however, he came to his employer again, and said that although he thought his owner was mean to set so high a price upon him, he had been thinking that if he was to be an old man he would rather be his own master, and if he did not live long, his money would not be of any use to him at any rate, and so he had concluded he would make the purchase.

He did so, and upon collecting the various sums that he had loaned to white people in the vicinity, he was found to have several hundred dollars more than was necessary. With the surplus, he paid for his passage to Liberia, and bought a handsome outfit. When he was about to leave, my informant had made him a present, and, in thanking him for it, the free man had said that the first thing he should do, on reaching Liberia, would be to learn to write, and, as soon as he could, he would write to him how he liked the country: he had been gone yet scarce a year, and had not been heard from.

Deep River, Jan. 18th.—The shad and herring fisheries upon the sounds and inlets of the North Carolina coast are an important branch of industry, and a source of considerable wealth. The men employed in them are mainly negroes, slave and free; and the manner in which they are conducted is interesting, and in some respects novel.

The largest sweep seines in the world are used. The gentleman to whom I am indebted for the most of my information, was the proprietor of a seine over two miles in length. It was manned by a force of forty negroes, most of whom were hired at a dollar a day, for the fishing season, which usually commences between the tenth and fifteenth of March, and lasts fifty days. In favourable years the profits are very great. In extremely unfavourable years many of the proprietors are made bankrupt.

Cleaning, curing, and packing houses are erected on the shore, as near as they conveniently may be to a point on the beach, suitable for drawing the seine. Six or eight windlasses, worked by horses, are fixed along the shore, on each side of this point. There are two large seine-boats, in each of which there is one captain, two seine-tenders, and eight or ten oarsmen. In making a cast of the net, one-half of it is arranged on the stern of each of the boats, which, having previously been placed in a suitable position—perhaps a mile off shore, in front of the buildings—are rowed from each other, the captains steering, and the seine-tenders throwing off, until the seine is all cast between them. This is usually done in such a way that it describes the arc of a circle, the chord of which is diagonal with the shore. The hawsers attached to the ends of the seine are brought first to the outer windlasses, and are wound in by the horses. As the operation of gathering in the seine occupies several hours, the boat hands, as soon as they have brought the hawsers to the shore, draw their boats up, and go to sleep.

As the wings approach the shore, the hawsers are from time to time carried to the other windlasses, to contract the sweep of the seine. After the gaff of the net reaches the shore, lines attached toward the bunt are carried to the windlasses, and the boats' crews are awakened, and arrange the wing of the seine, as fast as it comes in, upon the boat again. Of course, as the cast was made diagonally with the shore, one wing is beached before the other. By the time the fish in the bunt have been secured, both boats are ready for another cast, and the boatmen proceed to make it, while the shore gang is engaged in sorting and gutting the "take."

My informant, who had $50,000 invested in his fishing establishment, among other items of expenditure, mentioned that he had used seventy kegs of gunpowder the previous year, and amused himself for a few moments with letting me try to conjecture in what way villanous saltpetre could be put to use in taking fish.

There is evidence of a subsidence of this coast, in many places, at a comparatively recent period; many stumps of trees, evidently standing where they grew, being found some way below the present surface, in the swamps and salt marshes. Where the formation of the shore and the surface, or the strength of the currents of water, which have flowed over the sunken land, has been such as to prevent a later deposit, the stumps of great cypress trees, not in the least decayed, protrude from the bottom of the sounds. These would obstruct the passage of a net, and must be removed from a fishing-ground.

The operation of removing them is carried on during the summer, after the close of the fishing season. The position of a stump having been ascertained by divers, two large seine-boats are moored over it, alongside each other, and a log is laid across them, to which is attached perpendicularly, between the boats, a spar, fifteen feet long. The end of a chain is hooked to the log, between the boats, the other end of which is fastened by divers to the stump which it is wished to raise. A double-purchase tackle leads from the end of the spar to a ring-bolt in the bows of one of the boats, with the fall leading aft, to be bowsed upon by the crews. The mechanical advantages of the windlass, the lever, and the pulley being thus combined, the chain is wound on to the log, until either the stump yields, and is brought to the surface, or the boats' gunwales are brought to the water's edge.

When the latter is the case, and the stump still remains

firm, a new power must be applied. A spile, pointed with iron, six inches in diameter, and twenty feet long, is set upon the stump by a diver, who goes down with it, and gives it that direction which, in his judgment, is best, and driven into it by mauls and sledges, a scaffold being erected between the boats for men to stand on while driving it. In very large stumps, the spile is often driven till its top reaches the water; so that when it is drawn out, a cavity is left in the stump, ten feet in depth. A tube is now used, which is made by welding together three musket-barrels, with a breech at one end, in which is the tube of a percussion breech, with the ordinary position of the nipple reversed, so that when it is screwed on with a detonating cap, the latter will protrude within the barrel. This breech is then inserted within a cylindrical tin box, six inches in diameter, and varying in length, according to the supposed strength of the stump; and soap or tallow is smeared about the place of insertion to make it water tight. The box contains several pounds of gunpowder.

The long iron tube is elevated, and the diver goes down again, and guides it into the hole in the stump, with the canister in his arms. It has reached the bottom—the diver has come up, and is drawn into one of the boats—an iron rod is inserted in the mouth of the tube—all hands crouch low, and hold hard—the rod is let go—crack!—whoo—oosch! The sea swells, boils, and breaks upward. If the boats do not rise with it, they must sink; if they rise, and the chain does not break, the stump must rise with them. At the same moment the heart of cypress is riven; its furthest rootlets quiver; the very earth trembles, and loses courage to hold it; "up comes the stump, or down go the niggers!"

The success of the operation evidently depends mainly on the discretion and skill of the diver. My informant, who thought that he removed last summer over a thousand stumps, using for the purpose seventy kegs of gunpowder, employed several divers, all of them negroes. Some of them could remain under water, and work there to better advantage than others; but all were admirably skilful, and this, much in proportion to the practice and experience they had had. They wear, when diving, three or four pairs of flannel drawers and shirts. Nothing is required of them when they are not wanted to go to the bottom, and, while the other hands are at work, they may lounge, or go to sleep in the boat, which they do, in their wet garments. Whenever a diver displays unusual hardihood, skill, or perseverance, he is rewarded with whisky; or, as they are commonly allowed, while diving, as much whisky as they want, with money. Each of them would generally get every day from a quarter to half a dollar in this way, above the wages paid for them, according to the skill and industry with which they had worked. On this account, said my informant, "the harder the work you give them to do, the better they like it." His divers very frequently had intermittent fevers, but would very rarely let this keep them out of their boats. Even in the midst of a severe "shake," they would generally insist that they were "well enough to dive."

What! slaves eager to work, and working cheerfully, earnestly, and skilfully? Even so. Being for the time managed as freemen, their ambition stimulated by wages, suddenly they, too, reveal sterling manhood, and honour their Creator.

Norfolk, Jan. 19th.—The market gardens at Norfolk—which have been profitably supplying New York markets with poor early vegetables, and half-hardy luxuries for several years past—do not differ at all from market gardens elsewhere. They are situated in every direction for many miles from the city, offering a striking contrast, in all respects, to the large, old-fashioned Virginian farms, among which they are scattered.

On one of the latter, of over a thousand acres, a friend told me he had seen the negroes moving long, strawy manure with shovels, and upon inquiry found there was not a dungfork on the place.

The soil is a poor sandy loam, and manure is brought by shipping from Baltimore, as well as from the nearer towns, to enrich it. The proprietors of the market gardens are nearly all from New Jersey, and brought many of their old white labourers with them. Except at picking-time, when everything possessing fingers is in demand, they do not often employ slaves.

The *Norfolk Argus* says that, from about the 20th June to the 20th July, from 2,000 to 2,500 barrels of potatoes will be shipped daily from that city to Philadelphia and New York, together with 300 to 500 barrels of cucumbers, muskmelons, etc.

Norfolk, Jan. 20th.—While driving a chaise from Portsmouth to Deep River, I picked up on the road a jaded-looking negro, who proved to be a very intelligent and good-natured fellow. His account of the lumber business, and of the life of the lumbermen in the swamps, in answer to my questions, was clear and precise, and was afterwards verified by information obtained from his master.

He told me that his name was Joseph, that he belonged (as property) to a church in one of the inland counties, and that he was hired from the trustees of the church by his present master. He expressed contentment with his lot, but great unwillingness to be sold to go on to a plantation. He liked to "mind himself," as he did in the swamps. Whether he would still more prefer to be entirely his own master, I did not ask.

The Dismal Swamps are noted places of refuge for runaway negroes. They were formerly peopled in this way much more than at present; a systematic hunting of them with dogs and guns having been made by individuals who took it up as a business about ten years ago. Children were born, bred, lived, and died here. Joseph Church told me he had seen skeletons, and had helped to bury bodies recently dead. There were people in the swamps still, he thought, that were the children of runaways, and who had been runaways themselves "all their lives." What a life it must be! born outlaws; educated self-stealers; trained from infancy to be constantly in dread of the approach of a white man as a thing more fearful than wild cats or serpents, or even starvation.

There can be but few, however, if any, of these "natives" left. They cannot obtain the means of supporting life without coming often either to the outskirts to steal from the plantations, or to the neighbourhood of the camps of the lumbermen. They depend much upon the charity or the wages given them by the latter. The poorer white men, owning small tracts of the swamps, will sometimes employ them, and the negroes frequently. In the hands of either they are liable to be betrayed to the negro-hunters. Joseph said that they had huts in "back places," hidden by bushes, and difficult of access; he had, apparently, been himself quite intimate with them. When the shingle negroes employed them, he told me, they made them get up logs for them, and would give them enough to eat, and some clothes, and perhaps two dollars a month in money. But some, when they owed them money, would betray them, instead of paying them.

I asked if they were ever shot. "Oh, yes," he said; "when the hunters saw a runaway, if he tried to get from them, they would call out to him, that if he did not stop they would shoot, and if he did not, they would shoot, and sometimes kill him.

"*But some on 'em would rather be shot than be took, sir,*" he added, simply.

A farmer living near the swamp confirmed this account, and said he knew of three or four being shot in one day.

No particular breed of dogs is needed for hunting negroes: blood-hounds, fox-hounds, bull-dogs, and curs were used,* and one white man told me how they were trained for it, as if it were a common or notorious practice. They are shut up when puppies, and never allowed to see a negro except while training to catch him. A negro is made to run from them, and they are encouraged to follow him until he gets into a tree, when meat is given them. Afterwards they learn to follow any particular negro by scent, and then a shoe or a piece of clothing is taken off a negro, and they learn to find by scent who it belongs to, and to tree him, etc. All this the farmer told me. I don't think dogs are employed in the ordinary "driving" in the swamp, but only to overtake some particular slave, as soon as possible, after it is discovered that he has fled from a plantation. Joseph said that it was easy for the drivers to tell a fugitive from a regularly employed slave in the swamps.

"How do they know them?"

"How do you mean?"

"Oh, dey looks *strange*."

"*Skeared* like, you know, sir, and kind o' strange, cause

---

* I have since seen a pack of negro-dogs, chained in couples, and probably going to the field. They were all of a breed, and in appearance between a Scotch stag-hound and a fox-hound.

dey hasn't much to eat, and ain't decent [not decently clothed], like we is."

When the hunters take a negro who has not a pass, or "free papers," and they don't know whose slave he is, they confine him in jail, and advertise him. If no one claims him within a year he is sold to the highest bidder, at a public sale, and this sale gives title in law against any subsequent claimant.

The form of the advertisements used in such cases is shown by the following, which are cut from North Carolina newspapers, published in counties adjoining the Dismals. Such advertisements are quite as common in the papers of many parts of the Slave States as those of horses or cattle "Taken up" in those of the North:—

WAS TAKEN UP and committed to the Jail of Halifax County, on the 26th day of May, a dark coloured boy, who says his name is JORDAN ARTIS. Said boy says he was born free, and was bound out to William Beale, near Murfreesboro', Hertford County, N.C., and is now 21 years of age. The owner is requested to come forward, prove property, pay charges, and take the said boy away, within the time prescribed by law; otherwise he will be dealt with as the law directs.

O. P. SHELL, Jailer.

Halifax County, N.C., June 8, 1855.

TAKEN UP,

AND COMMITTED to the Jail of New Hanover County, on the 5th of March, 1855, a Negro Man, who says his name is EDWARD LLOYD. Said negro is about 35 or 40 years old, light complected, 5 feet 9½ inches high, slim built, upper fore teeth out; says he is a Mason by trade, that he is free, and belongs in Alexandria, Va., that he served his time at the Mason business under Mr. Wm. Stuart, of Alexandria. He was taken up and committed as a runaway. His owner is notified to come forward, prove property, pay charges, and take him away, or he will be dealt with as the law directs. E. D. HALL, Sheriff.

In the same paper with the last are four advertisements of Runaways: two of them, as specimens, I transcribe.

$200 REWARD.

RAN AWAY from the employ of Messrs. Holmes & Brown, on Sunday night, 20th inst., a negro man named YATNEY or MEDICINE, belonging to the undersigned. Said boy is stout built, about 5 feet 4 inches high, 22 years old, and dark complected, and has the appearance, when walking slow, of one leg being a little shorter than the other. He was brought from Chapel Hill, and is probably lurking either in the neighbourhood of that place, or Beatty's Bridge, in Bladen County.

The above reward will be paid for evidence sufficient to convict any white person of harbouring him, or a reward of $25 for his apprehension and confinement in any Jail in the State, so that I can get him, or for his delivery to me in Wilmington.

J. T. SCHONWALD.

RUNAWAY

FROM THE SUBSCRIBER, on the 27th of May, his negro boy ISOME. Said boy is about 21 years of age; rather light complexion; very coarse hair; weight about 150 lbs.; height about 5 feet 6 or 7 inches; rather pleasing countenance; quick and easy spoken; rather a downcast look. It is thought that he is trying to make his way to Franklin county, N.C., where he was hired in Jan. last, of Thomas J. Blackwell. A liberal Reward will be given for his confinement in any Jail in North or South Carolina, or to any one who will give information where he can be found.

W. H. PRIVETT,
Canwayboro', S.C.

Handbills, written or printed, offering rewards for the return of runaway slaves, are to be constantly seen at nearly every court-house, tavern, and post-office. The frequency with which these losses must occur, however, on large plantations, is most strongly evidenced by the following paragraph from the domestic-news columns of the *Fayetteville Observer*. A man who would pay these prices must anticipate frequent occasion to use his purchase.

"Mr. J. L. Bryan, of Moore county, sold at public auction, on the 20th instant, a pack of ten hounds, trained for hunting runaways, for the sum of $1,540. The highest price paid for any one dog was $301; lowest price, $75; average for the ten. $154. The terms of sale were six months' credit, with approved security, and interest from date."

The newspapers of the South-western States frequently contain advertisements similar to the following, which is taken from the *West Tennessee Democrat:*—

BLOOD-HOUNDS.—I have TWO of the FINEST DOGS for CATCHING NEGROES in the Southwest. They can take the trail TWELVE HOURS after the NEGRO HAS PASSED, and catch him with ease. I live just four miles southwest of Boliver, on the road leading from Boliver to Whitesville. I am ready at all times to catch runaway negroes.—March 2, 1853.

DAVID TURNER.

The largest and best "hotel" in Norfolk had been closed, shortly before I was there, from want of sufficient patronage to sustain it, and I was obliged to go to another house, which, though quite pretending, was shamefully kept. The landlord paid scarcely the smallest attention to the wants of his guests, turned his back when inquiries were made of him, and replied insolently to complaints and requests. His slaves were far his superiors in manners and morals; but, not being one quarter in number what were needed, and consequently not being able to obey one quarter of the orders that were given them, their only study was to disregard, as far as they would be allowed to, all requisitions upon their time and labour. The smallest service could only be obtained by bullying or bribing. Every clean towel that I got during my stay was a matter of special negotiation.

I was first put in a very small room, in a corner of the house, next under the roof. The weather being stormy, and the roof leaky, water was frequently dripping from the ceiling upon the bed and driving in at the window, so as to stand in pools upon the floor. There was no fire-place in the room; the ladies' parlour was usually crowded by ladies and their friends, among whom I had no acquaintance, and, as it was freezing cold, I was obliged to spend most of my time in the stinking bar-room, where the landlord, all the time, sat with his boon companions, smoking and chewing and talking obscenely.

This crew of old reprobates frequently exercised their indignation upon Mrs. Stowe, and other "Infidel abolitionists;" and, on Sunday, having all attended church, afterwards mingled with their ordinary ribaldry laudations of the "evangelical" character of the sermons they had heard.

On the night I arrived, I was told that I would be provided, the next morning, with a room in which I could have a fire, and a similar promise was given me every twelve hours, for five days, before I obtained it; then, at last, I had to share it with two strangers.

When I left, the same petty sponging operation was practised upon me as at Petersburg. The breakfast, for which half a dollar had been paid, was not ready until an hour after I had been called; and, when ready, consisted of cold salt fish; dried slices of bread and tainted butter; coffee, evidently made the day before and half re-warmed; no milk, the milkman not arriving so early in the morning, the servant said; and no sooner was I seated than the choice was presented to me, by the agitated book-keeper, of going without such as this, or of losing the train, and so being obliged to stay in the house twenty-four hours longer.

Of course I dispensed with the breakfast, and hurried off with the porter, who was to take my baggage on a wheelbarrow to the station. The station was across the harbour, in Portsmouth. Notwithstanding all the haste I could communicate to him, we reached the ferry-landing just as the boat left, too late by three seconds. I looked at my watch; it lacked but twenty minutes of the time at which the landlord and the book-keeper and the breakfast-table waiter and the railroad company's advertisements had informed me that the train left. "Nebber mine, massa," said the porter, "dey won't go widout 'ou—Baltimore boat haant ariv yet; dey doan go till dat come in, such."

Somewhat relieved by this assurance, and by the arrival of others at the landing, who evidently expected to reach the train, I went into the market and got a breakfast from the cake and fruit stalls of the negro-women.

In twenty minutes the ferry-boat returned, and after waiting some time at the landing, put out again; but when midway across the harbour, the wheels ceased to revolve, and for fifteen minutes we drifted with the tide. The fireman had been asleep, the fires had got low, and the steam given out. I observed that the crew, including the master or pilot, and the engineer, were all negroes.

We reached the railroad station about half an hour after the time at which the train should have left. There were several persons, prepared for travelling, waiting about it, but there was no sign of a departing train, and the ticket-office was not open. I paid the porter, sent him back, and was added to the number of the waiters.

The delay was for the Baltimore boat, which arrived in an hour after the time the train was advertised, unconditionally, to start, and the first forward movement was more than an hour and a half behind time. A brakeman told me this delay was not very unusual, and that an hour's waiting might be commonly calculated upon with safety.

The distance from Portsmouth to Welden, N.C., eighty miles, was run in three hours and twenty minutes—twenty-five miles an hour. The road, which was formerly a very poor and unprofitable one, was bought up a few years ago, mainly, I believe, by Boston capital, and reconstructed in a substantial manner. The grades are light, and there are few curves. Fare, 2¾ cents a mile.

At a way-station a trader had ready a company of negroes,

intended to be shipped South; but the "servants' car" being quite full already, they were obliged to be left for another train. As we departed from the station, I stood upon the platform of the rear car with two other men. One said to the other:—

"That's a good lot of niggers."

"Damn'd good; I only wish they belonged to me."

I entered the car, and took a seat, and presently they followed, and sat near me. Continuing their conversation thus commenced, they spoke of their bad luck in life. One appeared to have been a bar-keeper; the other an overseer. One said the highest wages he had ever been paid were two hundred dollars a year, and that year he hadn't laid up a cent. Soon after, the other, speaking with much energy and bitterness, said:—

"I wish to God, old Virginny was free of all the niggers."

"It would be a good thing if she was."

"Yes, sir; and, I tell you, it would be a damn'd good thing for us poor fellows."

"I reckon it would, myself."

When we stopped at Weldon, a man was shouting from a stage-coach, "Passengers for Gaston! Hurry up! Stage is waiting!" As he repeated this the third time, I threw up to him my two valises, and proceeded to climb to the box, to take my seat.

"You are in a mighty hurry, aint ye?"

"Didn't you say the stage was waiting?"

"If ye'r goin' ter get any dinner to-day, better get it here; won't have much other chance. Be right smart about it, too."

"Then you are not going yet?"

"You can get yer dinner, if ye want to."

"You'll call me, will you, when you are ready to go?"

"I shan't go without ye, ye needn't be afeard—go 'long in, and get yer dinner; this is the place, if anywar;—don't want to go without yer dinner, do ye?"

Before arriving at Weldon, a handbill, distributed by the proprietors of this inn, had been placed in my hands, from which I make the following extracts:—

"We pledge our word of honour, as gentlemen, that if the fare at our table be inferior to that on the table of our enterprising competitor, we will not receive a cent from the traveller, but relinquish our claims to pay, as a merited forfeit, for what we would regard as a wanton imposition upon the rights and claims of the unsuspecting traveller.

"We have too much respect for the Ladies of our House, to make even a remote allusion to their domestic duties in a public circular. It will not however, be regarded indelicate in us to say, that the duties performed by them have been, and are satisfactory to us, and, as far as we know, to the public. And we will only add, in this connection, that we take much pleasure in superintending both our "Cook-House" and Table in person, and in administering in person to the wants of our guests.

"We have made considerable improvements in our House of late, and those who wish to remain over at Weldon, will find, with us, airy rooms clean beds, brisk fires, and attentive and orderly servants, with abundance of FRESH OYSTERS during the season, and every necessary and luxury that money can procure.

"It is not our wish to deceive strangers nor others; and if, on visiting our House, they do not find things as here represented, they can publish us to the world as impostors, and the ignominy will be ours."

Going into the house, I found most of the passengers by the train at dinner, and the few negro boys and girls in too much of a hurry to pay attention to any one in particular. The only palatable viand within my reach was some cold sweet potatoes; of these I made a slight repast, paid the landlord, who stood like a sentry in the doorway, half a dollar, and in fifteen minutes, by my watch, from the time I had entered, went out, anxious to make sure of my seat on the box, for the coach was so small that but one passenger could be conveniently carried outside. The coach was gone.

"O, yes, sir," said the landlord, hardly disguising his

satisfaction; "gone—yes, sir, some time ago; you was in to dinner, was you, sir—pity! you'll have to stay over till to-morrow now, won't you?"

"I suppose so," said I, hardly willing to give up my intention to sleep in Raleigh that night, even to secure a clean bed and fresh oysters. "Which road does the stage go upon?"

"Along the county road."

"Which is that—this way through the woods?"

"Yes, sir.—Carried off your baggage did he?—Pity! Suppose he forgot you. Pity!"

"Thank you—yes, I suppose he did. Is it a pretty good road?"

"No, sir, 'taint first-rate—good many pretty bad slews. You might go round by the Petersburg Railroad, to-morrow. You'd overtake your baggage at Gaston."

"Thank you. It was not a very fast team, I know. I'm going to take a little run; and, if I shouldn't come back before night, you needn't keep a bed for me. Good day, sir."

In about half an hour I overhauled the coach: as I came up, the driver hailed me—

"Hallo! that you?"

"Why did not you wait for me, or call me when you wanted to go, as you promised?"

"Reckoned yer was inside—didn't look in, coz I asked if 'twas all right, and somebody, this 'ere gentleman here"—[who had got my seat]—"'Yes,' says he, 'all right;' so I reckoned 'twas, and driv along. Mustn't blame me. Ortn't to be so long swallerin' yer dinner—mind, next time!"

The road was as bad as anything under the name of a road can be conceived to be. Wherever the adjoining swamps, fallen trees, stumps, and plantation fences would admit of it, the coach was driven, with a great deal of dexterity, out of the road. When the wheels sunk in the mud, below the hubs, we were sometimes requested to get out and walk. An upset seemed every moment inevitable. At length, it came; and the driver, climbing on to the upper side, opened the door, and asked—

"Got mixed up some in here then, didn't ye? Ladies, hurt any? Well, come, get out here; don't want to stay here all night I reckon, do ye?—Aint nothing broke, as I see. We'll right her right up. Nary durn'd rail within a thousan' mile, I don't s'pose; better be lookin' roun'; got to get somethin' for a pry."

In four hours after I left the hotel at Weldon, the coach reached the bank of the Roanoke, a distance of fourteen miles, and stopped. "Here we are," said the driver, opening the door.

"Where are we—not in Gaston?"

"Durned nigh it. That ere's Gaston, over thar; and you jast holler, and they'll come over arter you in the boat."

Gaston was a mile above us, and on the other side of the river. Nearly opposite was a house, and a scow drawn up on the beach; the distance across the river was, perhaps, a quarter of a mile. When the driver had got the luggage off, he gathered his reins, and said—

"Seems to me them ther gol-durned lazy niggers aint a goin' to come over arter you now; if they won't you'd better go up to the railroad bridge, some of ye, and get a boat, or else go down here to Free Town; some of them cussed free niggers 'll be glad of the job, I no doubt."

"But, confound it, driver! you are not going to leave us here, are you? we paid to be carried to Gaston."

"Can't help it; you are clus to Gaston, any how, and if any man thinks he's goin' to hev me drive him up to the bridge to-night, he's damnably mistaken, he is, and I aint a goin' to do it not for no man, I ain't."

And away he drove, leaving us, all strangers, in a strange

country, just at the edge of night, far from any house, to "holler."

The only way to stop him was to shoot him; and, as we were all good citizens, and travelled with faith in the protection of the law, and not like knights-errant, armed for adventure, we could not do that.

Good citizens? No, we were not; for we have all, to this day, neglected to prosecute the fellow, or his employers. It would, to be sure, have cost us ten times any damages we should have been awarded; but, if we had been really good citizens, we should have been as willing to sacrifice the necessary loss, as knights-errant of old were to risk life to fight bloody giants. And, until many of us can have the nobleness to give ourselves the trouble and expense of killing off these impudent highwaymen of our time, at law, we have all got to suffer in their traps and stratagems.

We soon saw the "gol-durned lazy niggers" come to their scow, and after a scrutiny of our numbers, and a consultation among themselves, which evidently resulted in the conclusion that the job wouldn't pay, go back.

When it began to grow dark, leaving me as a baggage-guard, the rest of the coach's company walked up the bank of the river, and crossed by a railroad bridge to Gaston. One of them afterwards returned with a gang of negroes, whom he had hired, and a large freight-boat, into which, across the snags which lined the shore, we passed all the baggage. Among the rest, there were some very large and heavy chests, belonging to two pretty women, who were moving, with their effects; and, although they remained in our company all the next day, they not only neglected to pay their share of the boat and negro-hire, but forgot to thank us, or even gratefully to smile upon us, for our long toil in the darkness for them.

Working up the swollen stream of the Roanoke, with setting-poles and oars, we at length reached Gaston. When I bought my tickets at the station in Portsmouth, I said, "I will take tickets to any place this side of Raleigh at which I can arrive before night. I wish to avoid travelling after dark." "You can go straight through to Raleigh, before dark," said the clerk. "You are sure of that?" "Yes, sir." On reaching Gaston, I inquired at what time the train for Raleigh had passed: "At three o'clock."

According to the advertisement, it should have passed at two o'clock; and, under the most favourable circumstances, it could not have been possible for us, leaving Portsmouth at the time we did, to reach Gaston before four o'clock, or Raleigh in less than twenty-eight hours after the time promised. The next day, I asked one of the railroad men how often the connection occurred, which is advertised in the Northern papers, as if it were a certain thing to take place at Gaston. "Not very often, sir; it hain't been once, in the last two weeks." Whenever the connection is not made, all passengers whom these railroad freebooters have drawn into their ambush, are obliged to remain over a day, at Gaston; for, as is to be supposed, with such management, the business of the road will support but one train a day.

The route by sea, from Baltimore to Portsmouth, and thence by these lines, is advertised as the surest, cheapest, and most expeditious route to Raleigh. Among my stage companions, were some who lived beyond Raleigh. This was Friday. They would now not reach Raleigh till Saturday night, and such as could not conscientiously travel on Sunday, would be detained from home two days longer than if they had come the land route. One of them lived some eighty miles beyond Raleigh, and intended to proceed by a coach, which was to leave Saturday morning. He would probably be now detained till the following Wednesday, as the coach left Raleigh but twice a week.

The country from Portsmouth to Gaston, eighty miles, partly in Virginia, and partly in North Carolina, is almost all pine forest, or cypress swamp; and on the little land that is cultivated, I saw no indication of any other crop than maize. The soil is light and poor. Between Weldon and Gaston there are heavier soils, and we passed several cotton fields, and planters' mansions. On the low, flat lands bordering the banks of the Roanoke, the soil is of the character of that of James River, fine, fertile, mellow loam; and the maize crop seemed to have been heavy.

Gaston is a village of some twenty houses, shops, and cabins, besides the railroad storehouses, the hotel, and a nondescript building, which may be either a fancy barn, or a little church, getting high. From the manner in which passengers are forced, by the management of the trains arriving here, to patronize it, the hotel, I presume, belongs to the railroad companies. It is ill-kept, but affords some entertainment from its travesty of certain metropolitan vulgarities. I was chummed with a Southern gentleman, in a very small room. Finding the sheets on both our beds had been soiled by previous occupants, he made a row about it with the servants, and, after a long delay, had them changed; then observing that it was probably the mistress's fault, and not the servants', he paid the negro, whom he had been berating, for his trouble.

Among our inside passengers, in the stage-coach, was a free coloured woman; she was treated in no way differently from the white ladies. My room-mate said this was entirely customary at the South, and no Southerner would ever think of objecting to it. Notwithstanding which, I have known young Southerners to get very angry because negroes were not excluded from the public conveyances in which they had taken passage themselves, at the North; and I have always supposed that when they were so excluded, it was from fear of offending Southern travellers, more than anything else.*

Sitting near some men lounging on the river-bank, I took notes of the following interesting information, delivered in a high-keyed, blatant drawl:—

"The best medicine there is, is this here Idee of Potasun.

* *A South Carolina View of the Subject.* (*Correspondence of Willis's Musical World, New York.*)—" *Charlestown, Dec. 31.*—I take advantage of the season of compliments (being a subscriber to your invaluable sheet), to tender you this scrap, as a reply to a piece in your paper of the 17th ult., with the caption : 'Intolerance of coloured persons in New York.' The piece stated that up-town families (in New York) objected to hiring coloured persons as servants, in consequence of 'conductors and drivers refusing to let them ride in city cars and omnibuses,' and coloured boys, at most, may ride on the top. And after dwelling on this, you say, 'Shame on such intolerant and outrageous prejudice and persecution of the coloured race at the North !' You then say, 'Even the slaveholder would cry shame upon us.' You never made a truer assertion in your life. For you first stated that they were even rejected when they had white children in their arms. My dear friend, if this was the only persecution that your coloured people were compelled to yield submission to, then I might say nothing. Are they allowed (if they pay) to sit at the tables of your fashionable hotels ? Are they allowed a seat in the 'dress circle' at your operas ? Are they not subject to all kinds of ill-treatment from the whites ? Are they not pointed at, and hooted at, by the whites (natives of the city), when dressed up a little extra, and if they offer a reply, are immediately overpowered by gangs of whites ? You appear to be a reasonable writer, which is the reason I put these queries, knowing they can only be answered in the affirmative.

" We at the South feel proud to allow them to occupy seats in our omnibuses (public conveyances), while they, with the affection of mothers, embrace our white children, and take them to ride. And in our most fashionable carriages, you will see the slave sitting alongside of *their owner.* You will see the slave clothed in the most comfortable of wearing apparel. And more. Touch that slave, if you dare, and you will see the owner's attachment. And thus, in a very few words, you have the contrast between the situation of the coloured people at the North and South. Do teach the *detestable* Abolitionist of the North his duty, and open his eyes to the misery and starvation that surround his own home. *Teach him* to love his brethren of the South, and teach him to let Slavery alone in the South, while starvation and destitution surround him at the North; and oblige,

"BARON."

It's made out of two minerals; one on 'em they gets in the mountains of Scotland—that's the Idee; the other's steel-filings, and they mixes them eschemically until they works altogether into a solid stuff like saltpetre. Now, I tell you that's the stuff for medicine. It's the best thing a man can ever put into his self. It searches out every narve in his body."

The train by which we were finally able to leave Gaston arrived the next day an hour and a half after its advertised time. The road was excellent and the speed good, a heavy U rail having lately been substituted for a flat one. A new equipment of the road, throughout, is nearly complete. The cars of this train were very old, dirty, and with dilapidated and moth-eaten furniture. They furnished me with a comfort, however, which I have never been able to try before—a full-length lounge, on which, with my overcoat for a pillow, the car being warmed, and unintentionally well ventilated, I slept soundly after dark. Why night-trains are not furnished with sleeping apartments, has long been a wonder to me. We have now smoking-rooms and water-closets on our trains; why not sleeping, dressing, and refreshment rooms? With these additions, and good ventilation, we could go from New York to New Orleans, by rail, without stopping: as it is, a man of ordinary constitution cannot go a quarter that distance without suffering serious indisposition. Surely such improvements could not fail to be remunerative, particularly on lines competing with water communication.

The country passed through, so far as I observed, was almost entirely covered with wood; and such of it as was cultivated, very unproductive.

The city of Raleigh (old Sir Walter), the capital of North Carolina, is a pleasing town—the streets wide, and lined with trees, and many white wooden mansions, all having little court-yards of flowers and shrubbery around them. The State-house is, in every way, a noble building, constructed of brownish-gray granite, in Grecian style. It stands on an elevated position, near the centre of the city, in a square field, which is shaded by some tall old oaks, and could easily be made into an appropriate and beautiful little park; but which, with singular negligence, or more singular economy (while $500,000 has been spent upon the simple edifice), remains in a rude state of undressed nature, and is used as a hog-pasture. A trifle of the expense, employed with doubtful advantage, to give a smooth exterior face to the blocks of stone, if laid out in grading, smoothing, and dressing its ground base, would have added indescribably to the beauty of the edifice. An architect should always begin his work upon the ground.

It is hard to admire what is common; and it is, perhaps, asking too much of the citizens of Raleigh, that they should plant for ornament, or even cause to be retained about such institutions as their Lunatic Asylum, the beautiful evergreens that crowd about the town; but can any man walk from the Capitol oaks to the pine grove, a little beyond the Deaf and Dumb Institution, and say that he would not far rather have the latter than the former to curtain in his habitation? If he can, in summer, let him try it again, as I did, in a soft winter's day, when the evergreens fill the air with a balsamic odour, and the green light comes quivering through them, and the foot falls silently upon the elastic carpet they have spread, deluding one with all the feelings of spring.

The country, for miles about Raleigh, is nearly all pine forest, unfertile, and so little cultivated, that it is a mystery how a town of 2,500 inhabitants can obtain sufficient supplies from it to exist.

The public-house at which I stayed was, however, not only well supplied, but was excellently well kept, for a house of its class, in all other respects. The landlord superintended his business personally, and was always attentive and obliging to his guests; and the servants were sufficiently numerous, intelligent, and well instructed. Though I had no acquaintances in Raleigh, I remained, finding myself in such good quarters, several days. I think the house was called "The Burlinghame."

After this stay, rendered also partly necessary for the repair of damages to my clothing and baggage on the Weldon stage, I engaged a seat one day on the coach, advertised to leave at nine o'clock for Fayetteville. At half-past nine, tired of waiting for its departure, I told the agent, as it was not ready to start, I would walk on a bit, and let them pick me up. I found a rough road—for several miles a clayey surface and much water—and was obliged to pick my way a good deal through the woods on either side. Stopping frequently, when I came to cultivated land, to examine the soil and the appearance of the stubble of the maize—the only crop—in three different fields I made five measurements at random, of fifty feet each, and found the stalks had stood, on an average, five feet by two feet one inch apart, and that, generally, they were not over an inch in diameter at the butt. In one old-field, in process of clearing for new cultivation, I examined a most absurd little plough, with a share not more than six inches in depth, and eight in length on the sole, fastened by a socket to a stake, to which was fitted a short beam and stilts. It was drawn by one mule, and its work among the stumps could only be called scratching. A farmer told me that he considered twenty-five bushels of corn a large crop, and that he generally got only as much as fifteen. He said that no money was to be got by raising corn, and very few farmers here "made" any more than they needed for their own force. It cost too much to get it to market, and yet sometimes they had to buy corn at a dollar a bushel, and waggon it home from Raleigh, or further, enough not having been raised in the country for home consumption. Cotton was the only crop they got any money for. I, nevertheless, did not see a single cotton-field during the day. He said that the largest crop of corn that he knew of, reckoned to be fifty bushels to the acre, had been raised on some reclaimed swamp, while it was still so wet that horses would mire on it all the summer, and most of it had been tended entirely with hoes.

After walking a few miles, the country became more flat, and was covered with old forests of yellow pine, and, at nine miles south of Raleigh, there were occasionally young long-leaved pines: exceedingly beautiful they are while young, the colour being more agreeable than that of any other pine, and the leaves, or "straw," as its foliage is called here, long, graceful, and lustrous. As the tree gets older, it becomes of a stiffer character and darker colour.

I do not think I passed, in ten miles, more than half a dozen homesteads, and of these but one was at all above the character of a hut or cabin. The same remarkable appearance of listlessness, which I had noticed so often in Virginia, characterized the men who stood leaning against the logs of the hovels. They blinked at me as I passed, as if unable to withdraw their hands from their pockets to shade their eyes. Every dwelling sent its pack of curs to meet me, and as often as they opened cry, a woman, with a pipe in her mouth, would come to the door and call them off; the men and boys blinking on in rest and silence.

A little after one o'clock I reached "Banks's," a plantation where the stage horses are changed, eleven miles from

Raleigh. Here I waited nearly an hour, till the coach arrived, when, fresh horses having been put on, I took an outside seat.

"There ain't a man in North Car'lina could drive them horses up the hills without a whip," said the driver. "You ought to get yesef a whip, massa," said one of the negroes. "Durnation! think I'm going to buy whips! the best whip in North Car'lina wouldn't last a week on this road." "Dat's a fac—dat ar is a fac; but look yeah, massa, ye let me hab yer stick, and I'll make a whip for ye; ye nebber can make Bawley go widout it, no how." The stick was a sapling rod, of which two or three lay on the coach top; the negro fastened a long leather thong to it. "Dah! ye can fetch old Bawley wi' dat." "Bawley" had been tackled in as the leader of the "spike team;" but, upon attempting to start, it was found that he couldn't be driven in that way at all, and the driver took him out and put him to the pole, within reach of the butt of his stick, and another horse was put on the lead.

One negro now took the leader by the head, and applied a stick lustily to his flanks; another, at the near wheeler, did the same; and the driver belaboured Bawley from the box. But as soon as they began to move forward, and the negro let go the leader's head, he would face about. After this had been repeated many times, a new plan of operations was arranged that proved successful. Leaving the two wheelers to the care of the negroes, the driver was enabled to give all his attention to the leader. When the wheelers started, of course he was struck by the pole, upon which he would turn tail and start for the stable. The negroes kept the wheelers from following him, and the driver with his stick, and another negro with the bough of a tree, thrashed his face; he would then turn again, and, being hit by the pole, start ahead. So, after ten minutes of fearful outcry, we got off.

"How far is it to Mrs. Barclay's?" a passenger had asked. "Thirteen miles," answered a negro; "but I tell 'ou, massa, dais a heap to be said and talk 'bout 'fore 'ou see Missy Barclay's wid dem hosses." There was, indeed.

"Bawley—*you!* Bawley—Bawley! wha' 'bout?—ah!"

"*Rock!* wha' you doin'?—(durned sick horse—an't fit to be in a stage, nohow)."

"Bawley! you! g'up!"

"Oh! you dod-rotted Bob—*Bob!*—(he don't draw a pound, and he an't a gwine to)—*you,* Bob!—(well, he can't stop, can he, as long as the wheelers keep movin'?) Bob! I'll break yer legs, you don't git out the way."

"Oh, Bawley!—(no business to put such a lame hoss into the stage.) Blamnation, Bawley! Now, if you stop, I'll kill you."

"Wha' 'bout, Rock? Dod burn that Rock! You stop if you dare! (I'll be durned to Hux if that 'ere hoss arn't all used up.)"

"You, *Bob!* get out de way, or I'll be ——."

"Oh! d'rot yer soul, Bawley—y're gwine to stop! G'up! G'up! *Rock!* You all-fired ole villain! Wha' 'bout? (If they jus' git to stoppin', all hell couldn't git the mails through to-night.)"

After about three miles of this, they did stop. The driver threw the reins down in despair. After looking at the wheels, and seeing that we were on a good piece of road, nothing unusual to hinder progress, he put his hands in his pockets, and sat quietly a minute, and then began, in a business-like manner, to swear, no longer confining himself to the peculiar idiomatic profanity of the country, but using real, outright, old-fashioned, uncompromising English oaths, as loud as he could yell. Then he stopped, and after another pause, began to talk quietly to the horses:

"You, Bob, you won't draw? Didn't you git enough last night? (I jabbed my knife into his face twice when we got into that fix last night;" and the wounds on the horse's head showed that he spoke the truth.). "I swar, Bob, if I have to come down thar, I'll cut your throat."

He stopped again, and then sat down on the foot-board, and began to beat the wheelers as hard and as rapidly as possible with the butt of his stick. They started, and, striking Bob with the pole, he jumped and turned round; but a happy stroke on "the raw" in his face brought him to his place; and the stick being applied just in time to the wheelers, he caught the pole and jumped ahead. We were off again.

"Turned over in that 'ere mire hole last night," said the driver. "Couldn't do anythin' with 'em—passengers camped out—thar's were they had their fire, under that tree; didn't get to Raleigh till nine o'clock this mornin'. That's the reason I wern't along after you any sooner—hadn't got my breakfast; that's the reason the hosses don't draw no better to-day, too, I s'pose. *You*, Rock!—*Bawley!*—Bob!"

After two miles more, the horses stopped once more. The driver now quietly took the leader off (he had never drawn at all), and tied him behind the coach. He then began beating the near wheeler, a passenger did the same to Bawley—both standing on the ground—while I threw off my overcoat and walked on. For a time I could occasionally hear the cry, "Bawl—Rock!" and knew that the coach was moving again; gradually I outwalked the sound.

The road was a mere opening through a forest of the long-leafed pine; the trees from eight to eighteen inches in diameter, with straight trunks bare for nearly thirty feet, and their evergreen foliage forming a dense dark canopy at that height, the surface of the ground undulating with long swells, occasionally low and wet. In the latter case, there was generally a mingling of deciduous trees and a watercourse crossing the road, with a thicket of shrubs. The soil sandy, with occasionally veins of clay; the latter more commonly in the low ground, or in the descent to it. Very little grass, herbage, or underwood; and the ground covered, except in the road, with the fallen pine-leaves. Every tree, on one, two, or three sides, was scarified for turpentine. In ten miles, I passed half a dozen cabins, one or two small clearings, in which corn had been planted, and one turpentine distillery, with a dozen sheds and cabins clustered about it.

In about an hour after I left the coach, the driver, mounted on Bob, overtook me: he was going on to get fresh horses.

After dark, I had some difficulty in keeping the road, there being frequent forks, and my only guide the telegraph wire. I had to cross three or four brooks, which were now high, and had sometimes floated off the logs which, in this country, are commonly placed, for the teamsters, along the side of the road, where it runs through water. I could generally jump from stump to stump; and, by wading a little at the edges in my staunch Scotch shooting-boots, get across dry-shod. Where, however, the water was too deep, I always found, by going up or down stream, a short way, a fallen trunk across it, by which I got over.

I met the driver returning with two fresh horses; and at length, before eight o'clock, reached a long one-story cabin, which I found to be Mrs. Barclay's. It was right cheerful and comforting to open the door, from the dark, damp, chilly night, into a large room, filled with blazing light from a great fire of turpentine pine, by which two stalwart men were reading newspapers, a door opening into a background of supper-table and kitchen, and a nice, stout, kindly-looking, Quaker-like old lady coming forward to welcome me.

VOL. I.   N

As soon as I was warm, I was taken out to supper: seven preparations of swine's flesh, two of maize, wheat cakes, broiled quails, cold roast turkey, coffee, and tea.

My bed-room was a house by itself, the only connection between it and the main building being a platform, or gallery, in front. A great fire burned here also in a broad fire-place; a stuffed easy-chair had been placed before it, and a tub of hot water, which I had not thought to ask for, to bathe my weary feet.

And this was a piny-woods stage-house! But genius will find its development, no matter where its lot is cast; and there is as much genius for inn-keeping as for poetry. Mrs. Barclay is a Burns in her way, and with even more modesty; for, after twenty-four hours of the best entertainment that could be asked for, I was only charged one dollar. I paid two dollars for my stage-coach privileges—to wit, riding five miles and walking twenty-one.

At three o'clock in the morning, the three gentlemen that I had left ten miles back at four o'clock the previous day, were dragged, shivering in the stage-coach, to the door. They had had no meal since breakfasting at Raleigh; and one of them was now so tired that he could not eat, but dropt prone on the floor before the fire and slept the half-hour they were changing horses, or rather resting horses, for no relay was left.

I afterwards met one of the company in Fayetteville. Their night's adventure after I left them, and the continued cruelty to the horses, were most distressing. The driver once got off the box, and struck the poor, miserable, sick "Rock" with a rail, and actually knocked him down in the road. At another time, after having got fresh horses, when they, too, were "stalled," he took them out of the harness and turned them loose, and, refusing to give any answer to the inquiries of the passengers, looked about for a dry place, and laid down and went to sleep on the ground. One of the passengers had then walked on to Mrs. Barclay's, and obtained a pair of mules, with which the coach was finally brought to the house. The remainder kindled a fire, and tried to rest themselves by it. They were sixteen hours in coming thirty miles, suffering much from cold, and without food.

The next day I spent in visiting turpentine and rosin works, piny-wood farms, etc., under the obliging guidance of Mrs. Barclay's son-in-law, and in the evening again took the coach. The horses were better than on the previous stage: upon my remarking this to the driver, he said that the reason was, that they took care of this team themselves (the drivers); on the last stage the horses were left to negroes, who would not feed them regularly, nor take any decent care of them. " Why, what do you think?" said he; " when I got to Banks's, this morning, I found my team hadn't been fed all day; they hadn't been rubbed nor cleaned, nary durned thing done to 'em, and thar the cussed darkey was, fast asleep. Reckon I didn't gin him a wakin' up!"

" You don't mean the horses that you drove up?"

" Yes, I do, and they hadn't a cussed thing to eat till they got back to Barclay's!"

" How was it possible for you to drive them back?"

" Why, I don't suppose I could ha' done it if I'd had any passengers: (you *Suze!*) shall lose a mail again to-night, if this mare don't travel better, (durn ye, yer ugly, I believe). She's a good mare—a heap of go in her, but it takes right smart of work to get it out. *Suze!*"

So we toiled on, with incessant shouting, and many strange piny-wood oaths, and horrid belabouring of the poor horses' backs, with the butt-end of a hickory whip-stalk, till I really thought their spinal-columns must break. The country, the same undulating pine forest, the track tortuous among the trees, which frequently stood so close that it required some care to work between them. Often we made detours from the original road, to avoid a fallen tree, or a mire-hole, and all the time we were bouncing over protruding roots and small stumps. There was but little mud, the soil being sand, but now and then a deep slough. In one of these we found a waggon, heavily laden, stuck fast, and six mules and five negroes tugging at it. With our help it was got out of the way, and we passed on. Soon afterwards we met the return coach, apparently in a similar predicament; but one of the passengers, whom I questioned, replied: "No, not stalled, exactly, but somehow *the horses won't draw*. We have been more than three hours coming about four miles."

"How is it you have so many balky horses?" I asked the driver.

"The old man buys 'em up cheap, 'cause nobody else can do anything with 'em."

"I should not think you could do much with them, either—except to kill them."

"Well, that's what the old man says he buys 'em for. He was blowing me up for losing the mail t'other night; I told him, says I, 'You have to a'most kill them horses, 'fore you can make 'em draw a bit,' says I. 'Kill 'em, damn 'em, kill em, then; that's what I buy 'em for,' says he. 'I buy 'em a purpose to kill; that's all they are good for, ain't it?' says he. 'Don't s'pose they're going to last for ever, do ye?' says he."

We stopped once, nearly half an hour, for some unexplained reason, before a house on the road. The door of the house was open, an enormous fire was burning in it, and, at the suggestion of the driver, I went in to warm myself. It was a large log-cabin, of two rooms, with beds in each room, and with an apartment overhead, to which access was had by a ladder. Among the inmates were two women; one of them sat in the chimney-corner smoking a pipe, and rocking a cradle; the other sat directly before the fire, and full ten feet distant. She was apparently young, but her face was as dry and impassive as a dead man's. She was doing nothing, and said but little; but, once in about a minute, would suddenly throw up her chin, and spit with perfect precision into the hottest embers of the fire. The furniture of the house was more scanty and rude than I ever saw before in any house, with women living in it, in the United States. Yet these people were not so poor but that they had a negro woman cutting and bringing wood for their fire.

It must be remembered that this is a long-settled country, having been occupied by Anglo-Saxons as early as any part of the Free States, and that it is the main road between the capital of North Carolina and its chief sea-port.

There is nothing that is more closely connected, both as cause and effect, with the prosperity and wealth of a country, than its means and modes of travelling, and of transportation of the necessities and luxuries of life. I saw this day, as I shall hereafter describe, three thousand barrels of resin, worth a dollar and a half a barrel in New York, thrown away, a mere heap of useless offal, because it would cost more to transport it than it would be worth. There was a single waggon, with a ton or two of sugar, and flour, and tea, and axes, and cotton cloths, unable to move, with six mules, and five negroes at work upon it. Raleigh is a large distributing post-office, getting a very heavy mail from the North; here was all that is sent by one of its main radii, travelling one day two miles an hour, the next four miles, and on each occasion failing to connect with the conveyances which we pay to scatter further the intelligence and wealth transmitted by it. Barbarous is too mild a term to apply to the manner in which even this was done. The improvidence, if not the cruelty, no sensible barbarian could have been guilty of.

Afterwards, merely to satisfy my mind (for there is a satisfaction in seeing even scoundrelism consistently carried out, if attempted at all in a business), I called on the agent of the line at Fayetteville, stated the case, and asked if any part of what I had paid for my passage would be returned me, on account of the disappointment and delay which I had suffered from the inability of the proprietor to carry out his contract with me. The impudence of the suggestion, of course, only created amusement; and I was smilingly informed that the business was not so "lucky" that the proprietor could afford to pay back money that he had once got into his hands. What I had seen was regarded by no one, apparently, as at all unusual.

At one of the stations for changing horses, an old coloured man was taken into the coach. I ascertained from him that he was a blacksmith, and had been up the line to shoe the horses at the different stables. Probably he belonged (poor fellow!) to the man who bought horses to be killed in doing his work. After answering my inquiries, he lay down in the bottom of the coach, and slept until we reached Fayetteville. The next time we changed, the new driver inquired of the old one what passengers he had. "Only one gentleman, and old man Ned."

"Oh! is old man along—that's good—if we should turn over, or break down, or anything, reckon he could nigh about pray us up—he's right smart at prayin'."

"Well, I tell you, now, ole man can trot out as smart a prayer, when he's a mind to go in for't, as any man I ever heerd, durned if he can't."

The last ten miles we came over rapidly, smoothly, and

quietly, by a plank-road, reaching Fayetteville about twelve, of a fine, clear, frosty night.

Entering the office or bar-room of the stage-house, at which I had been advised to stay while in Fayetteville, I found it occupied by a group of old soakers, among whom was one of perhaps sixteen years of age. This lad, without removing the cigar which he had in his mouth, went to the bar, whither I followed him, and, without saying a word, placed an empty tumbler before me.

"I don't wish anything to drink," said I; "I am cold and tired, and I would like to go to a room. I intend to stay here some days, and I should be glad if you could give me a private room with a fire in it."

"Room with a fire in it?" he inquired, as he handed me the registry-book.

"Yes; and I will thank you to have it made immediately, and let my baggage be taken up."

He closed the book, after I had written my name, and returned to his seat at the stove, leaving me standing, and immediately engaged in conversation, without paying any attention to my request. I waited some time, during which a negro came into the room, and went out again. I then repeated my request, necessarily aloud, and in such a way as to be understood, not only by the boy, but by all the company. Immediately all conversation ceased, and every head was turned to look at me. The lad paused a moment, spit upon the stove, and then—

"Want a room to yourself?"

"Yes, if convenient."

No answer and no movement, all the company staring at me as if at a detected burglar.

"Perhaps you can't accommodate me?"

"Want a fire made in your room?"

"Why, yes, if convenient; but I should like to go to my room, at any rate; I am very tired."

After puffing and spitting for a moment, he rose and pulled a bell; then took his seat again. In about five minutes a negro came in, and during all this time there was silence.

"What'll you drink, Baker?" said the lad, rising and going to the bar, and taking no notice of the negro's entrance. A boozy man followed him, and made some reply; the lad turned out two glasses of spirits, added water to one, and drank it in a gulp.*

"Can this boy show me to my room?" I asked.

"Anybody in number eleven, Peter?"

"Not as I knows on, sar."

"Take this man's baggage up there."

I followed the negro up to number eleven, which was a large back room in the upper story, with four beds in it.

"Peter," said I, "I want a fire made here."

"Want a fire, sar?"

"Yes, I want you to make a fire."

"Want a fire, master, this time o' night?"

"Why, yes; I want a fire. Where are you going with the lamp?"

"Want a lamp, massa?"

"Want a lamp? Certainly, I do."

After about ten minutes, I heard a man splitting wood in the yard, and, in ten more, Peter brought in three sticks of green wood, and some chips; then, the little bed-lamp having burned out, he went into an adjoining room, where I heard him talking to some one, evidently awakened by his entrance

---

* The mother of this young man remonstrated with a friend of mine, for permitting his son to join a company of civil engineers, engaged, at the time, in surveying a route for a road—he would be subject to such fatiguing labour, and so much exposure to the elements; and congratulated herself that her own child was engaged in such an easy and gentleman-like employment as that of hotel-clerk and bar keeper.

to get a match; that failing, he went for another. By one o'clock, my fire was made.

"Peter," said I, "are you going to wait on me, while I stay here?"

"Yes, sar; I 'tends to dis room."

"Very well; take this, and, when I leave, I'll give you another, if you take good care of me. Now, I want you to get me some water."

"I'll get you some water in de morning, sar."

"I want some to-night—some water and some towels; don't you think you can get them for me?"

"I reckon so, massa, if you wants 'em. Want 'em 'fore you go to bed?"

"Yes; and get another lamp."

"Want a lamp?"

"Yes, of course."

"Won't the fire do you?"

"No; bring a lamp. That one won't burn without filling; you need not try it."

The water and the lamp came, after a long time.

In the morning, early, I was awakened by a knock at the door.

"Who's there?"

"Me, massa; I wants your boots to black."

I got up, opened the door, and returned to bed. Falling asleep, I was soon again awakened by Peter throwing down an armful of wood upon the floor. Slept again, and was again awakened, by Peter's throwing up the window, to empty out the contents of the wash bowl, etc. The room was filled with smoke of the fat light wood: Peter had already made a fire for me to dress by; but I again fell asleep, and, when I next awoke, the breakfast bell was ringing. Peter had gone off, and left the window and door open, and the fire had burned out. My boots had been taken away, and the bell-wire was broken. I dressed, and walking to the bar-room, asked the bar-keeper—a complaisant, full-grown man—for my boots. He did not know where they were, and rang the bell for Peter. Peter came, was reprimanded for his forgetfulness, and departed. Ten minutes elapsed, and he did not return. I again requested that he should be called; and this time he brought my boots. He had had to stop to black them; having, he said, been too busy to do it before breakfast.

The following evening, as it grew too cold to write in my room, I went down, and found Peter, and told him I wanted a fire again, and that he might get me a couple of candles. When he came up, he brought one of the little bed-lamps, with a capacity of oil for fifteen minutes' use. I sent him down again to the office, with a request to the proprietor that I might be furnished with candles. He returned, and reported that there were no candles in the house.

"Then, get me a larger lamp."

"Aint no larger lamps, nuther, sar;—none to spare."

"Then go out, and see if you can't buy me some candles, somewhere."

"Aint no stores open, Sunday, massa, and I don't know where I can buy 'em."

"Then go down, and tell the bar-keeper, with my compliments, that I wish to write in my room, and I would be obliged to him if he would send me a light, of some sort; something that will last longer, and give more light, than these little lamps."

"He won't give you none, massa—not if you hab a fire. Can't you see by da light of da fire? When a gentlemen hab a fire in his room, dey don't count he wants no more light 'n dat."

"Well, make the fire, and I'll go down and see about it."

As I reached the foot of the stairs, the bell rang, and I went in to tea. The tea table was moderately well lighted with candles. I waited till the company had generally left it, and then said to one of the waiters—

"Here are two dimes: I want you to bring me, as soon as you can, two of these candles to number eleven; do you understand?"

"Yes, sar; I'll fotch 'em, sar."

And he did.

About eight o'clock, there was an alarm of fire. Going into the street, I was surprised to observe how leisurely the people were walking toward the house in flames, standing very prominently, as it did, upon a hill, at one end of the town. As I passed a church, the congregation was coming out; but very few quickened their step above a strolling pace. Arrived near the house, I was still more astonished to see how few, of the crowd assembled, were occupied in restraining the progress of the fire, or in saving the furniture, and at the prevailing stupidity, confusion, and want of system and concert of action, in the labour for this purpose. A large majority of those engaged were negroes. As I returned toward the hotel, a gentleman, walking, with a lady, before me, on the side walk, accosted a negro whom he met:

"What! Moses! That you? Why were you not here sooner?"

"Why, Mass Richard, I was singing, an' I didn' her de bells and——I see twant in our ward, sar, and so I didn' see as dar was zactly 'casion for me to hurry myself to def. Ef eed a been in our ward, Mass Richard, I'd a rallied, you knows I would. Mose would ha rallied, ef eed a been in our ward—ha! ha! ha!—you knows it, Mass Richard!"

And he passed on, laughing comically, without further reproof.

Fayetteville.—The negroes employed in the turpentine business, to which during the last week I have been giving some examination, seem to me to be unusually intelligent and cheerful, decidedly more so than most of the white people inhabiting the turpentine forest. Among the latter there is a large number, I should think a majority, of entirely uneducated, poverty-stricken vagabonds. I mean by vagabonds, simply, people without habitual, definite occupation or reliable means of livelihood. They are poor, having almost no property but their own bodies; and the use of these, that is, their labour, they are not accustomed to hire out statedly and regularly, so as to obtain capital by wages, but only occasionally by the day or job, when driven to it by necessity. A family of these people will commonly hire, or "squat" and build, a little log cabin, so made that it is only a shelter from rain, the sides not being chinked, and having no more furniture or pretension to comfort than is commonly provided a criminal in the cell of a prison. They will cultivate a little corn, and possibly a few roods of potatoes, cow-peas, and coleworts. They will own a few swine, that find their living in the forest; and pretty certainly, also, a rifle and dogs; and the men, ostensibly, occupy most of their time in hunting. I am, mainly, repeating the statements of one of the turpentine distillers, but it was confirmed by others, and by my own observation, so far as it went.

A gentleman of Fayetteville told me that he had, several times, appraised, under oath, the whole household property of families of this class at less than $20. If they have need of money to purchase clothing, etc., they obtain it by selling their game or meal. If they have none of this to spare, or an insufficiency, they will work for a neighbouring farmer for a few days, and they usually get for their labour fifty cents a day, *finding themselves*. The farmers and distillers say, that that they do not like to employ them, because they cannot be relied upon to finish what they undertake, or to work according to directions; and because, being white men, they cannot "drive" them. That is to say, their labour is even more inefficient and unmanageable than that of slaves.

That I have not formed an exaggerated estimate of the proportion of such a class, will appear to the reader more probable from the testimony of a pious colporteur, given before a public meeting in Charleston, in February, 1855. I quote from a Charleston paper's report. The colporteur had been stationed at —— county, N.C. :—" *The larger portion* of the inhabitants seemed to be totally given up to a species of mental hallucination, which carried them captive at its will. They nearly all believed implicitly in witchcraft, and attributed everything that happened, good or bad, to the agency of persons whom they supposed possessed of evil spirits."

—The majority of what I have termed turpentine-farmers—. meaning the small proprietors of the long-leafed pine forest land—are people but a grade superior, in character or condition, to these vagabonds. They have habitations more like houses —log-cabins, commonly, sometimes chinked, oftener not— without windows of glass, but with a few pieces of substantial old-fashioned heir-loom furniture; a vegetable garden, in which, however, you will find no vegetable but what they call "collards" (colewort) for " greens ;" fewer dogs, more swine, and larger clearings for maize, but no better crops than the poorer class. Their property is, nevertheless, often of considerable money value, consisting mainly of negroes, who, associating intimately with their masters, are of superior intelligence to the slaves of the wealthier classes.

Some of the larger proprietors, who are also often cotton

planters, cultivating the richer low lands, are said to be gentlemen of good estate—intelligent, cultivated, and hospitable.

North Carolina has a proverbial reputation for the ignorance and torpidity of her people; being, in this respect, at the head of the Slave States. I do not find the reason of this in any innate quality of the popular mind; but, rather, in the circumstances under which it finds its development. Owing to the general poverty of the soil in the Eastern part of the State, and to the almost exclusive employment of slave labour on the soils productive of cotton; owing, also, to the difficulty and expense of reaching market with bulky produce from the interior and western districts, population and wealth is more divided than in the other Atlantic States; industry is almost entirely rural, and there is but little communication or concert of action among the small and scattered proprietors of capital. For the same reason, the advantages of education are more difficult to be enjoyed, the distance at which families reside apart preventing children from coming together in such numbers as to give remunerative employment to a teacher. The teachers are, generally, totally unfitted for their business; young men, as a clergyman informed me, themselves not only unadvanced beyond the lowest knowledge of the elements of primary school learning, but often coarse, vulgar, and profane in their language and behaviour, who take up teaching as a temporary business, to supply the demand of a neighbourhood of people as ignorant and uncultivated as themselves.

> The native white population of North Carolina is . . 550,267
> The whole white population under 20 years, is . . . 301,106
> Leaving white adults over 20 249,161
> Of these there are natives who cannot read and write . 73,226*

Being more than one-fourth of the native white adults.

* Official Census Report, pp. 309, 299, 317.

But the aspect of North Carolina with regard to slavery, is, in some respects, less lamentable than that of Virginia. There is not only less bigotry upon the subject, and more freedom of conversation, but I saw here, in the institution, more of patriarchal character than in any other State. The slave more frequently appears as a family servant—a member of his master's family, interested with him in his fortune, good or bad. This is a result of the less concentration of wealth in families or individuals, occasioned by the circumstances I have described. Slavery thus loses much of its inhumanity. It is still questionable, however, if, as the subject race approaches civilization, the dominant race is not proportionately detained in its onward progress. One is forced often to question, too, in viewing slavery in this aspect, whether humanity and the accumulation of wealth, the prosperity of the master, and the happiness and improvement of the subject, are not in some degree incompatible.

These later observations are made after having twice again passed through the State, once in a leisurely way on horseback. In some of the Western and Northern central parts of the State, there is much more enterprise, thrift, and comfort than in the Eastern part, where I had my first impressions.

I left Fayetteville in a steamboat (advertised for 8 o'clock, left at 8.45) bound down Cape Fear River to Wilmington. A description of the river, with incidents of the passage, will serve to show the character of most of the navigable streams of the cotton States, flowing into the Atlantic and the Gulf, and of the manner of their navigation.

The water was eighteen feet above its lowest summer stages; the banks steep, thirty feet high from the present water surface—from fifty to one hundred feet apart—and covered with large trees and luxuriant vegetation; the course crooked; the current very rapid; the trees overhanging the banks, and frequently falling into the channel—making the navigation hazardous. The river is subject to very rapid rising. The master told me that he had sometimes left his boat aground at night, and, on returning in the morning, found it floating in twenty-five feet water, over the same spot. The difference between the extremes of low stages and floods is as much as seventy feet. In summer, there are sometimes but eighteen inches of water on the bars: the boat I was in drew but fourteen inches, light. She was a stern-wheel craft—the boiler and engine (high pressure) being placed at opposite ends, to balance weights. Her burden was three hundred barrels, or sixty tons measurement. This is the character of most of the boats navigating the river—of which there are now twelve. Larger boats are almost useless in summer, from their liability to ground; and even the smaller ones, at low stages of water, carry no freight, but are employed to tow up "flats" or shallow barges. At this season of the year, however, the steamboats are loaded close to the water's edge.

The bulk of our freight was turpentine; and the close proximity of this to the furnaces suggested a danger fully equal to that from snags or grounding. On calling the attention of a fellow-passenger to it, he told me that a friend of his was once awakened from sleep, while lying in a berth on one of these boats, by a sudden, confused sound. Thinking the boiler had burst, he drew the bed-clothing over his head, and laid quiet, to avoid breathing the steam; until, feeling the boat ground, he ran out, and discovered that she was on fire near the furnace. Having some valuable freight near by, which he was desirous to save, and seeing no immediate danger, though left alone on the boat, he snatched a bucket, and, drawing water from alongside, applied it with such skill and rapidity as soon to quench the flames, and eventually to entirely extinguish the fire. Upon the return of the crew, a few repairs were made, steam was got up again, and the boat proceeded to her destination in safety. He afterwards ascertained that three hundred kegs of gunpowder were stowed beneath the deck that had been on fire—a circumstance which sufficiently accounted for the panic-flight of the crew.

Soon after leaving, we passed the Zephyr, wooding up: an hour later, our own boat was run to the bank, men jumped from her fore and aft, and fastened head and stern lines to the trees, and we also commenced wooding.

The trees had been cut away so as to leave a clear space to the top of the bank, which was some fifty feet from the boat, and moderately steep. Wood, cut, split, and piled in ranks, stood at the top of it, and a shoot of plank, two feet wide and thirty long, conveyed it nearly to the water. The crew rushed to the wood-piles—master, passengers, and all, but the engineer and chambermaid, deserting the boat—and the wood was first passed down, as many as could, throwing into the shoot, and others forming a line, and tossing it, from one to another, down the bank. From the water's edge it was passed, in the same way, to its place on board, with great rapidity—the crew exciting themselves with yells. They were all blacks, but one.

On a tree, near the top of the bank, a little box was nailed, on which a piece of paper was tacked, with this inscription:

"*Notic*
"*to all persons takin wood from this*
"*landin pleas to leav a ticket payable to*
"*the subscriber, at $1,75 a cord as*
"*heretofore.* "*Amos Sikes.*"

VOL. I. O

and the master—just before the wood was all on board—hastily filled a blank order (torn from a book, like a checkbook, leaving a memorandum of the amount, etc.) on the owner of the boat for payment, to Mr. Sikes, for two cords of pine-wood, at $1 75, and two cords of light-wood, at $2—and left it in the box. The wood used had been measured in the ranks with a rod, carried for the purpose, by the master, at the moment he reached the bank.

Before, with all possible haste, we had finished wooding, the Zephyr passed us; and, during the rest of the day, she kept out of our sight. As often as we met a steamboat, or passed any flats or rafts, our men were calling out to know how far ahead of us she was; and when the answer came back each time, in an increasing number of miles, they told us that our boat was more than usually sluggish, owing to an uncommonly heavy freight; but still, for some time, they were ready to make bets that we should get first to Wilmington.

Several times we were hailed from the shore, to take on a passenger, or some light freight; and these requests, as long as it was possible, were promptly complied with—the boat being run up, so as to rest her bow upon the bank, and then shouldered off by the men, as if she had been a skiff.

There were but three through-passengers, besides myself. Among them, was a glue-manufacturer, of Baltimore—getting orders from the turpentine-distillers,—and a turpentine-farmer and distiller. The glue-manufacturer said that, in his factory, they had formerly employed slaves; had since used Irishmen, and now employed Germans. Their operations were carried on night and day, and one gang of the men had to relieve another. The slaves they had employed never would be *on hand*, when the hour for relieving came. It was also necessary to be careful that certain operations should be performed at a certain time, and some judgment and watchfulness was necessary, to fix this time: the slaves never could be made to care enough for the matter, to be depended upon for discretion, in this respect; and great injury was frequently done in consequence. Some of the operations were disagreeable, and they would put one another up to thinking and saying that they ought not to be required to do such dirty work—and try to have their owners get them away from it.

Irishmen, he said, worked very well, and to a certain extent faithfully, and, for a time, they liked them very much; but they found that, in about a fortnight, an Irishman always thought he knew more than his master, and would exercise his discretion a little too much, as well as often directly disregard his orders. Irishmen were, he said, "*too* faithful"—that is, self-confident and officious.

At length, at a hurried time, they had employed one or two Germans. The Irishmen, of course, soon quarrelled with them, and threatened to leave, if they were kept. Whereupon, they were, themselves, all discharged, and a full crew of Germans, at much less wages, taken; and they proved excellent hands—steady, plodding, reliable, though they never pretended to know anything, and said nothing about what they could do. They were easily instructed, obeyed orders faithfully, and worked fairly for their wages, without boasting or grumbling.

The turpentine-distiller gave a good account of some of his men; but said he was sure they never performed half as much work as he himself could; and they sometimes would, of their own accord, do twice as much in a day, as could usually be got out of them. He employed a Scotchman at the "still;" but he never would have white people at ordinary work, because he couldn't drive them. He added, with the utmost simplicity—and I do not think any one present saw, at the time, how much the remark expressed more than it was intended to—"I never can drive a white man, for I know I could never bear to be driven, myself, by anybody."

The other passenger was "a North of England man," as I suspected from the first words I heard from him—though he had been in this country for about twenty years. He was a mechanic, and employed several slaves; but testified strongly of the expensive character of their labour; and declared, without any reserve, that the system was ruinous in its effects upon the character and value of all classes of working men.

The country on the river-bank was nearly all wooded, with, occasionally, a field of corn, which, even in the low alluvial meadows, sometimes overflowed by the river, and enriched by its deposit, had evidently yielded but a very meagre crop—the stalks standing singly, at great distances, and very small. The greater part, even of these once rich low lands, that had been in cultivation, were now "turned out," and covered either with pines or broom-sedge and brushwood.

At some seventy or eighty miles, I should think, below Fayetteville, the banks became lower, and there was much swamp land, in which the ground was often covered with a confusion of logs and sawn lumber, mingled with other rubbish, left by floods of the river. The standing timber was very large, and many of the trees were hung with the long, waving drapery of the tylandria, or Spanish moss, which, as well as the mistletoe, I here first saw in profusion. There was also a thick network among the trees, of beautiful climbing plants. I observed some very large grape-vines, and many trees of greater size than I ever saw of their species before. I infer that this soil, properly reclaimed, and protected from floods of the river, might be most profitably used in the culture of the various half-tropical trees and shrubs, of whose fruits we now import so large and costly an amount. The fig, I have been informed, grows and bears luxuriantly at Wilmington, seldom or never suffering in its wood, though a crop of fruit may be occasionally injured by a severe late spring frost. The almond, doubtless, would succeed equally well, so also the olive; but of none of these is there the slightest commercial value produced in North Carolina, or in all our country.

In the evening we passed many boats and rafts, blazing with great fires, made upon a thick bed of clay, and their crews singing at their sweeps. Twenty miles above Wilmington, the shores became marshy, the river wide, and the woody screen that had hitherto, in a great degree, hid the nakedness of the land, was withdrawn, leaving open to view only broad, reedy savannahs, on either side.

We reached Wilmington, the port at the mouth of the river, at half-past nine. Taking a carriage, I was driven first to one hotel and afterwards to another. They were both so crowded with guests, and excessive business duties so prevented the clerks from being tolerably civil to me, that I feared if I remained in either of them I should have another Norfolk experience. While I was endeavouring to ascertain if there was a third public-house, in which I might, perhaps, obtain a private room, my eye fell upon an advertisement of a new railroad line of passage to Charleston. A boat, to take passengers to the railroad, was to start every night, from Wilmington, at ten o'clock. It was already something past ten; but being pretty sure that she would not get off punctually, and having a strong resisting impulse to being packed away in a close room, with any chance stranger the clerk of the house might choose to couple me with, I shouldered my baggage and ran for the wharves. At half-past ten I was looking at Wilmington over the stern of another little wheelbarrow-steamboat, pushing back up the river. When or how I was to be taken to Charleston, I had not yet been able to ascertain. The captain assured me it was all right, and demanded twenty dollars. Being in his power I gave it to him, and received in return a pocketful of tickets, guaranteeing the bearer passage from place to place; of not one of which places had I ever heard before, except Charleston.

The cabin was small, dirty, crowded, close, and smoky. Finding a warm spot in the deck, over the furnace, and to leeward of the chimney, I pillowed myself on my luggage and went to sleep.

The ringing of the boat's bell awoke me, after no great lapse of time, and I found we were in a small creek, heading southward. Presently we reached a wharf, near which stood a locomotive and train. A long, narrow plank having been run out, half a dozen white men, including myself, went on shore. Then followed as many negroes, who appeared to be a recent purchase of their owner. Owing, probably, to an unusually low tide, there was a steep ascent from the boat to the wharf, and I was amused to see the anxiety of this gentleman for the safe landing of his property, and especially to hear him curse them for their carelessness, as if their lives were of much greater value to him than to themselves. One was a woman. All carried over their shoulders some little baggage, probably all their personal effects, slung in a blanket; and one had a dog, whose safe landing caused him nearly as much anxiety as his own did *his* owner.

"Gib me da dog, now," said the dog's owner, standing half way up the plank.

"Damn the dog," said the negro's owner; "give me your

hand up here. Let go of the dog; d'ye hear! Let him take care of himself."

But the negro hugged the dog, and brought him safely on shore.

After a short delay the train started : the single passenger car was a fine one (made at Wilmington, Delaware), and just sufficiently warmed. I should have slept again if it had not been that two of the six inmates were drunk—one of them uproariously.

Passing through long stretches of cypress swamps, with occasional intervals of either pine-barrens, or clear water ponds, in about two hours we came, in the midst of the woods, to the end of the rails. In the vicinity could be seen a small tent, a shanty of loose boards, and a large, subdued fire, around which, upon the ground, a considerable number of men were stretched out asleep. This was the camp of the hands engaged in laying the rails, and who were thus daily extending the distance which the locomotive could run.

The conductor told me that there was here a break of about eighty miles in the rail, over which I should be transferred by a stage coach, which would come as soon as possible after the driver knew that the train had arrived. To inform him of this, the locomotive trumpeted loud and long.

The negro property, which had been brought up in a freight car, was immediately let out on the stoppage of the train. As it stepped on to the platform, the owner asked, " Are you all here ?"

" Yes, massa, we is all heah," answered one. " Do dysef no harm, for we's all heah," added another, in an under tone.

The negroes immediately gathered some wood, and taking a brand from the railroad hands, made a fire for themselves ; then, all but the woman, opening their bundles, wrapped themselves in their blankets and went to sleep. The wom- bare-headed, and very inadequately clothed as she was, stood for a long time alone, erect and statue-like, her head bowed gazing in the fire. She had taken no part in the light ch— of the others, and had given them no assistance in ma: the fire. Her dress too was not the usual plantation apparel. It was all sadly suggestive.

The principal other freight of the train was one hundred and twenty bales of Northern hay. It belonged, as the conductor told me, to a planter who lived some twenty miles beyond here, and who had bought it in Wilmington at a dollar and a half a hundred weight, to feed his mules. Including the steamboat and railroad freight, and all the labour of getting it to his stables, its entire cost to him would not be much less than two dollars a hundred, or at least four times as much as it would have cost to raise and make it in the interior of New York or New England. There are not only several forage crops which can be raised in South Carolina, that cannot be grown on account of the severity of the winter in the Free States, but, on a farm near Fayetteville, a few days before, I had seen a crop of natural grass growing in half-cultivated land, dead upon the ground; which, I think, would have made, if it had been cut and well treated in the summer, three tons of hay to the acre. The owner of the land said that there was no better hay than it would have made, but he hadn't had time to attend to it. He had as much as his hands could do of other work at the period of the year when it should have been made.

Probably the case was similar with the planter who had bought this Northern hay at a price four times that which it would have cost a Northern farmer to make it. He had preferred to employ his slaves at other business.

The inference must be, either that there was most improbably-foolish, bad management, or that the slaves were more profitably employed in cultivating cotton, than they could have been in cultivating maize, or other forage crops.

I put the case, some days afterwards, to an English merchant, who had had good opportunities, and made it a part of his business to study such matters.

"I have no doubt," said he, " that if hay cannot be obtained here, other valuable forage can, with less labour than anywhere at the North ; and all the Southern agricultural journals sustain this opinion, and declare it to be purely bad management that neglects these crops, and devotes labour to cotton, so exclusively. Probably, it is so—at the present cost of forage. Nevertheless, the fact is also true, as the planters assert, that they cannot afford to apply their labour to anything else but cotton. And yet, they complain that the price of cotton is so low that there is no profit in growing it, which is evidently false. You see that they prefer buying hay to raising it at, to say the least, three times what it costs your Northern farmers to raise it. Of course, if cotton could be grown in New York and Ohio, it could be afforded at one-third the cost it is here—say at three cents per pound. And that is my solution of the slavery question. Bring cotton down to three cents a pound, and there would be more abolitionists in South Carolina than in Massachusetts. If that can be brought about, in any way—and it is not impossible that we may live to see it, as our railways are extended in India, and the French enlarge their free-labour plantations in Algiers—there will be an end of slavery."

It was just one o'clock when the stage-coach came for us. There was but one passenger beside myself—a Philadelphia gentleman, going to Columbia. We proceeded very slowly for about three miles, across a swamp, upon a "corduroy road;" then more rapidly, over rough ground, being tossed about in the coach most severely, for six or eight miles further. Besides the driver, there was on the box the agent or superintendent of the coach line, who now opened the doors, and we found ourselves before a log stable, in the midst of a forest of large pines. The driver took out a horse, and, mounting him, rode off, and we collected wood, splitting it with a hatchet that was carried on the coach, and, lighting it from the coach lamp, made a fire. It was very cold, ice half an inch thick, and a heavy hoar frost. We complained to the agent that there was no straw in the coach bottom, while there were large holes bored in it, that kept our feet excessively cold. He said there was no straw to be had in the country. They were obliged to bed their horses with pine leaves, which were damp, and would be of no service to us. The necessity for the holes he did not immediately explain, and we, in the exercise of our Yankee privilege, resolved that they were made with reference to the habit of expectoration, which we had observed in the car to be very general and excessive.

In about half an hour the driver of the new stage came to us on the horse that the first had ridden away. A new set of horses was brought out and attached to the coach, and we were driven on again. An hour later, the sun rose; we were still in pine-barrens, once in several miles passing through a clearing, with a log farm-house, and a few negro huts about it; often through cypress swamps, and long pools of water. At the end of ten miles we breakfasted, and changed horses and drivers at a steam saw-mill. A few miles further on, we were asked to get on the top of the coach, while it was driven through a swamp, in which the water was over the road, for a quarter of a mile, to such a depth that it covered the foot-board. The horses really groaned, as they pushed the thin ice away with their necks, and were very near swimming. The holes in the coach bottom, the agent now told us, were to allow the water that would here enter the body to flow out. At the end of these ten miles we changed again, at a cotton planter's house—a very neat, well-built house, having pine trees about it, but very poor, old, negro quarters.

Since the long ford we had kept the top, the inside of the coach being wet, and I had been greatly pleased with the driving—the coachman, a steady-going sort of a fellow, saying but little to his horses, and doing what swearing he thought necessary in English; driving, too, with great judgment and skill. The coach was a fine, roomy, old-fashioned, fragrant, leathery affair, and the horses the best I had seen this side of Virginia. I could not resist expressing my pleasure with the whole establishment. The new team was admirable; four sleek, well-governed, eager, sorrel cobs, and the driver, a staid, bronzed-faced man, keeping them tight in hand, drove quietly and neatly, his whip in the socket. After about fifteen minutes, during which he had been engaged in hushing down their too great impetuosity, he took out a large silver hunting-watch, and asked what time it was.

" Quarter past eleven," said the agent.

" Twelve minutes past," said the Philadelphian.

" Well, fourteen, only, I am," said the agent.

" Thirteen," said I.

" Just thirteen, I am," said the driver, slipping back his watch to its place, and then, to the agent, " ha'an't touched a hand of her since I left old Lancaster."

Suddenly guessing the meaning of what had been for some time astonishing me—" You are from the North ?" I asked.

"Yes, sir."

"And you, too, Mr. Agent?"

"Yes, sir."

"And the coach, and the cattle, and all?"

"All from Pennsylvania."

"How long have you been here?"

"We have been here about a fortnight, stocking the road. We commenced regular trips yesterday. You are the first passenger through, sir."

It was, in fact, merely a transfer from one of the old National Road lines, complete. After a little further conversation, I asked, "How do you like the country, here?"

'Very nice country," said the agent.

"It's the cussedest poor country God ever created," napped out the driver.

"You have to keep your horses on——"

"*Shucks!** damn it."

The character of the scenery was novel to me, the surface very flat, the soil a fine-grained, silvery white sand, shaded by a continuous forest of large pines, which had shed their lower branches, so that we could see from the coach-top, to the distance of a quarter of a mile, everything upon the ground. In the swamps, which were frequent and extensive, and on their borders, the pines gave place to cypresses, with great pedestal trunks, and protuberant roots, throwing up an awkward dwarf progeny of shrub, cypress, and curious bulbous-like stumps, called "cypress-knees." Mingled with these were a few of our common deciduous trees, the white-shafted sycamore, the gray beech, and the shrubby black-jack oak, with broad leaves, brown and dead, yet glossy, and reflecting the sunbeams. Somewhat rarely, the red cedar,

* Husks of maize.

and more frequently than any other except the cypress, the beautiful American holly. Added to these, there was often a thick undergrowth of evergreen shrubs. Vines and creepers of various kinds grew to the tops of the tallest trees and dangled beneath and between their branches, in intricate net-work. The tylandria hung in festoons, sometimes several feet in length, and often completely clothed the trunks, and every branch of the trees in the low ground. It is like a fringe of tangled hair, of a light gray pearly colour, and sometimes produces exquisite effects when slightly veiling the dark green, purple, and scarlet of the cedar, and the holly with their berries. The mistletoe also grew in large, vivid, green tufts, on the ends of the branches of the oldest and largest trees. A small fine and wiry dead grass, hardly perceptible, even in the most open ground, from the coach-tops, was the only sign of herbage. Large black buzzards were constantly in sight, sailing slowly, high above the tree-tops. Flocks of larks, quails, and robins were common, as were also doves, swiftly flying in small companies. The red-headed woodpecker could at any time be heard hammering the old tree-trunks, and would sometimes show himself, after his rat-tat, cocking his head archly, and listening to hear if the worm moved under the bark. The drivers told me that they had on previous days, as they went over the road, seen deer, turkeys, and wild hogs.

At every tenth mile, or thereabout, we changed horses; and, generally, were allowed half an hour to stroll in the neighbourhood of the stable—the agent observing that we could reach the end of the staging some hours before the cars should leave to take us further; and, as there were no good accommodations for sleeping there, we would pass the time quite as pleasantly on the road. We dined at "Marion

County House," a pleasant little village (and the only village we saw during the day), with a fine pine-grove, a broad street, a court-house, a church or two, a school-house, and a dozen or twenty dwellings. Towards night, we crossed the Great Pedee of the maps, the *Big* Pedee of the natives, in a flat boat. A large quantity of cotton, in bales, was upon the bank, ready for loading into a steamboat—when one should arrive—for Charleston.

The country was very thinly peopled; lone houses often being several miles apart. The large majority of the dwellings were of logs, and even those of the white people were often without glass windows. In the better class of cabins, the roof is usually built with a curve, so as to project eight or ten feet beyond the log-wall; and a part of this space, exterior to the logs, is enclosed with boards, making an additional small room—the remainder forms an open porch. The whole cabin is often elevated on four corner-posts, two or three feet from the ground, so that the air may circulate under it. The fire-place is built at the end of the house, of sticks and clay, and the chimney is carried up outside, and often detached from the log-walls; but the roof is extended at the gable, until in a line with its outer side. The porch has a railing in front, and a wide shelf at the end, on which a bucket of water, a gourd, and hand-basin, are usually placed. There are chairs, or benches, in the porch, and you often see women sitting at work in it, as in Germany.

The logs are usually hewn but little; and, of course, as they are laid up, there will be wide interstices between them —which are increased by subsequent shrinking. These, very commonly, are not "chinked," or filled up in any way; nor is the wall lined on the inside. Through the chinks, as you pass along the road, you may often see all that is going on in the house; and, at night, the light of the fire shines brightly out on all sides.

Cabins, of this class, would almost always be flanked by two or three negro huts. The cabins of the poor whites, much the largest in number, were of a meaner sort—being mere square pens of logs, roofed over, provided with a chimney, and usually with a shed of boards, supported by rough posts, before the door.

Occasionally, where, near the banks of a water-course, the silvery sand was darkened by a considerable intermixture of mould, there would be a large plantation, with negro-quarters, and a cotton-press and gin-house. We passed half a dozen of these, perhaps, during the day. Where the owners resided in them, they would have comfortable-looking residences, not unlike the better class of New England farm-houses. On the largest, however, there was no residence for the owner, at all, only a small cottage, or whitewashed cabin, for the overseer. The negro-cabins, here, were the smallest I had seen—I thought not more than twelve feet square, inside. They stood in two rows, with a wide street between them. They were built of logs, with no windows—no opening at all, except the doorway, with a chimney of sticks and mud; with no trees about them, no porches, or shades, of any kind. Except for the chimney—the purpose of which I should not readily have guessed if I had seen one of them in New England—I should have conjectured that it had been built for a powder-house, or perhaps an ice-house—never for an animal to sleep in.

We stopped, for some time, on this plantation, near where some thirty men and women were at work, repairing the road. The women were in majority, and were engaged at exactly the same labour as the men; driving the carts, loading them with dirt, and dumping them upon the road; cutting down trees, and drawing wood by hand, to lay across the miry places; hoeing, and shovelling. They were dressed in coarse gray gowns, generally very much burned, and very dirty; which, for greater convenience of working in the mud, were reefed up with a cord drawn tightly around the body, a little above the hips—the spare amount of skirt bagging out between this and the waist-proper. On their legs were loose leggins, or pieces of blanket or bagging wrapped about, and lashed with thongs; and they wore very heavy shoes. Most of them had handkerchiefs, only, tied around their heads, some wore men's caps, or old slouched hats, and several were bareheaded.

The overseer rode about among them, on a horse, carrying in his hand a raw-hide whip, constantly directing and encouraging them; but, as my companion and I, both, several times noticed, as often as he visited one end of the line of operations, the hands at the other end would discontinue their labour, until he turned to ride towards them again. Clumsy, awkward, gross, elephantine in all their movements; pouting, grinning, and leering at us; sly, sensual, and shameless, in all their expressions and demeanour; I never before had witnessed, I thought, anything more revolting than the whole scene.

At length, the overseer dismounted from his horse, and, giving him to a boy to take to the stables, got upon the coach, and rode with us several miles. From the conversation I had with him, as well as from what I saw of his conduct in the field, I judged that he was an uncommonly fit man for his duties; at least ordinarily amiable in disposition, and not passionate; but deliberate, watchful, and efficient. I thought he would be not only a good economist, but a firm and considerate officer or master.

If these women, and their children after them, were always

naturally and necessarily to remain of the character and capacity stamped on their faces—as is probably the opinion of their owner, in common with most wealthy South Carolina planters—I don't know that they could be much less miserably situated, or guided more for their own good and that of the world, than they were. They were fat enough, and didn't look as if they were at all overworked, or harassed by cares, or oppressed by a consciousness of their degradation. If that is all—as some think.

Afterwards, while we were changing at a house near a crossing of roads, strolling off in the woods for a short distance, I came upon two small white-topped waggons, each with a pair of horses feeding at its pole; near them was a dull camp fire, with a bake-kettle and coffee-pot, some blankets and a chest upon the ground, and an old negro sitting with his head bowed down over a meal sack, while a negro boy was combing his wool with a common horse-card. "Good evening, uncle," said I, approaching them. "Good evening, sar," he answered, without looking up.

"Where are you going?"

"Well, we ain't gwine nower, master; we's peddlin' tobacco roun."

"Where did you come from?"

"From Rockingham County, Norf Car'lina, master."

"How long have you been coming from there?"

"'Twill be seven weeks, to-morrow, sar, sin we leff home."

"Have you most sold out?"

"We had a hundred and seventy-five boxes in both waggons, and we's sold all but sixty. Want to buy some tobacco, master?" (Looking up.)

"No, thank you; I am only waiting here, while the coach changes. How much tobacco is there in a box?"

"Seventy-five pound."

"Are these the boxes?"

"No, them is our provision boxes, master. Show de gemman some of der tobacco, dah." (To the boy.)

A couple of negroes here passed along near us; the old man hailed them:

"Ho dah, boys! Doan you want to buy some backey?"

"No." (Decidedly.)

"Well, I'm sorry for it." (Reproachfully.)

"Are you bound homeward, now?" I asked.

"No, master; wish me was; got to sell all our backey fuss; you don't want none, master, does you? Doan you tink it pretty fair tobacco, sar? Juss try it: it's right sweet, reckon, you'll find."

"I don't wish any, thank you; I never use it. Is your master with you?"

"No, sar; he's gone across to Marion, to-day."

"Do you like to be travelling about, in this way?"

"Yes, master; I likes it very well."

"Better than staying at home, eh?"

"Well, I likes my country better dan dis; must say dat, master; likes my country better dan dis. I'se a free nigger in my country, master."

"Oh, you are a free man, are you! North Carolina is a better country than this, for free men, I suppose."

"Yes, master, I likes my country de best; I gets five dollar a month for dat boy." (Hastily, to change the subject.)

"He is your son, is he?"

"Yes, sar; he drives dat waggon, I drives dis; and I haant seen him fore, master, for six weeks, till dis mornin'."

"How were you separated?"

"We separated six weeks ago, sar, and we agreed to meet here, last night. We didn', dough, till dis mornin'."

The old man's tone softened, and he regarded his son with earnestness.

" 'Pears, dough, we was bofe heah, last night; but I couldn't find um till dis mornin'. Dis mornin' some niggars tole me dar war a niggar camped off yander in de wood ; and I knew 'twas him, and I went an' found him right off."

" And what wages do you get for yourself ?"

" Ten dollars a month, master."

" That's pretty good wages."

" Yes, master, any niggar can get good wages if he's a mind to be industrious, no matter wedder he's slave or free."

" So you don't like this country as well as North Carolina?"

" No, master. Fac is, master, 'pears like wite folks doan' ginerally like niggars in dis country ; day doan' ginerally talk so to niggars like as do in my country ; de niggars ain't so happy heah ; 'pears like de wite folks was kind o' different, somehow. I doan' like dis country so well ; my country suits me very well."

" Well, I've been thinking, myself, the niggars did not look so well here as they did in North Carolina and Virginia ; they are not so well clothed, and they don't appear so bright as they do there."

" Well, master, Sundays dey is mighty well clothed, dis country ; 'pears like dere an't nobody looks better Sundays dan dey do. But Lord ! workin' days, seems like dey haden no close dey could keep on 'um at all, master. Dey is a'mos' naked, wen deys at work, some on 'em. Why, master, up in our country, de wite folks—why, some on 'em has ten or twelve niggars ; dey doan' hev no real big plantation, like dey has heah, but some on 'em has ten or twelve niggars, may be, and dey juss lives and talks along wid 'em ; and dey treats 'um most as if dem was dar own chile. Dey doan'

P 2

keep no niggars dey can't treat so; dey won't keep 'em, wc be bodered wid 'em. If dey gets a niggar and he doan behave himself, day won't keep him; dey juss tell him, sar, he must look up anudder master, and if he doan' find hisself one, I tell 'ou, when de trader cum along, dey sells him, and he totes him away. Dey allers sell off all de bad niggars out of our country; dat's de way all de bad niggar and all dem no-account niggar keep a cumin' down heah; dat's de way on't, master."

"Yes, that's the way of it, I suppose; these big plantations are not just the best thing for niggers, I see that plainly."

"Master, you wan't raise in dis country, was 'ou?"

"No; I came from the North."

"I tort so, sar; I knew 'ou wan't one of dis country people; 'peared like 'ou was one o' my country people, way 'ou talks; and I loves dem kine of people. Won't you take some whisky, sar? Heah, you boy! bring dat jug of whisky dah, out o' my waggon; in dah,—in dat box under dem foddar."

"No, don't trouble yourself, I am very much obliged to you; but I don't like to drink whisky."

"Like to have you drink some, master, if you'd like it. You's right welcome to it. 'Pears like I knew you was one of my country people. Ever been in Greensboro,' master? dat's in Guilford."

"No, I never was there. I came from New York, further North than your country."

"New York, did 'ou, master? I heerd New York was what dey calls a Free State; all de niggars free dah."

"Yes, that is so."

"Not no slaves at all? well, I expec dat's a good ting, for all de niggars to be free. Greensboro' is a right comely town; tain't like dese heah Souf Car'lina towns."

"I have heard it spoken of as a beautiful town, and there are some fine people there."

"Yes, dere's Mr. —— ——, I knows him—he's a mighty good man."

"Do you know Mr. —— ?"

"O yes, sar, he's a mighty fine man, he is, master; ain't no better kind of man dan him."

"Well, I must go, or the coach will be kept waiting for me. Good-bye to you."

"Far'well, master, far'well; 'pears like it's done me good to see a man dat's cum out of my country again. Far'well, master."

We took supper at a neat log-cabin, standing a short distance off the road, with a beautiful evergreen oak, the first I had observed, in front of it. There was no glass in the windows, but drapery of white muslin restrained the currents of air; and during the day would let in sufficient light, while a blazing wood-fire both warmed and lighted the room by night. A rifle and powder-horn hung near the fire-place, and the master of the house, a fine, hearty, companionable fellow, said that he had lately shot three deer, and that there were plenty of cats, and foxes, as well as turkeys, hares, squirrels, and other small game in the vicinity. It was a perfectly charming little backwoods farm-house—good wife, supper, and all; but one disagreeable blot darkened the otherwise most agreeable picture of rustic civilization—we were waited upon at table by two excessively dirty, slovenly-dressed, negro girls. In the rear of the cabin were two hovels, each lighted by large fires, and apparently crowded with other slaves belonging to the family.

Between nine and ten at night, we reached the end of the completed railroad, coming up in search for that we had left the previous night. There was another camp and fire of the workmen, and in a little white frame-house we found a company of engineers. There were two trains and locomotives on the track, and a gang of negroes was loading cotton into one of them.

I strolled off until I reached an opening in the woods, in which was a cotton-field and some negro-cabins, and beyond it large girdled trees, among which were two negroes with dogs, barking, yelping, hacking, shouting, and whistling, after 'coons and 'possums. Returning to the railroad, I found a comfortable, warm passenger-car, and, wrapped in my blanket, went to sleep. At midnight I was awakened by loud laughter, and, looking out, saw that the gang of negroes had made a fire, and were enjoying a right merry repast. Suddenly, one raised such a sound as I never heard before; a long, loud, musical shout, rising and falling, and breaking into falsetto, his voice ringing through the woods in the clear, frosty night air, like a bugle-call. As he finished, the melody was caught up by another, and then another, and then by several in chorus. When there was silence again, one of them cried out, as if bursting with amusement: "Did yer see de dog?—when I began eeohing, he turn roun' an' look me straight into der face; ha! ha! ha!" and the whole party broke into the loudest peals of laughter, as if it was the very best joke they had ever heard.

After a few minutes I could hear one urging the rest to come to work again, and soon he stepped towards the cotton bales, saying, "Come, brederen, come; let's go at it; come now, coho! roll away! eeoho-eeoho-weeioho-i!"—and the rest taking it up as before, in a few moments they all had their shoulders to a bale of cotton, and were rolling it up the embankment.

About half-past three, I was awakened again by the whistle

of the locomotive, answering, I suppose, the horn of a stage-coach, which in a few minutes drove up, bringing a mail. A negro man and woman who had been sleeping near me, replenished the fire; two other passengers came in, and we started.

In the woods I saw a negro by a fire, while it was still night, shaving shingles very industriously. He did not even stop to look at the train. No doubt he was a slave, working by task, and of his own accord at night, that he might have the more daylight for his own purposes.

The negroes enjoy fine blazing fires in the open air, and make them at every opportunity. The train on this road was provided with a man and maid-servant to attend to the fire and wait on the passengers—a very good arrangement, by the way, yet to be adopted on our own long passenger trains. When we arrived at a junction where we were to change cars, as soon as all the passengers had left the train, they also left; but instead of going into the station-house with us, they immediately collected some pine branches and chips, and getting a brand from the locomotive, made a fire upon the ground, and seated themselves by it. Other negroes soon began to join them, and as they approached were called to: "Doan' yer cum widout som' wood! Doan' yer cum widout som' wood!" and every one had to make his contribution. At another place, near a cotton plantation, I found a woman collecting pine leaves into heaps, to be carted to the cattle-pens. She, too, had a fire near her. "What are you doing with a fire, aunty?" "Oh, jus' to warm my hans wen dey gits cold, massa." The weather was then almost uncomfortably warm.

We were running during the forenoon, for a hundred miles, or more, in a southerly direction, on nearly a straight course, through about the middle of the State of South Carolina. The greater part of this distance, the flat, sandy pine barrens continued, scarcely a foot of grading, for many miles at a time, having been required in the construction of the railroad. As the swamps, which were still frequent, were crossed on piles and tressel-work, the roads must have been built very cheaply —the land damages being nothing. We passed from the track of one company to that of another, several times during the day—the speed was from fifteen to twenty miles an hour, with long stoppages at the stations. A conductor said they could easily run forty miles, and had done it, including stoppages; but they were forbidden now to make fast time, from the injury it did the road—the superstructure being much more shaken and liable to displacement in these light sands than on our Northern roads. The locomotives that I saw were all made in Philadelphia; the cars were all from the Hartford, Conn., and Worcester, Mass., manufactories, and invariably, elegant and comfortable. The roads seemed to be doing a heavy freighting business with cotton. We passed at the turn-outs half a dozen trains, with nearly a thousand bales on each, but the number of passengers was always small. A slave country can never, it is evident, furnish a passenger traffic of much value. A majority of the passenger trains, which I saw used in the South, were not paying for the fuel and wages expended in running them.

For an hour or two we got above the sandy zone, and into the second, middle, or "wave" region of the State. The surface here was extremely undulating, gracefully swelling and dipping in bluffs and dells—the soil a mellow brown loam, with some indications of fertility, especially in the valleys. Yet most of the ground was occupied by pine woods (probably old-field pines, on exhausted cotton-fields). For a few miles, on a gently sloping surface of the same sort of soil, there were some enormously large cotton-fields.

I saw women working again, in large gangs with men. In

one case they were distributing manure—ditch scrapings it appeared to be—and the mode of operation was this: the manure had been already carted into heaps upon the ground; a number of the women were carrying it in from the heap in baskets, on their heads, and one in her apron, and spreading it with their hands between the ridges on which the cotton grew last year; the rest followed with great, long-handled, heavy, clumsy hoes, and pulled down the ridges over the manure, and so made new ridges for the next planting. I asked a young planter who continued with me a good part of the day, why they did not use ploughs. He said this was rather rough land, and a plough wouldn't work in it very well. It was light soil, and smooth enough for a parade ground. The fact is, in certain parts of South Carolina, a plough is yet an almost unknown instrument of tillage.

About noon we turned east, on a track running direct to Charleston. Pine barrens continued alternating with swamp, with some cotton and corn fields on the edges of the latter. A few of the pines were " boxed " for turpentine; and I understood that one or two companies from North Carolina had been operating here for several years. Plantations were not very often seen along the road through the sand; but stations, at which cotton was stored and loading, were comparatively frequent.

At one of the stations an empty car had been attached to the train; I had gone into it, and was standing at one end of it, when an elderly countryman with a young woman and three little children entered and took seats at the other. The old man took out a roll of deerskin, in which were bank-bills, and some small change.

"How much did he say 'twould be?" he inquired.

"Seventy cents."

"For both on us?"

"For each on us."

"Both on us, I reckon."

"Reckon it's each."

"I've got jess seventy-five cents in hard money."

"Give it to him, and tell him it's all yer got; reckon he'll let us go."

At this I moved, to attract their attention; the old man started, and looked towards me for a moment, and said no more. I soon afterwards walked out on the platform, passing him, and the conductor came in, and collected their fare; I then returned, and stood near them, looking out of the window of the door. The old man had a good-humoured, thin, withered, very brown face, and there was a speaking twinkle in his eye. He was dressed in clothes much of the Quaker cut—a broad-brimmed, low hat; white cotton shirt, open in front, and without cravat, showing his hairy breast; a long-skirted, snuff-coloured coat, of very coarse homespun; short trousers, of brown drilling; red woollen stockings, and heavy cow-hide shoes. He presently asked the time of day; I gave it to him, and we continued in conversation, as follows:—

"Right cold weather."

"Yes."

"G'wine to Branchville?"

"I am going beyond there—to Charleston."

"Ah—come from Hamburg this mornin'?"

"No—from beyond there."

"Did ye?—where 'd you come from?"

"From Wilmington."

"How long yer ben comin'?"

"I left Wilmington night before last, about ten o'clock. I have been ever since on the road."

"Reckon yer a night-bird."

"What?"

"Reckon you are a night-bird—what we calls a night-hawk; keeps a goin' at night, you know."

"Yes—I've been going most of two nights."

"Reckon so; kinder red your eyes is. Live in Charleston, do ye?"

"No, I live in New York."

"New York—that's a good ways, yet, ain't it?"

"Yes."

"Reckon yer arter a chicken, up here."

"No."

"Ah, ha—reckon ye are."

The young woman laughed, lifted her shoulder, and looked out of the window.

"Reckon ye'll get somebody's chicken."

"I'm afraid not."

The young woman laughed again, and tossed her head.

"Oh, reckon ye will—ah, ha! But yer mustn't mind my fun."

"Not at all, not at all. Where did *you* come from?"

"Up here to ——; g'wine hum; g'wine to stop down here, next deeper. How do you go, w'en you get to Charleston?"

"I am going on to New Orleans."

"Is New York beyond New Orleans?"

"Beyond New Orleans? Oh, no."

"In New Orleans, is't?"

"What?"

"New York is somewhere in New Orleans, ain't it?"

"No; it's the other way—beyond Wilmington."

"Oh! Been pretty cold thar?"

"Yes; there was a foot and a half of snow there, last week, I hear."

"Lord o'massy! why! have to feed all the cattle!—whew!—ha!—whew! don't wonner ye com' away."

"You are a farmer."

"Yes."

"Well, I am a farmer, too."

"Be ye—to New York?"

"Yes; how much land have you got?"

"A hundred and twenty-five acres; how much have you?"

"Just about the same. What's your land worth, here?"

"Some on't—what we call swamp-land—kinder low and wet like, you know—that's worth five dollars an acre; and mainly it's worth a dollar and a half or two dollars—that's takin' a common trac' of upland. What's yours worth?"

"A hundred and fifty to two hundred dollars."

"What!"

"A hundred and fifty to two hundred."

"Dollars?"

"Yes."

"Not an acre?"

"Yes."

"Good Lord! yer might as well buy niggers to onst. Do you work any niggers?"

"No."

"May be they don't have niggers—that is, slaves—to New York."

"No, we do not. It's against the law."

"Yes, I heerd 'twas, some place. How do yer get yer work done?"

"I hire white men—Irishmen generally."

"Do they work good?"

"Yes, better than negroes, I think, and don't cost nearly as much."

"What do yer have to give 'em?"

"Eight or nine dollars a month, and board, for common hands, by the year."

"Hi, Lordy! and they work up right smart, do they? Why, yer can't get any kind of a good nigger less'n twelve dollars a month."

"And board?"

"And board 'em? yes; and clothe, and blank, and shoe 'em, too."

He owned no negroes himself and did not hire any. "They," his family, "made their own crap." They raised maize, and sweet potatoes, and cow-peas. He reckoned, in general, they made about three barrels of maize to the acre; sometimes, as much as five. He described to me, as a novelty, a plough, with "a sort of a wing, like, on one side," that pushed off, and turned over a slice of the ground; from which it appeared that he had, until recently, never seen a mould-board; the common ploughs of this country being constructed on the same principles as those of the Chinese, and only rooting the ground, like a hog or a mole—not cleaving and turning. He had never heard of working a plough with more than one horse. He was frank and good-natured; embarrassed his daughter by coarse jokes about herself and her babies, and asked me if I would not go home with him, and, when I declined, pressed me to come and see them when I returned. That I might do so, he gave me directions how to get to his farm; observing that I must start pretty early in the day—because it would not be safe for a stranger to try to cross the swamp after dark. The moment the train began to check its speed, before stopping at the place at which he was to leave, he said to his daughter, "Come, gal! quick now; gather up yer young ones!" and stepped out, pulling her after him, on to the platform. As they walked off, I noticed that he strode ahead, like an Indian or a gipsy man, and she carried in her arms two of the children and a bundle, while the third child held to her skirts.

A party of fashionably-dressed people took the train for Charleston—two families, apparently, returning from a visit to their plantations. They came to the station in handsome coaches. Some minutes before the rest, there entered the car, in which I was then again alone, and reclining on a bench in the corner, an old nurse, with a baby, and two young negro women, having care of half a dozen children, mostly girls, from three to fifteen years of age. As they closed the door, the negro girls seemed to resume a conversation, or quarrel. Their language was loud and obscene, such as I never heard before from any but the most depraved and beastly women of the streets. Upon observing me, they dropped their voices, but not with any appearance of shame, and continued their altercation, until their mistresses entered. The white children, in the mean time, had listened, without any appearance of wonder or annoyance. The moment the ladies opened the door, they became silent.*

* *From the Southern Cultivator, June,* 1855.—" Children are fond of the company of negroes, not only because the deference shown them makes them feel perfectly at ease, but the subjects of conversation are on a level with their capacity; while the simple tales, and the witch and ghost stories, so common among negroes, excite the young imagination and enlist the feelings. If, in this association, the child becomes familiar with indelicate, vulgar, and lascivious manners and conversation, an impression is made upon the mind and heart, which lasts for years—perhaps for life. Could we, in all cases, trace effects to their real causes, I doubt not but many young men and women, of respectable parentage and bright prospects, who have made shipwreck of all their earthly hopes, have been led to the fatal step by the seeds of corruption which, in the days of childhood and youth, were sown in their hearts by the indelicate and lascivious manners and conversation of their father's negroes."

From an Address of Chancellor Harper, prepared for and read before the Society for the Advancement of Learning, of South Carolina.—" I have said the tendency of our institution is to elevate the female character, as well as that of the other sex, for similar reasons.

" And, permit me to say, that this elevation of the female character is no less important and essential to us, than the moral and intellectual cultivation of the other sex. It would, indeed, be intolerable, if, when one class of society is necessarily degraded in this respect, no compensation were made by the superior elevation and purity of the other. Not only essential purity of conduct, but the utmost purity of manners. And, I will add, though it may incur the formidable charge of affectation or prudery, *a greater severity of decorum than is required elsewhere, is necessary among us.* Always should be strenuously resisted the attempts, which have sometimes been made, to introduce among us the freedom of foreign European, and, especially, of continental manners. Let us say : we will not have *the manners* of South Carolina changed."

CHAPTER VI.

SOUTH CAROLINA AND GEORGIA, SURVEYED.

Savannah.—While riding, aimlessly, in the suburbs, I came upon a square field, in the midst of an open pine-wood, partially inclosed with a dilapidated wooden paling. It proved to be a grave-yard for negroes. Dismounting, and fastening my horse to a gate-post, I walked in, and found much in the monuments to interest me. Some of these were mere billets of wood, others were of brick and marble, and some were pieces of plank, cut in the ordinary form of tomb-stones. Many family-lots were inclosed with railings, and a few flowers or evergreen shrubs had sometimes been planted on the graves; but these were generally broken down and withered, and the ground was overgrown with weeds and briars. I spent some time in examining the inscriptions, the greater number of which were evidently painted by self-taught negroes, and were curiously illustrative both of their condition and character. I transcribed a few of them, as literally as possible, as follow:

"SACRED
TO THE MEMORY
OF HENRY. Gleve, ho
Dide JANUARY 19 1849
Age 44."

"BALDWING
In men of CHARLES
who died NOV
20. THE 1846
aged 62 years Blessed are the
dead who dieth
in the LORD
Even so said
the SPerit. For
the Rest From
Thair"

[The remainder rotted off.]

"DEAR
WIFE OF
JAMES DELBUG
BORN 1814 DIED 1852.'

In Memr
y, of,
M a
gare
-t. Born
August
29 and
died oc
tober 29 1852

[The following on marble.]
" To record the worth fidelity and virtue of Reynolda Watts, (who died on the 2d day of May 1829 at the age of 24 years, in giving birth to her 3d child).

" Reared from infancy by an affectionate mistress and trained by her in the paths of virtue, She was strictly moral in her deportment, faithful and devoted in her duty and heart and soul a

[Sand drifted over the remainder.]
There were a few others, of similar character to the above, erected by whites to the memory of favourite servants. The following was on a large brick tomb:—

"This tablet is erected to record the demise of Rev. HENRY CUNNINGHAM, Founder and subsequent pastor of the 2d African Church for 39 years, who yielded his spirit to its master the 29 of March 1842, aged 83 years."

[Followed by an inscription to the memory of Mrs. Cunningham.]

"This vault is erected by the 2d African Church, as a token of respect."

The following is upon a large stone table. The reader will observe its date; but I must add that, while in North Carolina, I heard of two recent occasions, in which public religious services had been interrupted, and the preachers—very estimable coloured men—publicly whipped.

"Sacred to the memory of Andrew Brian pastor of 1st colored Baptist church in Savannah. God was Pleased to lay his honour near his heart and impress the worth and weight of souls upon his mind that he was constrained to Preach the Gospel to dieng world, particularly to the sable sons of africa. though he labored under many disadvantage yet thought in the school of Christ, he was abie to bring out new and old out of the treasury And he has done more good among the poor slaves than all the learned Doctors in America, He was im prisoned for the Gospel without any ceremony was severely whipped. But while under the lash he told his prosecutor he rejoiced not only to be whipped but he was willing for to suffer death for the cause of CHRIST.

"He continued preaching the Gospel until Oct. 6 1812. He was supposed to be 96 years of age, his remains were interd with peculiar respect an address was delivered by the Rev. Mr Johnston Dr. Kolluck Thomas Williams and Henry Cunningham He was an honour to human nature an ornament to religion and a friend to mankind. His memory is still precious in the (hearts) of the living.

"Afflicted long he bore the rod
With calm submission to his maker God.
His mind was tranquil and serene
No terrors in his looks was seen
A SAVIOURS smile dispelled the gloom
And smoothed the passage to the tomb.

"I heard a voice from Heaven saying unto me, Write, Blessed are the dead which die in the Lord from henceforth! Yea saith the Spirit that they may rest from the labours.

"This stone is erected by the First Colored Church as a token of love for their most faithful pastor. A. D. 1821."

—*Plantation, February* —. I left town yesterday morning, on horseback, with a letter in my pocket to Mr. X., under whose roof I am now writing. The weather was fine, and, indeed, since I left Virginia, the weather for out-of-door purposes has been as fine as can be imagined. The exercise of walking or of riding warms one, at any time between sunrise and sunset, sufficiently to allow an overcoat to be dispensed with, while the air is yet brisk and stimulating. The public-houses are overcrowded with Northerners, who congratulate themselves on having escaped from the severe cold, of which they hear from home.

All, however, who know the country, out of the large towns, say that they have suffered more from cold here than ever at the North; because, except at a few first-class hotels, and in the better sort of mansions and plantation residences, any provision for keeping houses warm is so entirely neglected. It is, indeed, too cool to sit quietly, even at midday, out of sunshine, and at night it is often frosty. As a general rule, with such exceptions as I have indicated, it will be full two hours after one has asked for a fire in his room before the servants can be got to make it. The expedient of closing a door or window to exclude a draught of cold air seems really to be unknown to the negroes. From the time I left Richmond, until I arrived at Charleston, I never but once knew a servant to close the door on leaving a room, unless he was requested at the moment to do so.

The public houses of the smaller towns, and the country houses generally, are so loosely built, and so rarely have unbroken glass windows, that to sit by a fire, and to avoid remaining in a draught at the same time, is not to be expected.

As the number of Northerners, and especially of invalids, who come hither in winter, is every year increasing, more comfortable accommodations along the line of travel must soon be provided; if not by native, then by Northern enterprise. Some of the hotels in Florida, indeed, are already, I understand, under the management of Northerners; and this winter, cooks and waiters have been procured for them from the North. I observe, also, that one of them advertises that meats and vegetables are received by every steamer from New York.

Whenever comfortable quarters, and means of conveyance are extensively provided, at not immoderately great expense, there must be a great migration here every winter. The climate and the scenery, as well as the society of the more wealthy planters' families, are attractive, not to invalids alone, but even more to men and women who are able to enjoy invigorating recreations. Nowhere in the world could a man, with a sound body and a quiet conscience, live more pleasantly, at least as a guest, it seems to me, than here where I am. I was awakened this morning by a servant making a fire in my chamber. Opening the window, I found a clear, brisk air, but without frost—the mercury standing at 35° F. There was not a sign of winter, except that a few cypress trees, hung with seed attached to pretty pendulous tassels, were leafless. A grove which surrounded the house was all in dark verdure; there were green oranges on trees nearer the window; the buds were swelling on a jessamine-vine, and a number of camelia-japonicas were in full bloom; one of them, at least seven feet high, and a large compact shrub, must have had several hundred blossoms on it. Sparrows were chirping, doves cooing, and a mocking-bird whistling loudly. I walked to the stable, and saw clean and neatly-dressed negroes grooming thorough-bred horses, which pawed the ground, and tossed their heads, and drew deep inspirations, and danced as they were led out, in exuberance of animal spirits; and I felt as they did. We drove ten miles to church, in the forenoon, with the carriage-top thrown back, and with our overcoats laid aside; nevertheless, when we returned, and came into the house, we found a crackling wood fire, as comfortable as it was cheerful. Two lads, the sons of my host, had returned the night before from a "marooning party," with a boat-load of venison, wild fowl, and fish; and at dinner this evening there were delicacies which are to be had in perfection, it is said, nowhere else than on this coast. The woods and waters around us abound, not only with game, but with most interesting subjects of observation to the naturalist and the artist. Everything encourages cheerfulness, and invites to healthful life.

Now to think how people are baking in their oven-houses at home, or waddling out in the deep snow or mud, or across the frozen ruts, wrapped up to a Falstaffian rotundity in flannels and furs, one can but wonder that those, who have means, stay there, any more than these stay here in summer; and that my host would no more think of doing than the wild-goose.

But I must tell how I got here, and what I saw by the way.

A narrow belt of cleared land—"vacant lots"—only separated the town from the pine-forest—that great broad forest which extends uninterruptedly, and merely dotted with a few small corn and cotton fields, from Delaware to Louisiana.

Having some doubt about the road, I asked a direction of a man on horseback, who overtook and was passing me. In reply, he said it was a straight road, and we should go in company for a mile or two. He inquired if I was a stranger; and, when he heard that I was from the North, and now first visiting the South, he remarked that there was "no better place for me to go to than that for which I had inquired. Mr. X. was a very fine man—rich, got a splendid plantation, lived well, had plenty of company always, and there were a number of other show plantations near his. He reckoned I would visit some of them."

I asked what he meant by "show plantations." "Plantations belonging to rich people," he said, "where they had everything fixed up nice. There were several places that had that name; their owners always went out and lived on them part of the year, and kept a kind of open house, and were always ready to receive company. He reckoned I might go and stay a month round on them kind of places on —— river, and it would not cost me a cent. They always had a great many Northerners going to see them, those gentlemen had. Almost every Northerner that came here was invited right out to visit some of them; and, in summer, a good many of them went to the North themselves."

(It was not till long afterwards, long after the above paragraph was first printed, that I fully comprehended the significance of the statement, that on the show plantations it would not cost me a cent.)

During the forenoon my road continued broad and straight, and I was told that it was the chief outlet and thoroughfare of a very extensive agricultural district. There was very little land in cultivation within sight of the road, however; not a mile of it fenced, in twenty, and the only houses were log-cabins. The soil varied from a coarse, clean, yellow sand, to a dark, brown, sandy loam. There were indications that much of the land had, at some time, been under cultivation— had been worn out, and deserted.

Long teams of mules, driven by negroes, toiled slowly towards the town, with loads of rice or cotton. A stage-coach, with six horses to drag it through the heavy road, covered me, as it passed, with dust; and once or twice, I met a stylish carriage with fashionably-clad gentlemen and ladies, and primly-liveried negro-servants; but much the greates.

traffic of the road was done by small one-horse carts, driven by white men, or women.

These carts, all but their wheels, which come from the North, look as if they were made by their owners, in the woods, with no better tools than axes and jack-knives. Very little iron is used in their construction; the different parts being held together by wooden pins, and lashings of hide. The harness is made chiefly of ropes and undressed hide; but there is always a high-peaked riding-saddle, in which the driver prefers to sit, rather than on his cart. Once, I met a woman riding in this way, with a load of children in the cart behind her. From the axle-tree often hung a gourd, or an iron kettle. One man carried a rifle on his pommel. Sometimes, these carts would contain a single bale of cotton, more commonly, an assorted cargo of maize, sweet potatoes, poultry, game, hides, and peltry, with, always, some bundles of cornleaves, to be fed to the horse. Women and children were often passengers, or travelled on foot, in company with the carts, which were usually furnished with a low tilt. Many of them, I found, had been two or three days on the road, bringing down a little crop to market; whole families coming with it, to get reclothed with the proceeds.

The men with the carts were generally slight, with high cheek-bones and sunken eyes, and were of less than the usual stature of the Anglo-Saxon race. They were dressed in long-skirted homespun coats, wore slouched hats, and heavy boots, outside their trousers. As they met me, they usually bowed, and often offered a remark upon the weather, or the roads, in a bold, but not uncourteous manner—showing themselves to be, at least, in one respect, better off than the majority of European peasants, whose educated servility of character rarely fails to manifest itself, when they meet a well-dressed stranger.

The household markets of most of the Southern towns seem to be mainly supplied by the poor country people, who, driving in this style, bring all sorts of produce to exchange for such small stores and articles of apparel as they must needs obtain from the shops. Sometimes, owing to the great extent of the back country from which the supplies are gathered, they are offered in great abundance and variety : at other times, from the want of regular market-men, there will be a scarcity, and prices will be very high.

A stranger cannot but express surprise and amusement at the appearance and manners of these country traffickers in the market-place. The "wild Irish" hardly differ more from the English gentry than these rustics from the better class of planters and towns-people, with whom the traveller more commonly comes in contact. Their language even is almost incomprehensible, and seems exceedingly droll, to a Northern man. I have found it quite impossible to report it. I shall not soon forget the figure of a little old white woman, wearing a man's hat, smoking a pipe, driving a little black bull with reins; sitting herself bolt upright, upon the axle-tree of a little truck, on which she was returning from market. I was riding with a gentleman of the town at the time, and, as she bowed to him with an expression of ineffable self-satisfaction, I asked if he knew her. He had known her for twenty years, he said, and until lately she had always come into town about once a week, on foot, bringing fowls, eggs, potatoes, or herbs, for sale in a basket. The bull she had probably picked up astray, when a calf, and reared and broken it herself; and the cart and harness she had made herself; but he did not think anylady in the land felt richer than she did now, or prouder of her establishment.

In the afternoon, I left the main road, and, towards night, reached a much more cultivated district. The forest of pines still extended uninterruptedly on one side of the way, but on the other was a continued succession of very large fields, of rich dark soil—evidently reclaimed swamp-land—which had been cultivated the previous year, in Sea Island cotton. Beyond them, a flat surface of still lower land, with a silver thread of water curling through it, extended, Holland-like, to the horizon. Usually at as great a distance as a quarter of a mile from the road, and from half a mile to a mile apart, were the residences of the planters—white houses, with groves of evergreen trees about them; and between these and the road were little villages of slave-cabins.

My directions not having been sufficiently explicit, I rode in, by a private lane, to one of these. It consisted of some thirty neatly-whitewashed cottages, with a broad avenue, planted with Pride-of-China trees between them.

The cottages were framed buildings, boarded on the outside, with shingle roofs and brick chimneys; they stood fifty feet apart, with gardens and pig-yards, enclosed by palings, between them. At one, which was evidently the "sick house," or hospital, there were several negroes of both sexes, wrapped in blankets, and reclining on the door steps or on the ground, basking in the sunshine. Some of them looked ill, but all were chatting and laughing as I rode up to make an inquiry. I learned that it was not the plantation I was intending to visit, and received a direction, as usual, so indistinct and incorrect that it led me wrong.

At another plantation which I soon afterwards reached, I found the "settlement" arranged in the same way, the cabins only being of a slightly different form. In the middle of one row was a well-house, and opposite it, on the other row, was a mill-house, with stones, at which the negroes grind their corn. It is a kind of pestle and mortar; and I was informed afterwards that the negroes prefer to take their allowance of corn and crack it for themselves, rather than to receive meal, because they think the mill-ground meal does not make as sweet bread.

At the head of the settlement, in a garden looking down the street, was an overseer's house, and here the road divided, running each way at right angles; on one side to barns and a landing on the river, on the other toward the mansion of the proprietor. A negro boy opened the gate of the latter, and I entered.

On either side, at fifty feet distant, were rows of old live oak trees, their branches and twigs slightly hung with a delicate fringe of gray moss, and their dark, shining, green foliage, meeting and intermingling naturally but densely overhead. The sunlight streamed through, and played aslant the lustrous leaves, and fluttering pendulous moss; the arch was low and broad; the trunks were huge and gnarled, and there was a heavy groining of strong, rough, knotty, branches. I stopped my horse and held my breath; I thought of old Kit North's rhapsody on trees; and it was no rhapsody—it was all here, and real: "Light, shade, shelter, coolness, freshness, music, dew, and dreams dropping through their umbrageous twilight —dropping direct, soft, sweet, soothing, and restorative from heaven."

Alas! no angels; only little black babies, toddling about with an older child or two to watch them, occupied the aisle. At the upper end was the owner's mansion, with a circular court-yard around it, and an irregular plantation of great trees; one of the oaks, as I afterwards learned, seven feet in diameter of trunk, and covering with its branches a circle of one hundred and twenty feet in diameter. As I approached it, a smart servant came out to take my horse. I obtained from him a direction to the residence of the gentleman I was searching for, and rode away, glad that I had stumbled into so charming a place.

After riding a few miles further I reached my destination. Mr. X. has two plantations on the river, besides a large tract of poor pine forest land, extending some miles back upon the upland, and reaching above the malarious region. In the upper part of this pine land is a house, occupied by his overseer during the malarious season, when it is dangerous for any but negroes to remain during the night in the vicinity of the swamps or rice-fields. Even those few who have been born in the region, and have grown up subject to the malaria, are said to be generally weakly and short-lived. The negroes do not enjoy as good health on rice plantations as elsewhere; and the greater difficulty with which their lives are preserved, through infancy especially, shows that the subtle poison of the miasma is not innocuous to them; but Mr. X. boasts a steady increase of his negro stock, of five per cent. per annum, which is better than is averaged on the plantations of the interior.

The plantation which contains Mr. X.'s winter residence has but a small extent of rice land, the greater part of it being reclaimed upland swamp soil, suitable for the culture of Sea Island cotton. The other plantation contains over five hundred acres of rice-land, fitted for irrigation; the remainder is unusually fertile reclaimed upland swamp, and some hundred acres of it are cultivated for maize and Sea Island cotton.

There is a "negro settlement" on each; but both plantations, although a mile or two apart, are worked together as one, under one overseer—the hands being drafted from one to another as their labour is required. Somewhat over seven hundred acres are at the present time under the plough in the two plantations: the whole number of negroes is two hundred, and they are reckoned to be equal to about one hundred prime hands—an unusual strength for that number of all classes. The overseer lives, in winter, near the settlement of the larger plantation, Mr. X. near that of the smaller.

It is an old family estate, inherited by Mr. X.'s wife, who, with her children, were born and brought up upon it in close intimacy with the negroes, a large proportion of whom were also included in her inheritance, or have been since born upon the estate. Mr. X. himself is a New England farmer's son, and has been a successful merchant and manufacturer.

The patriarchal institution should be seen here under its most favourable aspects; not only from the ties of long family association, common traditions, common memories, and, if ever, common interests, between the slaves and their rulers, but, also, from the practical talent for organization and administration, gained among the rugged fields, the complicated looms, and the exact and comprehensive counting-houses of New England, which directs the labour.

The house-servants are more intelligent, understand and perform their duties better, and are more appropriately dressed, than any I have seen before. The labour required of them is light, and they are treated with much more consideration for their health and comfort than is usually given to that of free domestics. They live in brick cabins, adjoining the house and stables, and one of these, into which I have looked, is neatly and comfortably furnished. Several of the house-servants, as is usual, are mulattoes, and good-looking. The mulattoes are generally preferred for in-door occupations. Slaves brought up to house-work dread to be employed at field-labour; and those accustomed to the comparatively unconstrained life of the negro-settlement, detest the close control and careful movements required of the house-servants. It is a punishment for a lazy field-hand, to employ him in menial duties at the house, as it is to set a sneaking sailor to do the work of a cabin-servant; and it is equally a punishment to a neglectful house-servant, to banish him to the field-gangs. All the household economy is, of course, carried on in a style appropriate to a wealthy gentleman's residence—not more so, nor less so, that I observe, than in an establishment of similar grade at the North.

It is a custom with Mr. X., when on the estate, to look each day at all the work going on, inspect the buildings, boats, embankments, and sluice-ways, and examine the sick. Yesterday I accompanied him in one of these daily rounds.

After a ride of several miles through the woods, in the rear of the plantations we came to his largest negro-settlement. There was a street, or common, two hundred feet wide, on which the cabins of the negroes fronted. Each cabin was a framed building, the walls boarded and whitewashed on the outside, lathed and plastered within, the roof shingled; forty-two feet long, twenty-one feet wide, divided into two family tenements, each twenty-one by twenty-one; each tenement divided into three rooms—one, the common household apartment, twenty-one by ten; each of the others (bed-rooms), ten by ten. There was a brick fire-place in the middle of the long side of each living room, the chimneys rising in one, in the middle of the roof. Besides these rooms, each tenement had a cock-loft, entered by steps from the household room. Each tenement is occupied, on an average, by five persons. There were in them closets, with locks and keys, and a varying quantity of rude furniture. Each cabin stood two hundred feet from the next, and the street in front of them being two hundred feet wide, they were just that distance apart each way. The people were nearly all absent at work, and had locked their outer doors, taking the keys with them. Each cabin has a front and back door, and each room a window, closed by a wooden shutter, swinging outward, on hinges. Between each tenement and the next house, is a small piece of ground, inclosed with palings, in which are coops of fowl with chickens, hovels for nests, and for sows with pig. There were a great many fowls in the street. The negroes' swine are allowed to run in the woods, each owner having his own distinguished by a peculiar mark. In the rear of the yards were gardens—a half-acre to each family. Internally the cabins appeared dirty and disordered, which was rather a pleasant indication that their home-life was not much interfered with, though I found certain police regulations were enforced.

The cabin nearest the overseer's house was used as a nursery. Having driven up to this, Mr. X. inquired first of an old nurse how the children were; whether there had been any births since his last visit; spoke to two convalescent young mothers, who were lounging on the floor of the portico, with the children, and then asked if there were any sick people.

" Nobody, oney dat boy, Sam, sar."

" What Sam is that ?"

" Dat little Sam, sar ; Tom's Sue's Sam, sar."

" What's the matter with him ?"

"Don' 'spec dere's noting much de matter wid him now, sar. He came in Sa'dy, complainin' he had de stomach-ache, an' I gin him some ile, sar ; 'spec he mus' be well, dis time, but he din go out dis mornin'."

" Well, I'll see to him."

Mr. X. went to Tom's Sue's cabin, looked at the boy, and, concluding that he was well, though he lay abed, and pretended to cry with pain, ordered him to go out to work. Then, meeting the overseer, who was just riding away, on some business of the plantation, he remained some time in conversation with him, while I occupied myself in making a sketch of the nursery and street of the settlement in my note-book. On the verandah and the steps of the nursery, there were twenty-seven children, most of them infants, that had been left there by their mothers, while they were working their tasks in the fields. They probably make a visit to them once or twice during the day, to nurse them, and receive them to take to their cabins, or where they like, when they have finished their tasks—generally in the middle of the afternoon. The older children were fed with porridge, by the general nurse. A number of girls, eight or ten years old, were occupied in holding and tending the youngest infants. Those a little older—the crawlers—were in the-pen, and those big enough to toddle were playing on the steps, or before the house. Some of these, with two or three bigger ones, were singing and dancing about a fire that they had made on the ground. They were not at all disturbed or interrupted in their amusement by the presence of their owner and myself. At twelve years of age, the children are first put to regular field-work; until then no labour is required of them, except, perhaps, occasionally they are charged with some light kind of duty, such as frightening birds from corn. When first sent to the field, one quarter of an able-bodied hand's day's work is ordinarily allotted to them, as their task.

From the settlement, we drove to the "mill"—not a flouring mill, though I believe there is a run of stones in it—but a monster barn, with more extensive and better machinery for threshing and storing rice, driven by a steam-engine, than I have ever seen used for grain before. Adjoining the millhouse were shops and sheds, in which blacksmiths, carpenters, and other mechanics—all slaves, belonging to Mr. X. —were at work. He called my attention to the excellence of their workmanship, and said that they exercised as much ingenuity and skill as the ordinary mechanics that he was used to employ in New England. He pointed out to me some carpenter's work, a part of which had been executed by a New England mechanic, and a part by one of his own hands, which indicated that the latter was much the better workman.

I was gratified by this, for I had been so often told, in Virginia, by gentlemen anxious to convince me that the negro was incapable of being educated or improved to a condition in which it would be safe to trust him with himself—that no negro-mechanic could ever be taught, or induced to work carefully or nicely—that I had begun to believe it might be so.

We were attended through the mill-house by a respectable-looking, orderly, and quiet-mannered mulatto, who was called, by his master, "the watchman." His duties, however, as they were described to me, were those of a steward, or intendant. He carried, by a strap at his waist, a very large number of keys, and had charge of all the stores of provisions, tools, and materials of the plantations, as well as of all their produce, before it was shipped to market. He weighed and measured out all the rations of the slaves and the cattle; superintended the mechanics, and made and repaired, as was necessary, all the machinery, including the steam-engine.

In all these departments, his authority was superior to that of the overseer. The overseer received his private allowance of family provisions from him, as did also the head-servant at the mansion, who was his brother. His responsibility was much greater than that of the overseer; and Mr. X. said he would trust him with much more than he would any overseer he had ever known.

Anxious to learn how this trustworthiness and intelligence, so unusual in a slave, had been developed or ascertained, I inquired of his history, which was briefly as follows.

Being the son of a favourite house-servant, he had been, as

a child, associated with the white family, and received by chance something of the early education of the white children. When old enough, he had been employed, for some years, as a waiter; but, at his own request, was eventually allowed to learn the blacksmith's trade, in the plantation shop. Showing ingenuity and talent, he was afterwards employed to make and repair the plantation cotton-gins. Finally, his owner took him to a steam-engine builder, and paid $500 to have him instructed as a machinist. After he had become a skilful workman, he obtained employment as an engineer; and for some years continued in this occupation, and was allowed to spend his wages for himself. Finding, however, that he was acquiring dissipated habits, and wasting his earnings, Mr. X. eventually brought him, much against his inclinations, back to the plantations. Being allowed peculiar privileges, and given duties wholly flattering to his self-respect, he soon became contented; and, of course, was able to be extremely valuable to his owner.

I have seen another slave-engineer. The gentleman who employed him told me that he was a man of talent, and of great worth of character. He had desired to make him free, but his owner, who was a member of the Board of Brokers, and of Dr. ———'s Church, in New York, believed that Providence designed the negro race for slavery, and refused to sell him for that purpose. He thought it better that he (his owner) should continue to receive two hundred dollars a year for his services, while he continued able to work, because then, as he said, he should feel responsible that he did not starve, or come upon the public for a support, in his old age. The man himself, having light and agreeable duties, well provided for, furnished with plenty of spending money by his employer, patronized and flattered by the white people, honoured and looked up to by those of his own colour, was rather indifferent in the matter; or even, perhaps, preferred to remain a slave, to being transported for life to Africa.

The watchman was a fine-looking fellow: as we were returning from church, on Sunday, he had passed us, well dressed and well mounted, and as he raised his hat, to salute us, there was nothing in his manner or appearance, except his colour, to distinguish him from a gentleman of good breeding and fortune.

When we were leaving the house, to go to church, on Sunday, after all the white family had entered their carriages, or mounted their horses, the head house-servant also mounted a horse—as he did so, slipping a coin into the hands of the boy who had been holding him. Afterwards, we passed a family of negroes, in a light waggon, the oldest among them driving the horse. On my inquiring if the slaves were allowed to take horses to drive to church, I was informed that in each of these three cases, the horses belonged to the negroes who were driving or riding them. The old man was infirm, and Mr. X. had given him a horse, to enable him to move about. He was probably employed to look after the cattle at pasture, or at something in which it was necessary, for his usefulness, that he should have a horse: I say this, because I afterwards found, in similar cases on other plantations, that it was so. But the watchman and the house servant had bought their horses with money. The watchman was believed to own three horses; and, to account for his wealth, Mr. X.'s son told me that his father considered him a very valuable servant, and frequently encouraged his good behaviour with handsome gratuities. He receives, probably, considerably higher wages, in fact (in the form of presents), than the white overseer. He knew his father gave him two hundred dollars at once, a short time ago. The watchman has a private house, and, no doubt, lives in considerable luxury.

Will it be said, "therefore, Slavery is neither necessarily degrading nor inhumane?" On the other hand, so far as it is not, there is no apology for it. It is possible, though not probable, that this fine fellow, if he had been born a free man, would be no better employed than he is here; but, in that case, where is the advantage? Certainly not in the economy of the arrangement. And if he were self-dependent, if, especially, he had to provide for the present and future of those he loved, and was able to do so, would he not necessarily live a happier, stronger, better, and more respectable man?

After passing through tool-rooms, corn-rooms, mule-stables, store-rooms, and a large garden, in which vegetables to be distributed among the negroes, as well as for the family, are grown, we walked to the rice-land. It is divided by embankments into fields of about twenty acres each, but varying somewhat in size, according to the course of the river. The arrangements are such that each field may be flooded independently of the rest, and they are subdivided by open ditches into rectangular plats of a quarter acre each. We first proceeded to where twenty or thirty women and girls were engaged in raking together, in heaps and winrows, the stubble and rubbish left on the field after the last crop, and burning it. The main object of this operation is to kill all the seeds of weeds, or of rice, on the ground. Ordinarily it is done by tasks—a certain number of the small divisions of the field being given to each hand to burn in a day; but owing to a more than usual amount of rain having fallen lately, and some other causes, making the work harder in some places than others, the women were now working by the day, under the direction of a "driver," a negro man, who walked about among them, taking care that they left nothing unburned. Mr. X. inspected the ground they had gone over, to see whether the driver had done his duty. It had been sufficiently well burned, but not more than a quarter as much ground had been gone over, he said, as was usually burned in taskwork,—and he thought they had been very lazy, and reprimanded them. The driver made some little apology, but the women offered no reply, keeping steadily and, it seemed, sullenly, on at their work.

In the next field, twenty men, or boys, for none of them looked as if they were full-grown, were ploughing, each with a single mule, and a light, New-York-made plough. The soil was friable, the ploughing easy, and the mules proceeded at a smart pace; the furrows were straight, regular, and well turned. Their task was nominally an acre and a quarter a day; somewhat less actually, as the measure includes the space occupied by the ditches, which are two to three feet wide, running around each quarter of an acre. The ploughing gang was superintended by a driver, who was provided with a watch; and while we were looking at them he called out that it was twelve o'clock. The mules were immediately taken from the ploughs, and the plough-boys mounting them, leapt the ditches, and cantered off to the stables, to feed them. One or two were ordered to take their ploughs to the blacksmith, for repairs.

The ploughmen got their dinner at this time: those not using horses do not usually dine till they have finished their tasks; but this, I believe, is optional with them. They commence work, I was told, at sunrise, and at about eight o'clock have breakfast brought to them in the field, each hand having left a bucket with the cook for that purpose. All who are working in connection, leave their work together, and gather about a fire, where they generally spend about half an hour. The provisions furnished, consist mainly of meal, rice, and vegetables, with salt and molasses, and occasionally bacon, fish, and coffee. The allowance is a peck of meal, or an equivalent quantity of rice per week, to each working hand, old or young, besides small stores. Mr. X. says that he has lately given a less amount of meat than is now usual on plantations, having observed that the general health of the negroes is not as good as formerly, when no meat at all was customarily given them. (The general impression among planters is, that the negroes work much better for being supplied with three or four pounds of bacon a week.)

Leaving the rice-land, we went next to some of the upland fields, where we found several other gangs of negroes at work; one entirely of men engaged in ditching; another of women, and another of boys and girls, "listing" an old corn-field with hoes. All of them were working by tasks, and were overlooked by negro drivers. They all laboured with greater rapidity and cheerfulness than any slaves I have before seen; and the women struck their hoes as if they were strong, and well able to engage in muscular labour. The expression of their faces was generally repulsive, and their *ensemble* anything but agreeable. The dress of most was uncouth and cumbrous, dirty and ragged; reefed up, as I have once before described, at the hips, so as to show their heavy legs, wrapped round with a piece of old blanket, in lieu of leggings or stockings. Most of them worked with bare arms, but wore strong shoes on their feet, and handkerchiefs on their heads; some of them were smoking, and each gang had a fire burning on the ground, near where they were at work, by which to light their pipes and warm their breakfast. Mr. X. said this was always their custom, even in summer. To each gang a boy or girl was also attached, whose business it was to bring water for them to drink, and to go for anything required by the driver. The drivers would frequently call back a hand to go over again some piece of his or her task that had not been worked to his satisfaction, and were constantly calling to one or another, with a harsh and peremptory voice, to strike harder, or hoe deeper, and otherwise taking care that the work was well done. Mr. X. asked if Little Sam ("Tom's Sue's 'Sam") worked yet with the "three-quarter" hands, and learning that he did, ordered him to be put with the full hands, observing that though rather short, he was strong and stout, and, being twenty years old, well able to do a man's work.

The field-hands are all divided into four classes, according to their physical capacities. The children beginning as "quarter-hands," advancing to "half-hands," and then to "three-quarter hands;" and, finally, when mature, and able-bodied, healthy, and strong, to "full hands." As they decline in strength, from age, sickness, or other cause, they retrograde in the scale, and proportionately less labour is required of them. Many, of naturally weak frame, never are put among the full hands. Finally, the aged are left out at the annual classification, and no more regular field-work is required of them, although they are generally provided with some light, sedentary occupation. I saw one old woman picking "tailings" of rice out of a heap of chaff, an occupation at which she was probably not earning her salt. Mr. X. told me she was a native African, having been brought when a girl from the Guinea coast. She spoke almost unintelligibly; but after some other conversation, in which I had not been able to understand a word she said, he jokingly proposed to send her back to Africa. She expressed her preference to remain where she was, very emphatically. "Why?" She did not answer readily, but being pressed, threw up her palsied hands, and said furiously, "I lubs 'ou, mas'r, oh, I lubs 'ou. I don't want go 'way from 'ou."

The field-hands are nearly always worked in gangs, the strength of a gang varying according to the work that en gages it; usually it numbers twenty or more, and is directed by a driver. As on most large plantations, whether of rice or cotton, in Eastern Georgia and South Carolina, nearly all ordinary and regular work is performed *by tasks:* that is to say, each hand has his labour for the day marked out before him, and can take his own time to do it in. For instance, in making drains in light, clean meadow land, each man or woman of the full hands is required to dig one thousand cubic feet; in swamp-land that is being prepared for rice culture, where there are not many stumps, the task for a ditcher is five hundred feet: while in a very strong cypress swamp, only two hundred feet is required; in hoeing rice, a certain number of rows, equal to one-half or two-thirds of an acre, according to the condition of the land; in sowing rice (strewing in drills), two acres; in reaping rice (if it stands well), three-quarters of an acre; or, sometimes a gang will be required to reap, tie in sheaves, and carry to the stack-yard the produce of a certain area, commonly equal to one fourth the number of acres that there are hands working together. Hoeing cotton, corn, or potatoes; one half to one acre. Threshing; five to six hundred sheaves. In ploughing rice-land (light, clean, mellow soil) with a yoke of oxen, one acre a day, including the ground lost in and near the drains—the oxen being changed at noon. A cooper, also, for instance, is required to make barrels at the rate of eighteen a week. Drawing staves, 500 a day. Hoop poles, 120. Squaring timber, 100 ft. Laying worm-fence, 50 panels per hand. Post and rail do., posts set 2½ to 3 ft. deep, 9 ft. apart, nine or ten panels per hand. In getting fuel from the woods, (pine, to be cut and split,) one cord is the task for a day. In "mauling rails," the taskman selecting the trees (pine) that he judges will split easiest, one hundred a day, ends not sharpened.

These are the tasks for first-class able-bodied men; they are lessened by one quarter for three quarter hands, and proportionately for the lighter classes. In allotting the tasks, the drivers are expected to put the weaker hands where (if there is any choice in the appearance of the ground, as where certain rows in hoeing corn would be less weedy than others,) they will be favoured.

These tasks certainly would not be considered excessively hard, by a Northern labourer; and, in point of fact, the more industrious and active hands finish them often by two o'clock. I saw one or two leaving the field soon after one o'clock, several about two; and between three and four, I met a dozen women and several men coming home to their cabins, having finished their day's work.

Under this "Organization of Labour," most of the slaves work rapidly and well. In nearly all ordinary work, custom has settled the extent of the task, and it is difficult to increase it. The driver who marks it out, has to remain on the ground until it is finished, and has no interest in overmeasuring it; and if it should be systematically increased very much, there is danger of a general stampede to the "swamp"—a danger the slave can always hold before his master's cupidity. In fact, it is looked upon *in this region* as a proscriptive right of the negroes to have this incitement to diligence offered them; and the man who denied it, or who attempted to lessen it, would, it is said, suffer in his reputation, as well as experience much annoyance from the obstinate "rascality" of his negroes. Nothwithstanding this, I have heard a man assert, boastingly, that he made his negroes habitually perform double the customary tasks. Thus we get a glimpse again of the black side. If he is allowed the power to do this, what may not a man do?

It is the driver's duty to make the tasked hands do their

work well. If, in their haste to finish it, they neglect to do it properly, he "sets them back," so that carelessness will hinder more than it will hasten the completion of their tasks.

In the selection of drivers, regard seems to be had to size and strength—at least, nearly all the drivers I have seen are tall and strong men—but a great deal of judgment, requiring greater capacity of mind than the ordinary slave is often supposed to be possessed of, is certainly needed in them. A good driver is very valuable and usually holds office for life. His authority is not limited to the direction of labour in the field, but extends to the general deportment of the negroes. He is made to do the duties of policeman, and even of police magistrate. It is his duty, for instance, on Mr. X.'s estate, to keep order in the settlement; and, if two persons, men or women, are fighting, it is his duty to immediately separate them, and then to "whip them both."

Before any field of work is entered upon by a gang, the driver who is to superintend them has to measure and stake off the tasks. To do this at all accurately, in irregular-shaped fields, must require considerable powers of calculation. A driver, with a boy to set the stakes, I was told, would accurately lay out forty acres a day, in half-acre tasks. The only instrument used is a five-foot measuring rod. When the gang comes to the field, he points out to each person his or her duty for the day, and then walks about among them, looking out that each proceeds properly. If, after a hard day's labour, he sees that the gang has been overtasked, owing to a miscalculation of the difficulty of the work, he may excuse the completion of the tasks; but he is not allowed to extend them. In the case of uncompleted tasks, the body of the gang begin new tasks the next day, and only a sufficient number are detailed from it to complete, during the day, the unfinished tasks of the day before. The relation of the driver to the working hands seems to be similar to that of the boatswain to the seamen in the navy, or of the sergeant to the privates in the army.

Having generally had long experience on the plantation, the advice of the drivers is commonly taken in nearly all the administration, and frequently they are, *de facto*, the managers. Orders on important points of the plantation economy, I have heard given by the proprietor directly to them, without the overseer's being consulted or informed of them; and it is often left with them to decide when and how long to flow the rice-grounds—the proprietor and overseer deferring to their more experienced judgment. Where the drivers are discreet, experienced, and trusty, the overseer is frequently employed merely as a matter of form, to comply with the laws requiring the superintendence or presence of a white man among every body of slaves; and his duty is rather to inspect and report than to govern. Mr. X. considers his overseer an uncommonly efficient and faithful one, but he would not employ him, even during the summer, when he is absent for several months, if the law did not require it. He has sometimes left his plantation in care of one of the drivers for a considerable length of time, after having discharged an overseer; and he thinks it has then been quite as well conducted as ever. His overseer consults the drivers on all important points, and is governed by their advice.

Mr. X. said, that though overseers sometimes punished the negroes severely, and otherwise ill-treated them, it is their more common fault to indulge them foolishly in their disposition to idleness, or in other ways to curry favour with them, so they may not inform the proprietor of their own misconduct or neglect. He has his overseer bound to certain rules, by written contract; and it is stipulated that he can discharge him at any moment, without remuneration for his loss of time and inconvenience, if he should at any time be dissatisfied with him. One of the rules is, that he shall never punish a negro with his own hands, and that corporeal punishment, when necessary, shall be inflicted by the drivers. The advantage of this is, that it secures time for deliberation, and prevents punishment being made in sudden passion. His drivers are not allowed to carry their whips with them in the field; so that if the overseer wishes a hand punished, it is necessary to call a driver; and the driver has then to go to his cabin, which is, perhaps, a mile or two distant, to get his whip, before it can be applied.

I asked how often the necessity of punishment occurred?

"Sometimes, perhaps, not once for two or three weeks; then it will seem as if the devil had got into them all, and there is a good deal of it."

As the negroes finish the labour required of them by Mr. X., at three or four o'clock in the afternoon, they can employ the remainder of the day in labouring for themselves, if they choose. Each family has a half-acre of land allotted to it, for a garden; besides which, there is a large vegetable garden, cultivated by a gardener for the plantation, from which they are supplied, to a greater or less extent. They are at liberty to sell whatever they choose from the products of their own garden, and to make what they can by keeping swine and fowls. Mr. X.'s family have no other supply of poultry and eggs than what is obtained by purchase from his own negroes; they frequently, also, purchase game from them. The only restriction upon their traffic is a "liquor law." They are not allowed to buy or sell ardent spirits. This prohibition, like liquor laws elsewhere, unfortunately, cannot be enforced; and, of late years, grog shops, at which stolen goods are bought from the slaves, and poisonous liquors—

chiefly the worst whisky, much watered and made stupefying by an infusion of tobacco—are clandestinely sold to them, have become an established evil, and the planters find themselves almost powerless to cope with it. They have, here, lately organized an association for this purpose, and have brought several offenders to trial; but, as it is a penitentiary offence, the culprit spares no pains or expense to avoid conviction—and it is almost impossible, in a community of which so large a proportion is poor and degraded, to have a jury sufficiently honest and intelligent to permit the law to be executed.

A remarkable illustration of this evil has lately occurred. A planter, discovering that a considerable quantity of cotton had been stolen from him, informed the patrol of the neighbouring planters of it. A stratagem was made use of, to detect the thief, and, what was of much more importance—there being no question but that this was a slave—to discover for whom the thief worked. A lot of cotton was prepared, by mixing hair with it, and put in a tempting place. A negro was seen to take it, and was followed by scouts to a grog-shop, several miles distant, where he sold it—its real value being nearly ten dollars—for ten cents, taking his pay in liquor. The man was arrested, and, the theft being made to appear, by the hair, before a justice, obtained bail in $2,000, to answer at the higher court. Some of the best legal counsel of the State has been engaged, to obtain, if possible, his conviction.

This difficulty in the management of slaves is a great and very rapidly increasing one. Everywhere that I have been, I have found the planters provoked and angry about it. A swarm of Jews, within the last ten years, has settled in nearly every Southern town, many of them men of no character, opening cheap clothing and trinket shops; ruining, or driving out of business, many of the old retailers, and engaging in an unlawful trade with the simple negroes, which is found very profitable.*

The law which prevents the reception of the evidence of a negro in courts, here strikes back, with a most annoying force, upon the dominant power itself. In the mischief thus arising, we see a striking illustration of the danger which stands before the South, whenever its prosperity shall invite extensive immigration, and lead what would otherwise be a healthy competition to flow through its channels of industry. This injury to slave property, from grog-shops, furnishes the grand argument for the Maine Law at the South.†

---

* *From the Charleston Standard, Nov. 23rd, 1854.*—" This abominable practice of trading with slaves is not only taking our produce from us, but injuring our slave property. It is true the owner of slaves may lock, watch, and whip, as much as he pleases—the negroes will steal and trade as long as white persons hold out to them temptations to steal and bring to them. Three-fourths of the persons who are guilty, you can get no fine from ; and, if they have some property, all they have to do is to confess a judgment to a friend, go to jail, and swear out. It is no uncommon thing for a man to be convicted of offences against the State, and against the persons and property of individuals, and pay the fines, costs, and damages, by swearing out of jail, and then go and commit similar offences. The State, or the party injured, has the cost of all these prosecutions and suits to pay, besides the trouble of attending Court : the guilty is convicted, the injured prosecutor punished."

† *From an Address to the people of Georgia, by a Committee of the State Temperance Society, prior to the election of 1855.*—" We propose to turn the 2,200 *foreign* grog-shop keepers, in Georgia, out of office, and ask them to help us. They (the Know-Nothings) reply, ' We have no time for that now—we are trying to turn *foreigners* out of office ;' and when we call upon the Democratic party for aid, they excuse themselves, upon the ground that they have work enough to do in keeping these foreigners in office."

From the Penfield (Ga.) Temperance Banner, Sept. 29th, 1855.

" OUR SLAVE POPULATION.

" We take the following from the *Savannah Journal and Courier*, and would ask every candid reader if the evils referred to ought not to be corrected. How shall it be done ?

" ' By reference to the recent homicide of a negro, in another column, some facts

Mr. X. remarks that his arrangements allow his servants no excuse for dealing with these fellows. He has a rule to purchase everything they desire to sell, and to give them a high price for it himself. Eggs constitute a circulating medium on the plantation. Their par value is considered to be twelve for a dime, at which they may always be exchanged for cash, or left on deposit, without interest, at his kitchen. Whatever he takes of them that he cannot use in his own family, or has not occasion to give to others of his servants, is sent to town to be resold. The negroes do not commonly take money for the articles he has of them, but the value of them is put to their credit, and a regular account kept with them. He has a store, usually well supplied with articles that they most want, which are purchased in large quantities, and sold to them at wholesale prices; thus giving them a

---

will be seen suggestive of a state of things, in this part of our population, which should not exist, and which cannot endure without danger, both to them and to us. The collision, which terminated thus fatally, occurred at an hour past midnight— at a time when none but the evil-disposed are stirring, unless driven by necessity; and yet, at that hour, those negroes and others, as many as chose, were passing about the country, with ample opportunity to commit any act which might happen to enter their heads. In fact, they did engage, in the public highway, in a broil terminating in homicide. It is not difficult to imagine that their evil passions might have taken a very different direction, with as little danger of meeting control or obstacle.

"'But it is shown, too, that to the impunity thus given them by the darkness of midnight, was added the incitement to crime drawn from the abuse of liquor. They had just left one of those resorts where the negro is supplied with the most villanously-poisonous compounds, fit only to excite him to deeds of blood and violence. The part that this had in the slaughter of Saturday night, we are enabled only to imagine; but experience would teach us that its share was by no means small. Indeed, we have the declaration of the slayer, that the blow, by which he was exasperated so as to return it by the fatal stab, was inflicted by a bottle of brandy! In this fact, we fear, is a clue to the whole history of the transaction.'

"Here, evidently, are considerations deserving the grave notice of, not only those who own negroes, but of all others who live in a society where they are held."

great advantage in dealing with him rather than with the grog-shops. His slaves are sometimes his creditors to large amounts; at the present time he says he owes them about five hundred dollars. A woman has charge of the store, and when there is anything called for that she cannot supply, it is usually ordered, by the next conveyance, of his factors in town.

The ascertained practicability of thus dealing with slaves, together with the obvious advantages of the method of working them by tasks, which I have described, seem to me to indicate that it is not so impracticable as is generally supposed, if only it was desired by those having the power, to rapidly extinguish Slavery, and while doing so, to educate the negro for taking care of himself, in freedom. Let, for instance, any slave be provided with all things he will demand, as far as practicable, and charge him for them at certain prices— honest, market prices for his necessities, higher prices for harmless luxuries, and excessive, but not absolutely prohibitory, prices for everything likely to do him harm. Credit him, at a fixed price, for every day's work he does, and for all above a certain easily accomplished task in a day, at an increased price, so that his reward will be in an increasing ratio to his perseverance. Let the prices of provisions be so proportioned to the price of task-work, that it will be about as easy as it is now for him to obtain a bare subsistence. When he has no food and shelter due to him, let him be confined in solitude, or otherwise punished, until he asks for opportunity to earn exemption from punishment by labour.

When he desires to marry, and can persuade any woman to marry him, let the two be dealt with as in partnership. Thus, a young man or young woman will be attractive somewhat in proportion to his or her reputation for industry and providence. Thus industry and providence will become fashionable. Oblige them to purchase food for their children, and let them have the benefit of their children's labour, and they will be careful to teach their children to avoid waste, and to honour labour. Let those who have not gained credit while hale and young, sufficient to support themselves in comfort when prevented by age or infirmity from further labour, be supported by a tax upon all the negroes of the plantation, or of a community. Improvidence, and pretence of inability to labour, will then be disgraceful.

When any man has a balance to his credit equal to his value as a slave, let that constitute him a free man. It will be optional with him and his employer whether he shall continue longer in the relation of servant. If desirable for both that he should, it is probable that he will; for unless he is honest, prudent, industrious, and discreet, he will not have acquired the means of purchasing his freedom.

If he is so, he will remain where he is, unless he is more wanted elsewhere; a fact that will be established by his being called away by higher wages, or the prospect of greater ease and comfort elsewhere. If he is so drawn off, it is better for all parties concerned that he should go. Better for his old master; for he would not refuse him sufficient wages to induce him to stay, unless he could get the work he wanted him to do done cheaper than he would justly do it. Poor wages would certainly, in the long run, buy but poor work; fair wages, fair work.

Of course there will be exceptional cases, but they will always operate as cautions for the future, not only to the parties suffering, but to all who observe them. And be sure they will not be suffered, among ignorant people, to be lost. This is the beneficent function of gossip, with which wise and broad-working minds have nothing to do, such not being benefitted by the iteration of the lessons of life.

Married persons, of course, can only become free together.

In the appraisement of their value, let that of their young children be included, so that they cannot be parted from them; but with regard to children old enough to earn something more than their living, let it be optional what they do for them.

Such a system would simply combine the commendable elements of the emancipation law of Cuba,* and those of the reformatory punishment system, now in successful operation in some of the British penal colonies, with a few practical modifications. Further modifications would, doubtless, be needed, which any man who has had much practical experience in dealing with slaves might readily suggest. Much might be learned from the experience of the system pursued in the penal colonies, some account of which may be seen in the report of the Prisoners' Aid Society of New York, for 1854, or in a previous little work of my own. I have here only desired to suggest, apropos to my friend's experience, the practicability of providing the negroes an education in essential social morality, while they are drawing towards personal freedom; a desideratum with those who do not consider Slavery a purely and eternally desirable thing for both slave and slave-master, which the present system is calculated, as far as possible, in every direction to oppose.

Education in theology and letters could be easily combined with such a plan as I have hinted at; or, if a State should wish to encourage the improvement of its negro constituent—as, in the progress of enlightenment and Christianity, may be hoped to eventually occur—a simple provision of the law,

* In Cuba every slave has the privilege of emancipating himself, by paying a price which does not depend upon the selfish exactions of the masters; but it is either a fixed price, or else is fixed, in each case, by disinterested appraisers. The consequence is, that emancipations are constantly going on, and the free people of colour are becoming enlightened, cultivated, and wealthy. In no part of the United States do they occupy the high social position which they enjoy in Cuba.

making a certain standard of proficiency the condition of political freedom, would probably create a natural demand for education, which commerce, under its inexorable higher-laws, would be obliged to satisfy.

I do not think, after all I have heard to favour it, that there is any good reason to consider the negro, naturally and essentially, the moral inferior of the white; or, that if he is so, it is in those elements of character which should for ever prevent us from trusting him with equal social munities with ourselves.

So far as I have observed, slaves show themselves worthy of trust most, where their masters are most considerate and liberal towards them. Far more so, for instance, on the small farms of North Carolina than on the plantations of Virginia and South Carolina. Mr. X.'s slaves are permitted to purchase fire-arms and ammunition, and to keep them in their cabins; and his wife and daughters reside with him, among them, the doors of the house never locked, or windows closed, perfectly defenceless, and miles distant from any other white family.

Another evidence that negroes, even in slavery, when trusted, may prove wonderfully reliable, I will subjoin, in a letter written by Mr. Alexander Smets, of Savannah, to a friend in New York, in 1853. It is hardly necessary to say, that the "servants" spoken of were negroes, and the "suspicious characters," providentially removed, were whites. The letter was not written for publication:—

"The epidemic which spread destruction and desolation through our city, and many other places in most of the Southern States, was, with the exception of that of 1820, the most deadly that was ever known here. Its appearance being sudden, the inhabitants were seized with a panic, which caused an immediate *sauve qui peut* seldom witnessed before. I left, or rather fled, for the sake of my daughters, to Sparta, Hancock county. They were dreadfully frightened.

Of a population of fifteen thousand, six thousand, who could not get away, remained, nearly all of whom were more or less seized with the prevailing disease. The negroes, with very few exceptions, escaped.

"Amidst the desolation and gloom pervading the deserted streets, there was a feature that showed our slaves in a favourable light. There were entire blocks of houses, which were either entirely deserted—the owners in many instances having, in their flight, forgotten to lock them up—or left in charge of the servants. A finer opportunity for plunder could not be desired by thieves; and yet the city was remarkable, during the time, for order and quietness. There were scarcely any robberies committed, and as regards fires, so common in the winter, none! Every householder, whose premises had escaped the fury of the late terrific storm, found them in the same condition he had left them. Had not the yellow fever scared away or killed those suspicious characters, whose existence is a problem, and who prowl about every city, I fear that our city might have been laid waste. Of the whole board of directors of five banks, three or four remained, and these at one time were sick. Several of the clerks were left, each in the possession of a single one. For several weeks it was difficult to get anything to eat; the bakers were either sick or dead. The markets closed, no countryman dared venture himself into the city with the usual supplies for the table, and the packets had discontinued their trips. I shall stop, otherwise I could fill a volume with the occurrences and incidents of the dismal period of the epidemic."

On most of the large rice plantations which I have seen in this vicinity, there is a small chapel, which the negroes call their prayer-house. The owner of one of these told me that, having furnished the prayer-house with seats having a back-rail, his negroes petitioned him to remove it, because it did not leave them *room enough to pray*. It was explained to me that it is their custom, in social worship, to work themselves up to a great pitch of excitement, in which they yell and cry aloud, and finally, shriek and leap up, clapping their hands and dancing, as it is done at heathen festivals. The back-rail they found to seriously impede this exercise.

Mr. X. told me that he had endeavoured, with but little success, to prevent this shouting and jumping of the negroes at their meetings on his plantation, from a conviction that there was not the slightest element of religious sentiment in it. He considered it to be engaged in more as an exciting amusement than from any really religious impulse. In the town churches, except, perhaps, those managed and conducted almost exclusively by negroes, the slaves are said to commonly engage in religious exercises in a sober and decorous manner; yet, a member of a Presbyterian church in a Southern city told me, that he had seen the negroes in his own house of worship, during "a season of revival," leap from their seats, throw their arms wildly in the air, shout vehemently and unintelligibly, cry, groan, rend their clothes, and fall into cataleptic trances.

On almost every large plantation, and in every neighbourhood of small ones, there is one man who has come to be considered the head or pastor of the local church. The office among the negroes, as among all other people, confers a certain importance and power. A part of the reverence attaching to the duties is given to the person; vanity and self-confidence are cultivated, and a higher ambition aroused than can usually enter the mind of a slave. The self-respect of the preacher is also often increased by the consideration in which he is held by his master, as well as by his fellows; thus, the preachers generally have an air of superiority to other negroes; they acquire a remarkable memory of words, phrases, and forms; a curious sort of poetic talent is developed, and a habit is obtained of rhapsodizing and exciting furious emotions, to a great degree spurious and temporary, in themselves and others, through the imagination. I was introduced, the other day, to a preacher, who was represented to be quite distinguished among them. I took his hand, respectfully, and said I was happy to meet him. He seemed to take this for a joke, and laughed heartily. He was a "driver," and my friend said—

"He drives the negroes at the cotton all the week, and Sundays he drives them at the Gospel—don't you, Ned?"

He commenced to reply in some scriptural phrase, soberly; but before he could say three words, began to laugh again, and reeled off like a drunken man—entirely overcome with merriment. He recovered himself in a moment, and returned to us.

"They say he preaches very powerfully, too."

"Yes, massa! 'kordin' to der grace—*yah! yah!*"

And he staggered off again, with the peculiar hearty negro guffaw. My friend's tone was, I suppose, slightly humorous, but I was grave, and really meant to treat him respectfully, wishing to draw him into conversation; but he had got the impression that it was intended to make fun of him, and generously assuming a merry humour, I found it impossible to get a serious reply.

A majority of the public houses of worship at the South are small, rude structures of logs, or rough boards, built by the united labour or contributions of the people of a large neighbourhood or district of country, and are used as places of assembly for all public purposes. Few of them have any regular clergymen, but preachers of different denominations go from one to another, sometimes in a defined rotation, or "circuit," so that they may be expected at each of their stations at regular intervals. A late report of the Southern Aid Society states that hardly one-fifth of the preachers are regularly educated for their business, and that " you would starve a host of them if you debarred them from seeking additional support for their families by worldly occupation." In one presbytery of the Presbyterian Church, which is, perhaps, the richest, and includes the most educated body of people of all the Southern Churches, there are twenty-one ministers whose wages are not over two hundred and fifty dollars each. The proportion of ministers, of all sorts, to people, is estimated at one to thirteen hundred. (In the Free

States it is estimated at one to nine hundred.) The report of this Society also states, that "within the limits of the United States religious destitution lies comparatively at the South and South-west; and that from the first settlement of the country the North has preserved a decided religious superiority over the South, especially in three important particulars: in ample supply of Christian institutions; extensive supply of Christian truth; and thorough Christian regimen, both in the Church and in the community." It is added that, "while the South-western States have always needed a stronger arm of the Christian ministry to raise them up toward a Christian equality with their Northern brethren, their supply in this respect has always been decidedly inferior." The reason of this is the same with that which explains the general ignorance of the people of the South: The effect of Slavery in preventing social association of the whites, and in encouraging vagabond and improvident habits of life among the poor.

The two largest denominations of Christians at the South are the Methodists and Baptists—the last having a numerical superiority. There are some subdivisions of each, and of the Baptists especially, the nature of which I do not understand. Two grand divisions of the Baptists are known as the Hard Shells and the Soft Shells. There is an intense rivalry and jealousy among these various sects and sub-sects, and the controversy between them is carried on with a bitterness and persistence exceeding anything which I have known at the North, and in a manner which curiously indicates how the terms Christianity, piety, etc., are misapplied to partisanship and conditions of the imagination.

A general want of essential reverence of character seems to be evidenced in the frequent familiar and public use of expressions of rare reverence, and in high-coloured descriptions of personal feelings and sentiments, which, if actual, can only be among a man's dearest, most interior and secret, stillest, and most uncommunicable experiences. Men talk in public places, in the churches, and in bar-rooms, in the stage-coach, and at the fireside, of their personal communions with the Deity, and of the mutations of their harmony with His Spirit, just as they do about their family and business matters. The familar use of Scripture expressions by the negroes, I have already indicated. This is not confined to them. A dram-seller advertises thus :—

"'FAITH WITHOUT WORKS IS DEAD.'

IN order to engage in a more ' honorable ' business, I offer for sale, cheap for cash, my stock of
LIQUORS, BAR-FIXTURES, BILLIARD TABLE, &c., &c.
If not sold privately, by the 20th day of May, I will sell the same at public auction. 'Shew me thy faith without thy works, and I will shew thee my faith by my works.' E. KEYSER."

At a Sunday dinner-table, at a village inn in Virginia, two or three men had taken seats with me, who had, as they said, "been to the preachin'." A child had been baptized, and the discourse had been a defence of infant baptism.

"I'm damned," said one, "ef he teched on the primary significance of baptism, at all—buryin' with Jesus."

"They wus the weakest arguments for sprinklin' that ever I heerd," said another—a hot, red-faced, corpulent man—"and his sermon was two hours long, for when he stopped I looked at my watch. I thought it should be a lesson to me, for I couldn't help going to sleep. Says I to Uncle John, says I—he sot next to me, and I whispered to him—says I, 'When he gits to Bunker Hill, you wake me up,' for I see he was bound to go clean back to the beginnin' of things."

"Uncle John is an Episcopalian, aint he?"

"Yes."

"Well, there aint no religion in that, no how."

"No, there aint."

"Well now, you wouldn't think it, but I've studied into religion a heap in my life."

"Don't seem to have done you much good."

"No it aint, not yet, but I've studied into it, and I know what it is."

"There aint but one way, Benny."

"I know it."

"Repent of your sins, and believe in Christ, and be immersed—that's all."

"I know it."

"Well, I hope the Lord'll bring you to it, 'fore you die."

"Reckon he will—hope so, sure."

"You wouldn't hardly think that fat man was a preacher himself, would you?" said the landlady to me, after they left.

"Certainly not."

"He is, though, but I don't think much of that sort;" and the landlady immediately began to describe to me the religious history of the neighbourhood. It was some different here, she said she reckoned, in reply to a remark of mine, from what it was at the North. Most respectable people became pious here before they got to be very old, especially ladies. Young ladies were always gay and went to balls till they were near twenty years old, but from eighteen to twenty-five they generally got religion, and then they stopped right short, and never danced or carried on any after that. Sometimes it wasn't till after they were married, but there weren't many ladies who had children that warn't pious. She herself was an exception, for she had three children and had not got religion yet; sometimes she was frightened to think how old she was —her children growing up about her; but she did so like dancing—she hoped her turn would come—she knew it would

—she had a pious and praying mother, and she reckoned her prayers must be heard, and so on.

The religious service which I am about to describe, was held in a less than usually rude meeting-house, the boards by which it was enclosed being planed, the windows glazed, and the seats for the white people provided with backs. It stood in a small clearing of the woods, and there was no habitation within two miles of it. When I reached it with my friends, the services had already commenced. Fastened to trees, in a circle about the house, there were many saddled horses and mules, and a few attached to carts or waggons. There were two smouldering camp-fires, around which sat circles of negroes and white boys, roasting potatoes in the ashes.

In the house were some fifty white people, generally dressed in homespun, and of the class called "crackers," though I was told that some of them owned a good many negroes, and were by no means so poor as their appearance indicated. About one-third of the house, at the end opposite the desk, was covered by a gallery or cock-loft, under and in which, distinctly separated from the whites, was a dense body of negroes; the men on one side, the women on another. The whites were seated promiscuously in the body of the house. The negroes present outnumbered the whites, but the exercises at this time seemed to have no reference to them; there were many more waiting about the doors outside, and they were expecting to enjoy a meeting to themselves, after the whites had left the house. They were generally neatly dressed, more so than the majority of the whites present, but in a distinctly plantation or slave style. A few of them wore somewhat expensive articles, evidently of their own selection and purchase; but I observed, with some surprise, that not one of the women had a bonnet upon her head, all wearing handkerchiefs, generally of gay patterns, and becomingly arranged. I inquired if this was entirely a matter of taste, and was told that it, no doubt, was generally so, though the masters would not probably allow them to wear bonnets, if they should be disposed to, and should purchase them themselves, as it would be thought presuming. In the towns, the coloured women often, but not generally, wear bonnets.

During all the exercises, people of both classes were frequently going out and coming in; the women had brought their babies with them, and these made much disturbance. A negro girl would sometimes come forward to take a child out; perhaps the child would prefer not to be taken out, and would make loud and angry objections; it would then be fed. Several were allowed to crawl about the floor, carrying handfuls of corn-bread and roasted potatoes about with them; one had a fancy to enter the pulpit; which it succeeded in climbing into three times, and was as often taken away, in spite of loud and tearful expostulations, by its father. Dogs were not excluded; and outside, the doors and windows all being open, there was much neighing and braying, unused as were the mules and horses to see so many of their kind assembled.

The preliminary devotional exercises—a Scripture reading, singing, and painfully irreverential and meaningless harangues nominally addressed to the Deity, but really to the audience —being concluded, the sermon was commenced by reading a text, with which, however, it had, so far as I could discover, no further association. Without often being violent in his manner, the speaker nearly all the time cried aloud at the utmost stretch of his voice, as if calling to some one a long distance off; as his discourse was extemporaneous, however, he sometimes returned with curious effect to his natural conversational tone; and as he was gifted with a strong imagination, and possessed of a good deal of dramatic power, he kept the attention of the people very well. There was no argument upon any point that the congregation were likely to have much difference of opinion upon, nor any special connection between one sentence and another; yet there was a constant, sly, sectarian skirmishing, and a frequently recurring cannonade upon French infidelity and socialism, and several crushing charges upon Fourier, the Pope of Rome, Tom Paine,-Voltaire, "Roosu," and Joe Smith. The audience were frequently reminded that the preacher did not want their attention for any purpose of his own; but that he demanded a respectful hearing as "the ambassador of Christ." He had the habit of frequently repeating a phrase, or of bringing forward the same idea in a slightly different form, a great many times. The following passage, of which I took notes, presents an example of this, followed by one of the best instances of his dramatic talent that occurred. He was leaning far over the desk, with his arm stretched forward, gesticulating violently, yelling at the highest key, and catching breath with an effort:—

"A—ah! why don't you come to Christ? ah! what's the reason? ah! Is it because he was of *lowly birth?* ah! Is that it? *Is it* because he was born in a manger? ah! Is it because he was of a humble origin? ah! Is it because he was lowly born? a-ha! Is it because, ah!—is it because, ah!— because he was called a Nazarene? Is it because he was born in a stable?—or is it because—because he was of humble origin? Or is it—is it because"——He drew back, and after a moment's silence put his hand to his chin, and began walking up and down the platform of the pulpit, soliloquizing. "It can't be – it can't be— ?" Then lifting his eyes and gradually turning towards the audience, while he continued to speak in a low, thoughtful tone: "Perhaps you don't like the messenger—is that the reason? I'm the ambassador of the great and glorious King; it's his invitation, 'taint mine. You musn't mind me. I ain't no account. Suppose a ragged, insignificant little boy should come running in here and tell you, 'Mister, your house's a-fire!' would you mind the ragged, insignificant little boy, and refuse to listen to him, because he didn't look respectable?"

At the end of the sermon he stepped down from the pulpit, and, crossing the house towards the negroes, said, quietly, as he walked, "I take great interest in the poor blacks; and this evening I am going to hold a meeting specially for you." With this he turned back, and without re-entering the pulpit, but strolling up and down before it, read a hymn, at the conclusion of which, he laid his book down, and speaking for a moment with natural emphasis, said—

"I don't want to create a tumultuous scene, now;—that isn't my intention. I don't want to make an excitement,—that aint what I want,—but I feel that there's some here that I may never see again, ah! and, as I may never have another opportunity, I feel it my duty as an ambassador of Jesus Christ, ah! before I go——" By this time he had returned to the high key and whining yell. Exactly what he felt it his duty to do, I did not understand; but evidently to employ some more powerful agency of awakening than arguments and appeals to the understanding; and, before I could conjecture, in the least, of what sort this was to be, while he was yet speaking calmly, deprecating excitement, my attention was attracted to several men, who had previously appeared sleepy and indifferent, but who now suddenly began to sigh, raise their heads, and *shed tears*—some standing up, so that they might be observed in doing this by the whole congregation—the tears running down their noses without any interruption. The speaker, presently, was crying aloud, with a mournful, distressed, beseeching shriek, as if he were himself suffering torture : " Oh, any of you fond parents, who know that any of your dear, sweet, little ones may be, oh! at any moment snatched right away from your bosom, and cast into hell fire, oh! there to suffer torment for ever and ever, and ever and ever—Oh! come out here and help us pray for them! Oh, any of you wives that has got an unconverted husband, that won't go along with you to eternal glory, but is set upon being separated from you, oh! and taking up his bed in hell —Oh! I call upon you, if you love him, now to come out here and jine us in praying for him. Oh, if there's a husband here, whose wife is still in the bond of iniquity," etc., through a long category.

It was immediately evident that a large part of the audience, understood his wish to be the reverse of what he had declared, and considered themselves called upon to assist him; and it was astonishing to see with what readiness the faces of those who, up to the moment he gave the signal, had appeared drowsy and stupid, were made to express distressing excitement, sighing, groaning, and weeping. Rising in their seats, and walking up to the pulpit, they grasped each other's hands agonizingly, and remained, some kneeling, others standing, with their faces towards the remainder of the assembly. There was great confusion and tumult, and the poor children, evidently impressed by the terrified tone of the howling preacher, with the expectation of some immediately impending calamity, shrieked, and ran hither and thither, till negro girls came forward, laughing at the imposition, and carried them out.

At length, when some twenty had gathered around the preacher, and it became evident that no more could be drawn out, he stopped a moment for breath, and then repeated a verse of a hymn, which being sung, he again commenced to cry aloud, calling now upon all the unconverted, who were *willing* to be saved, to kneel. A few did so, and another verse was sung, followed by another more fervent exhortation. So it went on; at each verse his entreaties, warnings, and threats, and the responsive groans, sobs, and ejaculations of his coterie grew louder and stronger. Those who refused to kneel were addressed as standing on the brink of the infernal pit, into which a diabolical divinity was momentarily on the point of satisfying the necessities of his character by hurling them off.

All this time about a dozen of the audience remained standing, many were kneeling, and the larger part had taken their seats—all having risen at the commencement of the singing. Those who continued standing were mainly wild-looking young fellows, who glanced with smiles at one another, as if they needed encouragement to brazen it out. A few young women were evidently fearfully excited, and perceptibly trembled, but for some reason dared not kneel, or compromise, by sitting. One of these, a good-looking and gaily-dressed girl, stood near, and directly before the preacher, her lips compressed, and her eyes fixed fiercely and defiantly upon him. He for some time concentrated his force upon her; but she was too strong for him, he could not bring her down. At length, shaking his finger toward her, with a terrible expression, as if he had the power, and did not lack the inclination, to damn her for her resistance to his will, he said: "I tell you this is *the last call!*" She bit her lips, and turned paler, but still stood erect, and defiant of the immense magnetism concentrated upon her; and he gave it up himself, quite exhausted with the effort.

The last verse of the hymn was sung. A comparatively quiet and sober repetition of Scripture phrases, strung together heterogeneously and without meaning, in the form of prayer, followed, a benediction was pronounced, and in five minutes all the people were out of the door, with no trace of the previous excitement left, but most of the men talking eagerly of the price of cotton, and negroes, and other news.

The negroes kept their place during all of the tumult; there may have been a sympathetic groan or exclamation uttered by one or two of them, but generally they expressed only the interest of curiosity in the proceedings, such as Europeans might at a performance of the dancing dervishes, an Indian pow-wow, or an exhibition of "psychological" or "spiritual" phenomena, making it very evident that the emotion of the performers was optionally engaged in, as an appropriate part of divine service. There was generally a self-satisfied smile upon their faces; and I have no doubt they felt that they could do it with a good deal more energy and abandon, if they were called upon. I did not wish to detain my companion to witness how they succeeded, when their turn came; and I can only judge from the fact, that those I saw the next morning were so hoarse that they could scarcely speak, that the religious exercises they most enjoy are rather hard upon the lungs, whatever their effect may be upon the soul.

CHAPTER VII.

THE SOUTH-WEST, ALABAMA AND MISSISSIPPI.

Mobile.—I left Savannah for the West, by the Macon road; the train started punctually to a second, at its advertised time; the speed was not great, but regular, and less time was lost unnecessarily, at way-stations, than usually on our Northern roads.

I have travelled more than five hundred miles on the Georgia roads, and I am glad to say that all of them seem to be exceedingly well managed. The speed upon them is not generally more than from fifteen to twenty miles an hour; but it is made, as advertised, with considerable punctuality. The roads are admirably engineered and constructed, and their equipment will compare favourably with that of any other roads on the continent. There are now upwards of twelve hundred miles of railroad in the State, and more building. The Savannah and Macon line—the first built—was commenced in 1834. The increased commerce of the city of Savannah, which followed its completion, stimulated many other railroad enterprises, not only within the State, but elsewhere at the South, particularly in South Carolina. Many of these were rashly pushed forward by men of no experience, and but little commercial judgment; the roads were injudiciously laid out, and have been badly managed, and, of course, have occasioned disastrous losses. The Savannah and Macon road has, however, been very successful. The receipts are now over $1,000,000 annually; the road is well stocked, is out of debt, and its business is constantly increasing; the stock is above par, and the stockholders are receiving eight per cent. dividends, with a handsome surplus on hand. It has been always, in a great degree, under the management of Northern men — was engineered, and is still worked chiefly by Northern men, and a large amount of its stock is owned at the North. I am told that most of the mechanics, and of the successful merchants and tradesmen of Savannah came originally from the North, or are the sons of Northern men.

Partly by rail and partly by rapid stage-coaching (the coaches, horses, and drivers again from the North), I crossed the State in about twenty-four hours. The railroad is since entirely completed from Savannah to Montgomery, in Alabama, and is being extended slowly towards the Mississippi; of course with the expectation that it will eventually reach the Pacific, and thus make Savannah "the gate to the commerce of the world." Ship-masters will hope that, when either it or its rival in South Carolina has secured that honour, they will succeed, better than they yet have done, in removing the bars, physical and legal, by which commerce is now annoyed in its endeavours to serve them.

At Columbus, I spent several days. It is the largest manufacturing town, south of Richmond, in the Slave States. It is situated at the Falls, and the head of steamboat navigation of the Chatahooche, the western boundary of Georgia. The water-power is sufficient to drive two hundred thousand spindles, with a proportionate number of looms. There are, probably, at present from fifteen to twenty thousand spindles running. The operatives in the cotton-mills are said to be mainly "Cracker girls" (poor whites from the country), who earn, in good times, by piece-work, from $8 to $12 a month.

VOL. I.   T

There are, besides the cotton-mills, one woollen-mill, one paper-mill, a foundry, a cotton-gin factory, a machine-shop, etc. The labourers in all these are mainly whites, and they are in such a condition that, if temporarily thrown out of employment, great numbers of them are at once reduced to a state of destitution, and are dependent upon credit or charity for their daily food. Public entertainments were being held at the time of my visit, the profits to be applied to the relief of operatives in mills which had been stopped by the effects of a late flood of the river. Yet Slavery is constantly boasted to be a perfect safeguard against such distress.

I had seen in no place, since I left Washington, so much gambling, intoxication, and cruel treatment of servants in public, as in Columbus. This, possibly, was accidental; but I must caution persons, travelling for health or pleasure, to avoid stopping in the town. The hotel in which I lodged was disgustingly dirty; the table rovolting; the waiters stupid, inattentive, and annoying. It was the stage-house; but I was informed that the other public-house was no better. There are very good inns at Macon, and at Montgomery, Alabama; and it will be best for an invalid proceeding from Savannah westward, if possible, not to spend a night between those towns.

A day's journey took me from Columbus, through a hilly wilderness, with a few dreary villages, and many isolated cotton farms, with comfortless habitations for black and white upon them, to Montgomery, the capital of Alabama.

Montgomery is a prosperous town, with pleasant suburbs, and a remarkably enterprising population, among which there is a considerable proportion of Northern and foreign-born business-men and mechanics.

I spent a week here, and then left for Mobile, on the

steamboat Fashion, a clean and well-ordered boat, with polite and obliging officers. We were two days and a half making the passage, the boat stopping at almost every bluff and landing to take on cotton, until she had a freight of nineteen hundred bales, which was built up on the guards, seven or eight tiers in height, and until it reached the hurricane deck. The boat was thus brought so deep that her guards were in the water, and the ripple of the river constantly washed over them. There are two hundred landings on the Alabama river, and three hundred on the Bigby (Tombeckbee of the geographers), at which the boats advertise to call, if required, for passengers or freight. This, of course, makes the passage exceedingly tedious. The so-called landings, however, have not in many cases the slightest artificial accommodations for the purpose of a landing. The boat's hawser, if used, is made fast to a living tree ; there is not a sign of a wharf, often no house in sight, and sometimes no distinct road.

The principal town at which we landed was Selma, a pleasant village, in one corner of which I came upon a tall, ill-proportioned, broken-windowed brick barrack ; it had no grounds about it, was close upon the highway, was in every way dirty, neglected, and forlorn in expression. I inquired what it was, and was answered, the "Young Ladies' College." There were a number of pretty private gardens in the town, in which I noticed several evergreen oaks, the first I had seen since leaving Savannah.

At Claiborne, another village upon the river, we landed at nine o'clock on a Sunday night. It is situated upon a bluff, a hundred and fifty feet high, with a nearly perpendicular bank, upon the river. The boat came to the shore at the foot of a plank slide-way, down which cotton was sent to it, from a warehouse at the top.

There was something truly Western in the direct, reckless way in which the boat was loaded. A strong gang-plank being placed at right angles to the slide-way, a bale of cotton was let slide from the top, and, coming down with fearful velocity, on striking the gang-plank, it would rebound up and out on to the boat, against a barricade of bales previously arranged to receive it. The moment it struck this barricade, it would be dashed at by two or three men, and jerked out of the way, and others would roll it to its place for the voyage, on the tiers aft. The mate, standing near the bottom of the slide, as soon as the men had removed one bale to what he thought a safe distance, would shout to those aloft, and down would come another. Not unfrequently, a bale would not strike fairly on its end, and would rebound off, diagonally, overboard; or would be thrown up with such force as to go over the barricade, breaking stanchions and railings, and scattering the passengers on the berth deck. Negro hands were sent to the top of the bank, to roll the bales to the side, and Irishmen were kept below to remove them, and stow them. On asking the mate (with some surmisings) the reason of this arrangement, he said—

"The niggers are worth too much to be risked here; if the Paddies are knocked overboard, or get their backs broke, nobody loses anything!"

There were about one hundred passengers on the Fashion, besides a number of poor people and negroes on the lower deck. They were, generally, cotton-planters, going to Mobile on business, or emigrants bound to Texas or Arkansas. They were usually well dressed, but were a rough, coarse style of people, drinking a great deal, and most of the time under a little alcoholic excitement. Not sociable, except when the topics of cotton, land, and negroes, were started; interested, however, in talk about theatres and the turf; very profane; often showing the handles of concealed weapons about their persons, but not quarrelsome, avoiding disputes and altercations, and respectful to one another in forms of words; very ill-informed, except on plantation business; their language ungrammatical, idiomatic, and extravagant. Their grand characteristics—simplicity of motives, vague, shallow, and purely objective habits of thought; and bold, self-reliant movement.

With all their individual independence, I soon could perceive a very great homogeneousness of character, by which they were distinguishable from any other people with whom I had before been thrown in contact; and I began to study it with interest, as the Anglo-Saxon development of the South-west.

I found that, more than any people I had ever seen, they were unrateable by dress, taste, forms, and expenditures. I was perplexed by finding, apparently united in the same individual, the self-possession, confidence, and the use of expressions of deference, of the well-equipped gentleman, and the coarseness and low tastes of the uncivilized boor—frankness and reserve, recklessness and self-restraint, extravagance, and penuriousness.

There was one man, who "lived, when he was to home," as he told me, "in the Red River Country," in the north-eastern part of Texas, having emigrated thither from Alabama, some years before. He was a tall, thin, awkward person, and wore a suit of clothes (probably bought "ready-made") which would have better suited a short, fat figure. Under his waistcoat he carried a large knife, with the hilt generally protruding at the breast. He had been with his family to his former home, for a business purpose, and was now returning to his plantation. His wife was a pale and harassed-looking woman; and he scarce ever paid her the smallest attention, not even sitting near her at the public table. Of his children, however, he seemed very fond; and they had a negro servant in attendance upon them, whom he was constantly scolding and threatening. Having been from home for six weeks, his impatience to return was very great, and was constantly aggravated by the frequent and long-continued stoppages of the boat. "Time's money, time's money!" he would be constantly saying, while we were taking on cotton—"time's worth more'n money to me now; a hundred per cent. more, 'cause I left my niggers all alone; not a dam white man within four mile on 'em."

I asked how many negroes he had.

"I've got twenty on 'em to home, and thar they ar! and thar they ar! and thar aint a dam soul of a white fellow within four mile on 'em."

"They are picking cotton, I suppose?"

"No, I got through pickin' 'fore I left."

"What work have they to do, then, now?"

"I set 'em to clairin', but they aint doin' a dam thing—not a dam thing, they aint; that's wat they are doin', that is—not a dam thing. I know that, as well as you do. That's the reason time's an object. I told the capting so, wen I came aboard: says I, 'capting,' says I, 'time is in the objective case with me.' No, sir, they aint doin' a dam solitary thing; that's what they are up to. I know that as well as anybody; I do. But I'll make it up, I'll make it up, when I get thar, now you'd better believe."

Once, when a lot of cotton, baled with unusual neatness, was coming on board, and some doubt had been expressed as to the economy of the method of baling, he said very loudly:

"Well, now, I'd be willin' to bet my salvation, that them thar's the heaviest bales that's come on to this boat."

"I'll bet you a hundred dollars of it," answered one.

"Well, if I was in the habit of bettin', I'd do it. I aint a bettin' man. But I am a cotton man, I am, and I don't car who knows it. I know cotton, I do. I'm dam if I know anythin' but cotton. I ought to know cotton, I had. I've been at it ever sin' I was a chile."

"Stranger," he asked me once, "did you ever come up on the Leweezay? She's a right smart pretty boat, she is, the Leweezay; the best I ever see on the Alabamy river. They wanted me to wait and come down on her, but I told 'em time was in the objective case to me. She is a right pretty boat, and her capting's a high-tone gentleman; haint no objections to find with him—he's a high-tone gentleman, that's what he is. But the pilot—well, damn him! He run her right out of the river, up into the woods—didn't run her in the river, at all. When I go aboard a steamboat, I like to keep in the river, somewar; but that pilot, he took her right up into the woods. It was just clairin' land. Clairin' land, and playin' hell ginerally, all night; not follering the river at all. I believe he was drunk. He must have been drunk, for I could keep a boat in the river myself. I'll never go in a boat where the pilot's drunk all the time. I take a glass too much myself, sometimes; but I don't hold two hundred lives in the holler of my hand. I was in my berth, and he run her straight out of the river, slap up into the furest. It threw me clean out of my berth, out onter the floor; I didn't sleep any more while I was aboard. The Leweezay's a right smart pretty little boat, and her capting's a high-tone gentleman. They hev good livin' aboard of her, too. Haan't no objections on that score; weddin' fixins all the time; but I won't go in a boat war the pilot's drunk. I set some vally on the life of two hundred souls. They wanted to hev me come down on her, but I told 'em time was in the objective case."

There were three young negroes, carried by another Texan, on the deck, outside the cabin. I don't know why they were not allowed to be with the other emigrant slaves, carried on the lower deck, unless the owner was afraid of their trying to get away, and had no handcuffs small enough for them. They were boys; the oldest twelve or fourteen years old, the youngest not more than seven. They had evidently been bought lately by their present owner, and probably had just been taken from their parents. They lay on the deck and slept, with no bed but the passengers' luggage, and no cover but a single blanket for each. Early one morning, after a very stormy night, when they must have suffered much from the driving rain and cold, I saw their owner with a glass of spirits, giving each a few swallows from it. The older ones smacked their lips, and said, "Tank 'ou massa;" but the little one couldn't drink it, and cried aloud, when he was forced to. The older ones were very playful and quarrelsome, and continually teasing the younger, who seemed very sad, or homesick and sulky. He would get very angry at their mischievous fun, and sometimes strike them. He would then be driven into a corner, where he would lie on his back, and kick at them in a perfect frenzy of anger and grief. The two boys would continue to laugh at him, and frequently the passengers would stand about, and be amused by it. Once, when they had plagued him in this way for some time, he jumped up on to the cotton-bales, and made as if he would have plunged overboard. One of the older boys caught him by the ankle, and held him till his master came and hauled him in, and gave him a severe flogging with a rope's end. A number of passengers collected about them, and I heard several say, "That's what he wants." Red River said to me, "I've been a watchin' that ar boy, and I see what's the matter with him; he's got the devil in him right bad, and he'll hev to take a right many of them warmins before it'll be got out."

The crew of the boat, as I have intimated, was composed partly of Irishmen, and partly of negroes; the latter were slaves, and were hired of their owners at $40 a month—the same wages paid to the Irishmen. A dollar of their wages was given to the negroes themselves, for each Sunday they were on the passage. So far as convenient, they were kept at work separately from the white hands; they were also messed separately. On Sunday I observed them dining in a group, on the cotton-bales. The food which was given to them in tubs, from the kitchen, was various and abundant, consisting of bean-porridge, bacon, corn bread, ship's biscuit, potatoes, duff (pudding), and gravy. There was one knife used only, among ten of them; the bacon was cut and torn into shares; splinters of the bone and of fire-wood were used for forks; the porridge was passed from one to another, and drank out of the tub; but though excessively dirty and beast-like in their appearance and manners, they were good-natured and jocose as usual.

"Heah! you Bill," said one to another, who was on a higher tier of cotton, "pass down de dessart. You! up dar on de hill; de dessart! Augh! don't you know what de dessart be? De duff, you fool."

"Does any of de gemmen want some o' dese potatum?" asked another; and no answer being given, he turned the tub full of potatoes overboard, without any hesitation. It was evident he had never had to think on one day how he should be able to live the next.

Whenever we landed at night or on Sunday, for wood or cotton, there would be many negroes come on board from the neighbouring plantations, to sell eggs to the steward.

Sunday was observed by the discontinuance of public gambling in the cabin, and in no other way. At midnight gambling was resumed, and during the whole passage was never at any other time discontinued, night or day, so far as I saw. There were three men that seemed to be professional sharpers, and who probably played into each other's hands. One young man lost all the money he had with him—several hundred dollars.

Mobile, in its central, business part, is very compactly built, dirty, and noisy, with little elegance, or evidence of taste or public spirit, in its people. A small, central, open square—the only public ground that I saw—was used as a horse and hog pasture, and clothes drying-yard. Out of the busier quarter, there is a good deal of the appearance of a thriving New England village—almost all the dwelling-houses having plots of ground enclosed around them, planted with trees and shrubs. The finest trees are the magnolia and live oak; and the most valuable shrub is the Cherokee rose, which is much used for hedges and screens. It is evergreen, and its leaves are glossy and beautiful at all seasons, and in March it blooms profusely. There is an abundance, also, of the Cape jessamine. It is as beautiful as a camelia; and, when in blossom, scents the whole air with a most delicate and delicious fragrance. At a market-garden, near the town which I visited, I found most of the best Northern and Belgian pears fruiting well, and apparently healthy, and well suited in climate, on quince-stocks. Figs are abundant, and bananas and oranges are said to be grown with some care, and slight winter protection.

The Battle House, kept by Boston men, with Irish servants, I found an excellent hotel; but with higher charge than I had ever paid before. Prices, generally, in Mobile, range very high. There are large numbers of foreign merchants in the population; but a great deficiency of tradesmen and mechanics.

While I was at Montgomery, my hat was one day taken from the dining-room, at dinner-time, by some one who left in its place for me a very battered and greasy substitute, which I could not wear, if I had chosen to. I asked the landlord what I should do. "Be before him, to-morrow." Following this cool advice, and, in the mean time, wearing a cap, I obtained my hat the next day; but so ill used, that I should not have known it, but for the maker's name, stamped within it. Not succeeding in fitting myself with a new hat, I desired to have my old one pressed, when in Mobile; but I could not find a working hatter in the place, though it has a population of thirty thousand souls. Finally, a hat-dealer, a German Jew, I think he was, with whom I had left it while looking further, returned it to me, with a charge of one dollar, for brushing it—the benefit of which brushing I was unable, in the least, to perceive. A friend informed me that he found it cheaper to have all his furniture and clothing made for him, in New York, to order, when he needed any, and sent on by express, than to get it in Mobile.

The great abundance of the best timber for the purpose, in the United States, growing in the vicinity of the town, has lately induced some persons to attempt ship-building at Mobile. The mechanics employed are all from the North.

The great business of the town is the transfer of cotton, from the producer to the manufacturer, from the waggon and the steamboat to the sea-going ship. Like all the other cotton-ports, Mobile labours under the disadvantage of a shallow harbour. At the wharves, there were only a few small craft and steamboats. All large sea-going vessels lie some thirty miles below, and their freights are transhipped in lighters.

There appears to be a good deal of wealth and luxury, as well as senseless extravagance in the town. English merchants affect the character of the society, considerably; some very favourably—some, very much otherwise. Many of them own slaves, and, probably, all employ them; but Slavery seems to.be of more value to them from the amusement it affords, than in any other way. "So-and-so advertises 'a valuable drayman, and a good blacksmith and horse-shoer, for sale, on reasonable terms;' an acclimated double-entry book-keeper, kind in harness, is what I want," said one; "those Virginia patriarchs haven't any enterprise, or they'd send on a stock of such goods every spring, to be kept over through the fever, so they could warrant them."

"I don't know where you'll find one," replied another; "but if you are wanting a private chaplain, there's one I have heard, in —————— street, several times, that could probably be bought for a fair price; and I will warrant him sound enough in wind, if not in doctrine."

"I wouldn't care for his doctrine, if I bought him; I don't care how black he is; feed him right, and in a month he will be as orthodox as an archbishop."

CHAPTER VIII.

MISSISSIPPI AND LOUISIANA.

New Orleans.—The steamboat by which I made the passage along the north shore of the Mexican Gulf to New Orleans, was New York built, and owned by a New-Yorker; and the Northern usage of selling passage tickets, to be returned on leaving the boat, was retained upon it. I was sitting near a group of Texans and emigrating planters, when a waiter passed along, crying the usual request, that passengers who had not obtained tickets would call at the captain's office for that purpose. "What's that? What's that?" they shouted; "What did he mean? What is it?" "Why, it's a dun," said one. "He is dunnin' on us, sure," continued one and another; and some started from the seats, as if they thought it insulting. "Well, it's the first time I ever was dunned by a nigger, I'll swar," said one. This seemed to place it in a humorous aspect; and, after a hearty laugh, they resumed their discussion of the advantages offered to emigrants in different parts of Texas, and elsewhere.

There was a young man on the boat who had been a passenger with me on the boat from Montgomery. He was bound for Texas; and while on board the Fashion I had heard him saying that he had met with "a right smart bad streak of luck" on his way, having lost a valuable negro.

"I thought you were going on with those men to Texas, the other day," said I.

"No," he replied; "I left my sister in Mobile, when I

went back after my nigger, and when I came down again, I found that she had found an old acquaintance there, and they had concluded to get married; so I stayed to see the wedding."

"Rather quick work."

"Well, I reckon they'd both thought about it when they knew each other before; but I didn't know it, and it kind o' took me by surprise. So my other sister, she concluded Ann had done so well stopping in Mobile, she'd stop and keep company with her a spell; and so I've got to go 'long alone. Makes me feel kind o' lonesome—losing that nigger too."

"Did you say that you went back after the nigger? I thought he died?"

"Well, you see I had brought him along as far as Mobile, and he got away from me there, and slipped aboard a steamboat going back, and hid himself. I found out that he was aboard of her pretty soon after she got off, and I sent telegraphic despatches to several places along up the river, to the captain, to put him in a jail, ashore, for me. I know he got one of them at Cahawba, but he didn't mind it till he got to Montgomery. Well, the nigger didn't have any attention paid to him. They just put him in irons; likely enough he didn't get much to eat, or have anything to cover himself, and he took cold, and got sick—got pneumonia—and when they got to Montgomery, they made him walk up to the jail, and there wan't no fire, and nothin' to lie on, nor nothin' for him in the jail, and it made quick work with him. Before I could get up there he was dead. I see an attorney here to Mobile, and he offered to take the case, and prosecute the captain; and he says if he don't recover every red cent the man was worth, he won't ask me for a fee. It comes kinder hard on me. I bought the nigger up, counting I should make a speculation on him; reckoned I'd take him to

Texas if I couldn't turn him to good advantage at Mobile. As niggers is goin' here now, I expect 'twas a dead loss of eight hundred dollars, right out of pocket."

There were a large number of steerage passengers occupying the main deck, forward of the shaft. Many of them were Irish, late immigrants, but the large majority were slaves, going on to New Orleans to be sold, or moving with their masters, to Texas. There was a fiddle or two among them, and they were very merry, dancing and singing. A few, however, refused to join in the amusement, and looked very disconsolate. A large proportion of them were boys and girls, under twenty years of age.

On the forecastle-deck there was a party of emigrants, moving with waggons. There were three men, a father and his two sons, or sons-in-law, with their families, including a dozen or more women and children. They had two waggons, covered with calico and bed-ticks, supported by hoops, in which they carried their furniture and stores, and in which they also slept at night, the women in one, and the men in the other. They had six horses, two mules, and two pair of cattle with them. I asked the old man why he had taken his cattle along with him, when he was going so far by sea, and found that he had informed himself accurately of what it would cost him to hire or buy cattle at Galveston; and that taking into account the probable delay he would experience in looking for them there, he had calculated that he could afford to pay the freight on them, to have them with him, to go on at once into the country on his arrival, rather than to sell them at Mobile.

"But," said he, "there was one thing I didn't cakulate on, and I don't understand it; the capting cherged me two dollars and a half for 'wherfage.' I don't know what that means, do you? I want to know, because I don't car' to be imposed upon by nobody. I payed it without sayin' a word, 'cause I never travelled on the water before; next time I do, I shall be more sassy." I asked where he was going. "Didn't know much about it," he said, "but reckoned he could find a place where there was a good range, and plenty of game. If 'twas as good a range (pasture) as 'twas to Alabama when he first came there, he'd be satisfied." After he'd got his family safe through acclimating this time, he reckoned he shouldn't move again.. He had moved about a good deal in his life. There was his littlest boy, he said, looking kindly at a poor, thin, blue-faced little child—he reckoned they'd be apt to *leave* him; he had got *tropsical*, and was of mighty weak constitution, nat'rally; 'twouldn't take much to carry him off, and, of course, a family must be exposed a good deal, moving so this time of year. They should try to find some heavy timbered land—good land, and go to clearing; didn't calculate to make any crops the first year—didn't calculate on it, though perhaps they might if they had good luck. They had come from an eastern county of Alabama. Had sold out his farm for two dollars an acre; best land in the district was worth four; land was naturally kind of thin, and now 'twas pretty much all worn out there. He had moved first from North Carolina, with his father. They never made anything to sell but cotton; made corn for their own use. Never had any negroes; reckoned he'd done about as well as if he had had them; reckoned a little better on the whole. No, he should not work negroes in Texas. "Niggers is so kerless, and want so much lookin' arter; they is so monstrous lazy; they won't do no work, you know, less you are clus to 'em all the time, and I don't feel like it. I couldn't, at my time of life, begin a-using the lash; and you know they do have to take that, all on 'em—and a heap on't, sometimes."

"I don't know much about it; they don't have slaves where I live."

"Then you come from a Free State; well, they've talked some of makin' Alabamy a Free State."

"I didn't know that."

"O, yes, there was a good deal of talk one time, as if they was goin' to do it right off. O, yes; there was two or three of the States this way, one time, come pretty nigh freein' the niggers—lettin' 'em all go free."

"And what do you think of it?"

"Well, I'll tell you what I think on it; I'd like it if we could get rid on 'em to yonst. I wouldn't like to hev 'em freed, if they was gwine to hang 'round. They ought to get some country, and put 'em war they could be by themselves. It wouldn't do no good to free 'em, and let 'em hang round, because they is so monstrous lazy; if they hadn't got nobody to take keer on 'em, you see they wouldn't do nothin' but juss nat'rally laze round, and steal, and pilfer, and no man couldn't live, you see, war they was—if they was free, no man couldn't live. And then, I've two objections; that's one on 'em—no man couldn't live—and this ere's the other: Now suppose they was free, you see they'd all think themselves just as good as we; of course they would, if they was free. Now, just suppose you had a family of children: how would you like to hev a niggar feelin' just as good as a white man? how'd you like to hev a niggar steppin' up to your darter? Of course you wouldn't; and that's the reason I wouldn't like to hev 'em free; but I tell you, I don't think it's right to hev 'em slaves so; that's the fac—taant right to keep 'em as they is."

I was awakened, in the morning, by the loud ringing of a hand-bell; and, turning out of my berth, dressed by dim lamp-light. The waiters were serving coffee and collecting baggage; and, upon stepping out of the cabin, I found that the boat was made fast to a long wooden jetty, and the passengers were going ashore. A passage-ticket for New Orleans was handed me, as I crossed the gang-plank. There was a rail-track and a train of cars upon the wharf, but no locomotive; and I got my baggage checked, and walked on toward the shore.

It was early daylight—a fog rested on the water, and only the nearest point could be discerned. There were many small buildings near the jetty, erected on piles over the water—bathing-houses, bowling-alleys, and billiard-rooms, with other indications of a place of holiday resort—and, on reaching the shore, I found a slumbering village. The first house from the wharf had a garden about it, with complex alleys, and tables, and arbours, and rustic seats, and cut shrubs, and shells, and statues, and vases, and a lamp was feebly burning in a large lantern over the entrance gate. I was thinking how like it was to a rural restaurant in France or Germany, when a locomotive backed, screaming hoarsely, down the jetty; and I returned to get my seat.

Off we puffed, past the restaurant, into the village—the name of which I did not inquire, everybody near me seemed so cold and cross,—through the little village of white houses —whatever it was—and away into a dense, gray cypress forest. For three or four rods, each side of the track, the trees had all been felled and removed, leaving a dreary strip of swamp, covered with stumps. This was bounded and intersected by broad ditches, or narrow and shallow canals, with a great number of very small punts in them. So it continued, for two or three miles; then the ground became dryer, there was an abrupt termination of the gray wood; the fog was lifting and drifting off, in ragged, rosy clouds, disclosing a flat country, skirted still, and finally bounded, in the background, with the swamp-forest. A few low houses, one story high, all having verandahs before them, were scattered thinly over it.

At length, a broad road struck in by the side of the track; the houses became more frequent; soon forming a village street, with smoke ascending from breakfast fires; windows and doors opening, maids sweeping steps, bakers' waggons passing, and broad streets, little built upon, breaking off at right angles.

At the corners of these streets, were high poles, connected at the top by a rope, and furnished with blocks and halyards, by which great square lanterns were slung over the middle of the carriage-way. I thought again of France, ("*à la lanterne!*") and turning to one of my cold and cross companions—a man wrapped in a loose coat, with a cowl over his head—I asked the name of the village, for my geography was at fault. I had expected to be landed at New Orleans by the boat, and had not been informed of the railroad arrangement, and had no idea in what part of Louisiana we might be. "Note Anglische, sare," was the gruff reply.

There was a sign, "*Café du Faubourg*," and, putting my head out of the window, I saw that we must have arrived at New Orleans. We reached the terminus, which was surrounded with *fiacres*, in the style of Paris. "To the Hotel St. Charles," I said to a driver, confused with the loud French and quiet English of the crowd about me. "*Oui*, yer 'onor," was the reply of my Irish-born fellow-citizen: another passenger was got, and away we rattled through narrow dirty streets, among grimy old stuccoed walls; high arched windows and doors, balconies and entresols, and French noises and French smells, French signs, ten to one of English, but with funny polygomatic arrangements, sometimes, from which less influential families were not excluded.

The other fare to whom I had not ventured to speak was

set down at a *salle pour la vente des* somethings, and soon after the *fiacre* turned out upon a broad place, covered with bales of cotton, and casks of sugar, and weighing scales, and disclosing an astonishing number of steamboats, lying all close together in a line, the ends of which were lost in the mist, which still hung upon the river.

Now the signs became English, and the new brick buildings American. We turned into a broad street, in which shutters were being taken from great glass store-fronts, and clerks were exercising their ingenuity in the display of muslin, and silks, and shawls. In the middle of the broad street there was an open space of waste ground, looking as if the corporation had not been able to pave the whole of it at once, and had left this interval to be attended to when the treasury was better filled. Crossing through a gap in this waste, we entered a narrow street of high buildings, French, Spanish, and English signs, the latter predominating; and at the second block, I was landed before the great Grecian portico of the stupendous, tasteless,. ill-contrived, and inconvenient St. Charles Hotel.

After a bath and breakfast, I returned, with great interest, to wander in the old French town, the characteristics of which I have sufficiently indicated. Among the houses, one occasionally sees a relic of ancient Spanish builders, while all the newer edifices have the characteristics of the dollar-pursuing Yankees.

I was delighted when I reached the old Place d'Armes, now a public garden, bright with the orange and lemon trees, and roses, and myrtles, and laurels, and jessamines of the south of France. Fronting upon it is the ancient Hotel de Ville, still the city court-house, a quaint old French structure, with scaly and vermiculated surface, and deep-worn door-sills, and smooth-rubbed corners; the most picturesque and historic-looking public building, except the highly preserved, little old court-house at Newport, that I can now think of in the United States.

Adjoining it is an old Spanish cathedral, damaged by paint, and late alterations and repairs, but still a fine thing in our desert of the reverend in architecture. Enough, that while it is not new, it is not shabby, and is not tricked out with much frippery,* gingerbread and confectionery work. The door is open; coaches and crippled beggars are near it. A priest, with a face the expression of which first makes one think of an ape and then of an owl, is coming out. If he were not otherwise to be heartily welcomed to fresh air and sunlight, he should be so, for the sake of the Sister of Charity who is following him, probably to some death-bed, with a corpse-like face herself, haggard but composed, pensive and absorbed, and with the eyes of a broken heart. I think that I may yet meet them looking down compassionately and soothingly, in some far distant pestilent or war-hospital. In lieu of holy-water, then, here is money for the poor-box, though the devil share it with good angels.

Dark shadows, and dusky light, and deep, subdued, low organ strains pervade the interior; and, on the bare floor, here are the kneeling women—" good" and " bad" women— and, ah! yes, white and black women, bowed in equality before their common Father. " Ridiculously absurd idea," say democratic Governors Mc Duffie and Hammond; " Self-evident," said our ancestors, and so must say the voice of conscience, in all free, humble hearts.

In the crowded market-place, there were not only the pure old Indian Americans, and the Spanish, French, English, Celtic, and African, but nearly all possible mixed varieties of these, and no doubt of some other breeds of mankind.

* Contemptible; from the root Fripper, to wear out.—WEBSTER.

The various grades of the coloured people are designated by the French as follows, according to the greater or less predominance of negro blood :—

Sacatra	griffe and negress.
Griffe	negro and mulatto.
Marabon	mulatto and griffe.
Mulatto	white and negro.
Quarteron	white and mulatto.
Metif	white and quarteron.
Meamelouc	white and metif.
Quarteron	white and meamelouc.
Sang-mele	white and quarteron.

And all these, with the sub-varieties of them, French, Spanish, English, and Indian, and the sub-sub-varieties, such as Anglo-Indian-mulatto, I believe experts pretend to be able to distinguish. Whether distinguishable or not, it is certain they all exist in New Orleans.

They say that the cross of the French and Spanish with the African produces a finer and a healthier result than that of the more Northern European races. Certainly, the French quadroons are very handsome and healthy in appearance; and I should not be surprised if really thorough and sufficient scientific observation should show them to be—contrary to the common assertion—more vigorous than either of the parent races.

Some of the coloured women spoke French, Spanish, and English, as their customers demanded.*

*[From the New Orleans Picayune.]
" FIFTY DOLLARS REWARD.—Ran away from the subscriber, about two months ago, a bright mulatto girl, named Mary, about twenty-five years of age, almost white, and reddish hair, front teeth out, a cut on her upper lip; about five feet five inches high; has a scar on her forehead; she passes for free; talks *French, Italian, Dutch, English, and Spanish.*

" ANDRE GRASSO.
" Upper side of St. Mary's Market."

Three taverns, bearing the sign of "The Pig and Whistle," indicated the recent English, a cabaret to the Universal Republic, with a red flag, the French, and the Gasthaus zum Rheinplatz, the Teutonic contributions to the strength of our nation. A policeman, with the richest Irish brogue, directed me back to the St. Charles.

In front of a large New York clothing store, twenty-two negroes were standing in a row. Each wore a blue suit, and a black hat, and each held a bundle of additional clothing, and a pair of shoes, in his hands. They were all, but one, who was probably a driver having charge of them, young men, not over twenty-five, and the majority, I should think, between eighteen and twenty-two years of age. Their owner was probably in the clothing store, settling for the outfit he had purchased for them, and they were waiting to be led to the steamboat, which should convey them to his plantation. They were silent and sober, like a file of soldiers standing at ease ; and, perhaps, were gratified by the admiration their fine manly figures and uniform dress obtained from the passers by.

"Well, now, that ar's the likeliest lot of niggers I ever see," said one, to me. "Some feller's bin roun', and just made his pick out o' all the jails* in Orleens. Must ha' cost him a heap o' rocks. I don't reckon thar's a nigger in that crowd that wouldn't fetch twelve hundred dollars, at a vandue. Twenty thousand dollars wouldn' be no banter for 'em. Dam'd if they aint just the best gang o' cotton-hands ever I see. Give me half on 'em, and I'd sign off—wouldn' ask nothing more."

· Louisiana or Texas, thought I, pays Virginia twenty odd thousand dollars for that lot of bone and muscle. Virginia's interest in continuing the business may be imagined, especially

* The private establishments, in which stocks of slaves are kept for sale in New Orleans, are called jails.

if, in their place, could come free labourers, to help her people at the work she needs to have done; but where is the advantage of it to Louisiana, and especially to Texas? Yonder is a steamboat load of the same material—bone and muscle—which, at the same sort of valuation, is worth two hundred and odd thousand dollars; and off it goes, past Texas, through Louisiana—far away yet, up the river, and Wisconsin or Iowa will get it, two hundred thousand dollars' worth, to say nothing of the thalers and silver groschen, in those strong chests—all for nothing.

In ten years' time, how many mills, and bridges, and schoolhouses, and miles of railroad, will the Germans have built? And how much cloth and fish will they want from Massachusetts, iron from Pennsylvania, and tin from Banca, hemp from Russia, tea from China, and coffee from Brazil, fruit from Spain, wine from Ohio, and oil and gold from the Pacific, silk from France, sugar from Louisiana, cotton from Texas, and rags from Italy, lead from Illinois, notions from Connecticut, and machines from New Jersey, and intelligence from everywhere?

And how much of all these things will the best two hundred Virginians that Louisiana can buy, at any price, demand of commerce, in ten years?

A mechanic, English by birth, who had lived in New Orleans for several years, always going up the river in the summer, to escape the danger of fever in the city, told me that he could lay up money much more rapidly than in New York. The expenses of living were not necessarily greater than in New York. If a man kept house, and provided for himself, he could live much cheaper than at boarding-houses. Many unmarried mechanics, therefore, lived with coloured mistresses, who were commonly vile and dishonest. He was at a boarding-house, where he paid four dollars a week. In

New York he had paid three dollars, but the board was not as good as in New Orleans. "The reason," said he, "that people say it costs so much more to live here than in New York is, that what they think treats in New York, they consider necessaries here. Everybody lives freer, and spends their money more willingly here." When he first came to New Orleans, a New England mechanic came with him. He supposed him to have been previously a man of sober habits; but almost immediately after he got to New Orleans, he got into bad ways, and in a few months he was so often drunk, and brought so much scandal on their boarding-house, that he was turned out of it. Soon after this, he called on him, and borrowed two dollars. He said he could not live in New Orleans, it was too expensive, and he was going to Texas. This was several years before, and he had not heard from him since. And this he said was a very common course with New England boys, who had been "too carefully brought up at home," when they came to New Orleans. The master mechanics, who bought up slaves, and took contracts for work, he said, made more money than any others. They did so because they did very poor work—poorer than white mechanics could generally be got to do. But nearly all work was done in New Orleans more hastily and carelessly than in New York, though he thought it was bad enough there. The slave-holding bosses could get no white men to work with their slaves, except Irishmen or Germans—no man who had any regard for his position among his fellow-craftsmen would ever let himself be seen working with a negro. He said I could see any day in Canal Street, "a most revolting sight"—Irishmen waiting on negro masons. He had seen, one morning as he was going to his work, a negro carrying some mortar, when another negro hailed him with a loud laugh: "Hallo! you is turned Irishman, is 'ou?" White working men were rapidly displacing the slaves in all sorts of work, and he hoped and believed it would not be many years before every negro would be driven out of the town. He thought acclimated white men could do more hard work than negroes, even in the hottest weather, if they were temperate, and avoided too stimulating food. That, he said, was the general opinion among those of them who stayed over summer. Those who drank much whisky and cordials, and kept up old habits of eating, just as if they were in England, were the ones who complained most of the climate, and who thought white men were not made to work in it. He had stayed as late as July, and returned in September, and he never saw the day in which he could not do as much work as he did in London.

A New-Yorker, whom I questioned about this, said: "I have worked through the very hottest weather, steadily, day after day, and done more work than any three niggers in the State, and been no worse for it. A man has only to take some care of himself."

Going to Lafayette, on the top of an omnibus, I heard an Irishman, somewhat over-stimulated, as Irishmen are apt to be, loudly declare himself an abolitionist: a companion endeavoured in vain to stop him, or make him recant, and finally declared he would not ride any further with him if he could not be more discreet.

The *Morehouse* (Louisiana) *Advocate*, in an article abusive of foreigners, thus describes what, if foreign born working men were not generally so ignorant and easily imposed upon as they are, would undoubtedly be (although they certainly have not yet generally been) their sentiments with regard to Slavery:

"The great mass of foreigners who come to our shores are labourers, and consequently come in competition with slave labour. It is to their interest to abolish Slavery; and we know full well the disposition of man to promote all things which advance his own interests. These men come from nations where Slavery is not allowed, and they drink in abolition sentiments from their mothers' breasts; they (all the white race) entertain an utter abhorrence of being put on a level with blacks, whether in the field or in the workshop. Could Slavery be abolished, there would be a greater demand for labourers, and the prices of labour must be greatly enhanced. These may be termed the internal evidences of the abolitionism of foreigners.

"But we may find near home facts to corroborate these 'internal' evidences: It is well known that there exists a great antipathy among the draymen and rivermen of·New Orleans (who are almost to a man foreigners) to the participation of slaves in these branches of industry."

It is obvious that free men have very much gained the field of labour in New Orleans to themselves. The majority of the cartmen, hackney-coach men, porters, railroad hands, public waiters, and common labourers, as well as of skilled mechanics, appear to be white men; and of the negroes employed in those avocations a considerable proportion are free.

This is the case here more than in any other town in the South, although the climate is torrid, and inconvenient or dangerous to strangers; because New Orleans is more extensively engaged in commerce than they are, and because there is, by the passing and sojourning immigration from Europe, constantly in the city a sufficient number of free labourers to sustain, by competition and association with each other, the habits of free-labour communities. It is plainly perceptible that the white working men in. New Orleans have more business-like manners, and more assured self-respect, than those of smaller towns. They are even not without some *esprit du corps*.

As Commerce, or any high form of industry requires intelligence in its labourers, slaves can never be brought together in dense communities, but their intelligence will increase to a degree dangerous to those who enjoy the benefit of their labour. The slave must be kept dependent, day by day, upon his master for his daily bread, or he will find, and will declare his independence, in all respects, of him. This condition disqualifies the slave for any but the simplest and rudest forms of labour; and every attempt to bring his labour into competition with free labour can only be successful at the hazard of insurrection. Hundreds of slaves in New Orleans must be constantly reflecting and saying to one another, " I am as capable of taking care of myself as this Irish hod-carrier, or this German market-gardener; why can't I have the enjoyment of my labour as well as they? I am as capable of taking care of my own family as much as they of theirs; why should I be subject to have them taken from me by those other men who call themselves our owners? Our children have as much brains as the children of these white neighbours of ours, who not long ago were cooks and waiters at the hotels; why should they be spurned from the school-rooms? I helped to build the school-house, and have not been paid for it. One thing I know, if I can't have my rights, I can have my pleasures; and if they won't give me wages I can take them."

That this influence of association in labour with free-men cannot fail to be appreciated by intelligent observers, will be evident from the following paragraph from the *New Orleans Crescent*, although it was probably written to show only the amusing and picturesque aspect of the slave community:—

"GUINEA-LIKE.—Passing along Baronne street, between Perdido and Poydras streets, any Sunday afternoon, the white passer-by might easily suppose himself in Guinea, Caffraria, or any other thickly-peopled region in the land of Ham. Where the darkies all come from, what they do there, or where they go to, constitute a problem somewhat beyond our algebra. It seems to be a sort of nigger exchange. We know there are in that vicinity a coloured church, coloured ice-cream saloon, coloured restaurant, coloured coffee-houses, and a coloured barber-shop, which, we have heard say, has a back communication with one of the groggeries, for the benefit of slaves; but as the police haven't found it out yet, we suppose it ain't so. However, if the ebony dandies who attend Sunday evening 'change, would keep within their various retreats, or leave a path about three feet wide on the side-walk, for the free passage of people who are so unlucky as to be white, we wouldn't complain; but to have to elbow one's way through a crowd of woolly-heads on such a day as yesterday, their natural muskiness made more villanous by the fumes of whisky, is too much for delicate olfactories like ours. A fight, last evening, between two white men at one of the groggeries, afforded much edification to the darkies standing around, and seemed to confirm them in their opinion, that white folks, after all, ain't much."

Similar complaints to the following, which I take from the *New Orleans Crescent*, I have heard, or seen in the journals, at Richmond, Savannah, Louisville, and most other large manufacturing, or commercial towns of the South.

"PASSES TO NEGROES.—Something must be done to regulate and prescribe the manner in which passes shall be given to slaves. This is a matter that should no longer be shirked or avoided. The Common Council should act promptly. The slave population of this city is already demoralized to a deplorable extent, all owing to the indiscriminate licence and indulgence extended them by masters, mistresses, and guardians, and to the practice of *forging passes*, which has now become a regular business in New Orleans. The greater portion of the evil flows from forged passes. As things now stand, any negro can obtain a pass for four bits or a dollar, from miserable wretches who obtain a living by such infamous practices. The consequence is that hundreds spend their nights drinking, carousing, gambling, and contracting the worst of habits, which not only make them *useless to their owners*, but dangerous pests to society. We know of many negroes, completely ruined, morally and physically, by such causes. The inherent vice in the negro character always comes out when unrestrained, and there is no degradation too low for him to descend.

"Well, for the remedy to cure this crying evil. Prosecuting the forgers is out of the question; for where one conviction could be obtained, thousands of fraudulent passes would be written. *Slave evidence weighs nothing against white forgers and scoundrels.* Hence the necessity of adopting some other mode of prevention. It has been suggested to us, that if the Council would adopt a form for passes, different each month, to be obtained by masters from the Chief of Police, exclusively, that a great deal of good would be at once accomplished. We have no doubt of it. Further, we believe that all owners and guardians would cheerfully submit to the inconvenience in order to obtain so desirable an end. We trust the Common Council will pay some little attention to these suggestions."

How many men, accustomed to the close calculations necessary to successful enterprises, can listen to these suggestions, without asking themselves whether a system, that requires to be sustained by such inconvenient defences, had not better be thrown up altogether?

First and last, I spent some weeks in New Orleans and its vicinity. I doubt if there is a city in the world, where the resident population has been so divided in its origin, or where there is such a variety in the tastes, habits, manners, and moral codes of the citizens. Although this injures civic enterprise—which the peculiar situation of the city greatly demands to be directed to means of cleanliness, convenience, comfort, and health—it also gives a greater scope to the working of individual enterprise, taste, genius, and conscience; so that nowhere are the higher qualities of man—as displayed in generosity, hospitality, benevolence, and courage—better developed, or the lower qualities, likening him to a beast, less interfered with, by law or the action of public opinion.

There is one, among the multitudinous classifications of society in New Orleans, which is a very peculiar and characteristic result of the prejudices, vices, and customs of the various elements of colour, class, and nation, which have been there brought together.

I refer to a class composed of the illegitimate offspring of white men and coloured women (mulattoes or quadroons), who, from habits of early life, the advantages of education, and the use of wealth, are too much superior to the negroes, in general, to associate with them, and are not allowed by law, or the popular prejudice, to marry white people. The girls are frequently sent to Paris to be educated, and are very accomplished. They are generally pretty, often handsome. I have rarely, if ever, met more beautiful women than one or two whom I saw by chance, in the streets. They are better formed, and have a more graceful and elegant carriage than Americans in general, while they seem to have commonly inherited or acquired much of the taste and skill, in the selection and arrangement, and the way of wearing dresses and ornaments, that is the especial distinction of the women of Paris. Their beauty and attractiveness being their fortune, they cultivate and cherish with diligence every charm or accomplishment they are possessed of.

Of course, men are attracted by them, associate with them, are captivated, and become attached to them, and, not being able to marry them legally, and with the usual forms and securities for constancy, make such arrangements "as can be agreed upon." When a man makes a declaration of love to a girl of this class, she will admit or deny, as the case may be, her happiness in receiving it; but, supposing she is favourably disposed, she will usually refer the applicant to her mother. The mother inquires, like the "Countess of Kew," into the circumstances of the suitor; ascertains whether he is able to maintain a family, and, if satisfied with him, in these and other respects, requires from him security that he will support her daughter in a style suitable to the habits in which she has been bred, and that, if he should ever leave her, he will give her a certain sum for her future support, and a certain additional sum for each of the children she shall then have.

The wealth, thus secured, will, of course, vary—as in society with higher assumptions of morality—with the value of the lady in the market; that is, with her attractiveness, and the number and value of other suitors she may have, or may reasonably expect. Of course, I do not mean that love has nothing at all to do with it; but love is sedulously restrained, and held firmly in hand, until the road of competency is seen to be clear, with less humbug than our English custom requires about it. Everything being satisfactorily arranged, a tenement in a certain quarter of the town is usually taken, and the couple move into it and go to housekeeping

—living as if they were married. The woman is not, of course, to be wholly deprived of the society of others—her former acquaintances are continued, and she sustains her relations as daughter, sister, and friend. Of course, too, her husband (she calls him so) will be likely to continue, also, more or less in, and form a part of, this kind of society. There are parties and balls—*bals masqués*—and all the movements and customs of other fashionable society, which they can enjoy in it, if they wish.* The women of this sort are represented to be exceedingly affectionate in disposition, and constant beyond reproach.

During all the time a man sustains this relation, he will commonly be moving, also, in reputable society on the other side of the town; not improbably, eventually he marries, and has a family establishment elsewhere. Before doing this, he may separate from his *placée* (so she is termed). If so, he pays her according to agreement, and as much more, perhaps, as his affection for her, or his sense of the cruelty of the proceeding, may lead him to; and she has the world before her again, in the position of a widow. Many men continue for a

* "THE GLOBE BALL ROOM,
Corner of St. Claude and St. Peter Streets, abreast of the Old Basin,
WILL OPEN THIS EVENING, October 16, when a Society Ball will be given.
No ladies admitted without masks.
Gentlemen, fifty cents—Ladies, gratis.
Doors open at 9½ o'clock. Ball to commence at 10 o'clock.
No person admitted with weapons, by order of the Council.
A superior orchestra has been engaged for the season.
The public may be assured of the most strict order, as there will be at all times an efficient police in attendance.
Attached to the establishment is a superior Bar, well stocked with wines and liquors; also, a Restaurant, where may be had all such delicacies as the market affords.
All ladies are requested to procure free tickets in the Mask Room, as no lady will be admitted into the ball-room without one.
A. WHITLOCK, Manager."

long time, to support both establishments—particularly if their legal marriage is one *de convenance*. But many others form so strong attachments, that the relation is never discontinued, but becomes, indeed, that of marriage, except that it is not legalized or solemnized. These men leave their estate, at death, to their children, to whom they may have previously given every advantage of education they could command. What becomes of the boys, I am not informed; the girls, sometimes, are removed to other countries, where their colour does not prevent their living reputable lives; but, of course, mainly continue in the same society, and are fated to a life similar to that of their mothers.

I have described this custom as it was described to me; I need hardly say, in only its best aspects. The crime and heart-breaking sorrow that must frequently result from it, must be evident to every reflective reader.

A gentleman, of New England education, gave me the following account of his acquaintance with the quadroon society. On first coming to New Orleans, he was drawn into the social circles usually frequented by New England people, and some time afterwards was introduced by a friend to a quadroon family, in which there were three pretty and accomplished young women. They were intelligent and well informed; their musical taste was especially well cultivated; they were well read in the literature of the day, and their conversation upon it was characterized by good sense and refined discrimination. He never saw any indication of a want of purity of character or delicacy of feeling. He was much attracted by them, and for some time visited them very frequently. Having then discontinued his intimacy, at length one of the girls asked him why he did not come to see them as often as he had formerly done. He frankly replied, that he had found their society so fascinating, that he had thought it best to restrict himself in the enjoyment of it, lest it should become necessary to his happiness; and out of regard to his general plans of life, and the feelings of his friends, he could not permit himself to indulge the purpose to be united to one of them, according to the usual custom with their class. The young woman was evidently much pained, but not at all offended, and immediately acknowledged and commended the propriety and good sense of his resolution.

One reason which leads this way of living to be frequently adopted by unmarried men, who come to New Orleans to carry on business, is, that it is much cheaper than living at hotels and boarding-houses. As no young man ordinarily dare think of marrying, until he has made a fortune to support the extravagant style of housekeeping, and gratify the expensive tastes of young women, as fashion is now educating them, many are obliged to make up their minds never to marry. Such a one undertook to show me that it was cheaper for him to *placer* than to live in any other way which could be expected of him in New Orleans. He hired, at a low rent, two apartments in the older part of the town; his *placée* did not, except occasionally, require a servant; she did the marketing, and performed all the ordinary duties of housekeeping herself; she took care of his clothes, and in every way was economical and saving in her habits; it being her interest, if her affection for him were not sufficient, to make him as much comfort and as little expense as possible, that he might be the more strongly attached to her, and have the less occasion to leave her. He concluded by assuring me that whatever might be said against it, it certainly was better than the way in which most young men lived who depended on salaries in New York.

It is asserted by Southerners who have lived at the North, and Northerners who lived at the South, that although the facilities for licentiousness are much greater at the South, the evil of licentiousness is much greater at the North. Not because the average standard of "respectable position" requires a less expenditure at the South, for the contrary is the case.* But it is said licentiousness at the North is far more captivating, irresistible, and ruinous than at the South. Its very intrigues, cloaks, hazards, and expenses, instead of repressing the passions of young men, exasperate them, and increase its degrading effect upon their character, producing hypocrisy, interfering with high ambitions, destroying self-respect, causing the worst possible results to their health, and giving them habits which are inimical to future domestic contentment and virtue.

Possibly there is some ground for this assertion with regard to young men in towns, though in rural life the advantage of the North, I believe, is incomparable.

Mrs. Douglass, a Virginia woman, who was tried, convicted, and punished, a year or two since, for teaching a number of slaves to read, contrary to law, says in a letter from her jail—

"This subject demands the attention, not only of the religious population, but of statesmen and law-makers. It is one great evil hanging over the Southern Slave States, destroying domestic happiness and the peace of thousands. It is summed up in the single word—*amalgamation*. This, and this only, causes the vast extent of ignorance, degradation, and crime that lies like a black cloud over the whole South. And the practice is more general than even the Southerners are willing to allow.

"Neither is it to be found only in the lower order of the white population. It pervades the entire society. Its followers are to be found among all ranks, occupations, and professions. The white mothers and daughters of the South have suffered under it for years—have seen their dearest affections trampled upon—their hopes of domestic happiness destroyed, and

---

* A gentleman in an inland Southern town said to me, "I have now but one servant; if I should marry, I should be obliged to buy three more, and that alone would withdraw from my capital at least three thousand dollars."

their future lives embittered, even to agony, by those who should be all in all to them, as husbands, sons, and brothers. I cannot use too strong language in reference to this subject, for I know that it will meet with a heartfelt response from every Southern woman."

A negress was hung this year in Alabama, for the murder of her child. At her trial she confessed her guilt. She said her owner was the father of the child, and that her mistress knew it, and treated it so cruelly in consequence, that she had killed it to save it from further suffering, and also to remove a provocation to her own ill-treatment.

A large planter told, as a reason for sending his boys to the North to be educated, that there was no possibility of their being brought up in decency at home. Another planter told me that he was intending to move to a free country on this account. He said that the practice was not occasional or general, it was universal. "There is not," he said, "a likely-looking black girl in this State that is not the concubine of a white man. There is not an old plantation in which the grandchildren of the owner are not whipped in the field by his overseer. I cannot bear that the blood of the —— should run in the veins of slaves." He was of an old Scotch family.

New Orleans, Sunday.—Walking this morning through a rather mean neighbourhood I was attracted, by a loud chorus singing, to the open door of a chapel or small church. I found a large congregation of negroes assembled within, and the singing being just then concluded, and a negro preacher commencing a sermon, I entered an empty pew near the entrance. I had no sooner taken a seat than a negro usher came to me, and, in the most polite manner, whispered—

"Won't you please to let me give you a seat higher up, master, 'long o' tudder white folks?"

I followed him to the uppermost seat, facing the pulpit, where there were three other white persons. One of them was a woman—old, very plain, and not as well dressed as many of the negroes ; another looked like a ship's officer, and was probably a member of the police force in undress—what we call a spy, when we detect it in Europe ; both of these remained diligently and gravely attentive during the service ; the third was a foreign-looking person, very flashily dressed and sporting a yellow-headed walking-stick, and much cheap jewelry.

The remainder of the congregation consisted entirely of coloured persons, many of them, however, with light hair and hardly any perceptible indications of having African blood. On the step of the chancel were a number of children, and among these one of the loveliest young girls that I ever saw. She was a light mulatto, and had an expression of unusual intelligence and vivacity. During the service she frequently smiled, I thought derisively, at the emotions and excitement betrayed by the older people about her. She was elegantly dressed, and was accompanied by a younger sister, who was also dressed expensively and in good taste, but who was a shade darker, though much removed from the blackness of the true negro, and of very good features and pleasant expression.

The preacher was nearly black, with close woolly hair. His figure was slight, he seemed to be about thirty years of age, and the expression of his face indicated a refined and delicately sensitive nature. His eye was very fine, bright, deep, and clear ; his voice and manner generally quiet and impressive.

The text was, " I have fought the good fight, I have kept the faith ; henceforth there is laid up for me a crown of glory ;" and the sermon was an appropriate and generally correct explanation of the customs of the Olympian games, and a proper and often eloquent application of the figure to the Christian course of life. Much of the language was highly metaphorical; the figures long, strange, and complicated, yet sometimes, however, beautiful. Words were frequently misplaced, and their meaning evidently misapprehended, while the grammar and pronunciation were sometimes such as to make the idea intended to be conveyed by the speaker incomprehensible to me. Vulgarisms and slang phrases occasionally occurred, but evidently without any consciousness of impropriety on the part of the speaker or his congregation.

As soon as I had taken my seat, my attention was attracted by an old negro near me, whom I supposed for some time to be suffering under some nervous complaint; he trembled, his teeth chattered, and his face, at intervals, was convulsed. He soon began to respond aloud to the sentiments of the preacher, in such words as these: "Oh, yes!" "That's it, that's it!" "Yes, yes—glory—yes!" and similar expressions could be heard from all parts of the house whenever the speaker's voice was unusually solemn, or his language and manner eloquent or excited.

Sometimes the outcries and responses were not confined to ejaculations of this kind, but shouts, and groans, terrific shrieks, and indescribable expressions of ecstacy—of pleasure or agony—and even stamping, jumping, and clapping of hands were added. The tumult often resembled that of an excited political meeting; and I was once surprised to find my own muscles all stretched, as if ready for a struggle—my face glowing, and my feet stamping—having been infected unconsciously, as men often are, with instinctive bodily sympathy with the excitement of the crowd. So wholly unintellectual was the basis of this excitement, however, that I could not, when my mind retroverted to itself, find any connection or meaning in the phrases of the speaker that remained in my memory; and I have no doubt it was his "action" rather than his sentiments, that had given rise to the excitement of the congregation.

I took notes as well as I could of a single passage of the sermon. The preacher having said that among the games of the arena, were "raaslin" (wrestling) and boxing, and described how a combatant, determined to win the prize, would come boldly up to his adversary and stand square before him, looking him straight in the eyes, and while he guarded himself with one hand, would give him a "lick" with the other, continued in these words: " Then would he stop, and turn away his face, and let the adversary hit back? No, my brethren, no, no! he'd follow up his advantage, and give him another lick; and if he fell back, he'd keep close after him, and not stop!—and not faint!—not be content with merely driving him back!—but he'd *persevere!* (yes, glory!) and hit him again! (that's it, hit him again! hit him again! oh, glory! hi! hi! glory!) drive him into the corner! and never, never stop till he had him *down!* (glory, glory, glory!) and he had got his foot on his neck, and the crown of wild olive leaves was placed upon his head by the lord of the games. (Ha! ha! glory to the Lord! etc.) It was the custom of the Olympian games, my brethren, for the victor to be crowned with a crown of wild olive leaves; but sometimes, after all, it wouldn't be awarded right, because the lord of the games was a poor, frail, erroneous man, and maybe he couldn't see right, or maybe he wasn't an honest man, and would have his favourites among the combatants, and if his favourite was beaten, he would not *allow* it, but would declare that he was the victor, and the crown would descend on *his* head (*glory!*) But there ain't no danger of that with our fight with the world, for our Lord is throned in justice. (Glory!—oh, yes! yes!—sweet Lord! sweet Lord!) He seeth in secret, and he knoweth all things, and there's no chance for a mistake.

and if we only will just persevere and conquer, and conquer and persevere (yes, sir! oh, Lord, yes!) and persevere—not for a year, or for two year, or ten year; nor for seventy year, perhaps; but if we persevere—(yes! yes!)—if we persevere —(oh! Lord! help us!)—if we persevere unto the end— (oh! oh! glory! glory! glory!)—until he calls us home! (Frantic shouting.) Henceforth there is laid up for us a crown of immortal glory—(Ha! ha! HA!)—not a crown of wild olive leaves that begin to droop as soon as they touch our brow, (oh! oh! oh!) but a crown of immortal glory! That fadeth not away! Never begins to droop! But is immortal in the heavens!" (Tremendous uproar, many of the congregation on their feet, and uttering cries and shrieks impossible to be expressed in letters.) The shabby gentleman by my side, who had been asleep, suddenly awakened, dropped his stick, and shouted with all his might, "Glory to the Lord!"

The body of the house was filled by the audience; there were galleries, but few persons were in them; on one side, two or three boys, and on the other, on the seat nearest the pulpit, about a dozen women.

The preacher was drawing his sermon to a close, and offering some sensible and pertinent advice, soberly and calmly, and the congregation was attentive and comparatively quiet, when a small old woman, perfectly black, among those in the gallery, suddenly rose, and began dancing and clapping her hands; at first with a slow and measured movement, and then with increasing rapidity, at the same time beginning to shout "*ha! ha!*" The women about her arose also, and tried to hold her, as there appeared great danger that she would fall out of the gallery, and those below left their pews that she might not fall upon them.

The preacher continued his remarks—much the best part

of his sermon—but it was plain that they were wasted; every one was looking at the dancing woman in the gallery, and many were shouting and laughing aloud (in joyful sympathy, I suppose). His eye flashed as he glanced anxiously from the woman to the people, and then stopping in the middle of a sentence, a sad smile came over his face; he closed the book and bowed his head upon his hands to the desk. A voice in the congregation struck into a tune, and the whole congregation rose and joined in a roaring song. The woman was still shouting and dancing, her head thrown back and rolling from one side to the other. Gradually her shout became indistinct, she threw her arms wildly about instead of clapping her hands, fell back into the arms of her companions, then threw herself forward and embraced those before her, then tossed herself from side to side, gasping, and finally sunk to the floor, where she remained at the end of the song, kicking, as if acting a death struggle.

Another man now rose in the pulpit, and gave out a hymn, naming number and page, and holding a book before him, though I thought he did not read from it, and I did not see another book in the house. Having recited seven verses, and repeated the number and page of the hymn, he closed the book and commenced to address the congregation. He was a tall, full-blooded negro, very black, and with a disgusting expression of sensuality, cunning, and vanity in his countenance, and a pompous, patronizing manner—a striking contrast, in all respects, to the prepossessing, quiet, and modest young preacher who had preceded him. He was dressed in the loosest form of the fashionable sack overcoat, which he threw off presently, showing a white vest, gaudy cravat, and a tight cut-away coat, linked together at the breast with jet buttons. He commenced by proposing to further elucidate the meaning of the apostle's words; they had an important bearing, he said, which his brother had not had time to bring out adequately before the congregation. At first he leaned carelessly on the pulpit cushion, laughing-cunningly, and spoke in a low, deep, hoarse, indistinct, and confidential tone; but soon he struck a higher key, drawling his sentences like a street salesman, occasionally breaking out into a yell with all the strength of extraordinarily powerful lungs, at the same time taking a striking attitude and gesturing in an extraordinary manner: This would create a frightful excitement in the people, and be responded to with the loudest and most terrific shouts. I can compare them to nothing else human I ever heard. Sometimes he would turn from the audience and assume a personal opponent to be standing by his side in the pulpit. Then, after battling for a few minutes in an awful and majestic manner with this man of Belial, whom he addressed constantly as "sir!" he would turn again to the admiring congregation, and in a familiar, gratulatory, and conversational tone explain the difficulty into which he had got him, and then again suddenly turn back upon him, and in a boxing attitude give another knock-down reply to his heretical propositions.

His language was in a great part unintelligible to me, but the congregation seemed to enjoy it highly, and encouraged and assisted him in his combat with "Sir" Knight of his imagination most tumultuously; and I soon found that this poor gentleman, over whom he rode his high horse so fiercely, was one of those "who take unto themselves the name of Baptist," and that the name of his own charger was "*Perseverance-of-the-Saints.*"

The only intelligible argument that I could discover, was presented under the following circumstances. Having made his supposed adversary assert that "if a man would only just believe, and let him bury him under de water, he would be saved,"—he caught up the big pulpit Bible, and using it as a catapult, pretended to hurl from it the reply—"Except ye persevere and fight de good fight unto de end, ye shall be damned!" "That's it, that's it!" shouted the delighted audience. "Yes! you shall be damned! Ah! you've got it now, have ye! Pooh!—Wha's de use o' his tellin' us dat ar?" he continued, turning to the congregation with a laugh; "wha's de use on't, when we know dat a month arter he's buried 'em under de water—whar do we find 'em? Ha? ah ha! Whar? In de grog-shop! (ha! ha! ha! ha!) Yes we do, don't we? (Yes! yes!) In de rum-hole! (Ha! ha! ha! Yes! yes! oh Lord!) and we know de spirit of rum and de Spirit of God hasn't got no 'finities. (Yah! ha! ha! yes! yes! dat's it! dat's it! oh, my Jesus! Oh! oh! glory! glory!) Sut'nly, sah! You may launch out upon de ocean a drop of oil way up to Virginny, and we'll launch annudder one heah to Lusiana, and when dey meets—no matter how far dey been gone—dey'll unite! Why, sah? Because dey's got de 'finities, sah! But de spirit of rum haint got nary sort o' 'finity with de Spirit," etc.

Three of the congregation threw themselves into hysterics during this harangue, though none were so violent as that of the woman in the gallery. The man I had noticed first from his strange convulsive motions, was shaking as if in a violent ague, and frequently snatched the sleeve of his coat in his teeth as if he would rend it. The speaker at length returned to the hymn, repeated the number and page and the first two lines. These were sung, and he repeated the next, and so on, as in the Scotch Presbyterian service. The congregation sang; I think every one joined, even the children, and the collective sound was wonderful. The voices of one or two women rose above the rest, and one of these soon began to introduce variations, which consisted mainly of shouts of Oh! oh! at a piercing height. Many of the singers kept time with their feet, balancing themselves on each alternately, and swinging their bodies accordingly. The reading of the lines would be accompanied also by shouts, as during the previous discourse.

When the preacher had concluded reading the last two lines, as the singing again proceeded, he raised his own voice above all, turned around, clapped his hands, and commenced to dance, and laughed aloud—first with his back, and then with his face to the audience.

The singing ceased, but he continued his movements, leaping, with increasing agility, from one side of the pulpit to the other. The people below laughed and shouted, and the two other preachers who were shut in the pulpit with the dancer, tried hard to keep out of his way, and threw forward their arms or shoulders, to fend off his powerful buffets as he surged about between them. Swinging out his arms at random, with a blow of his fist he knocked the great Bible spinning off the desk, to the great danger of the children below; then threw himself back, jamming the old man, who was trying to restrain him, against the wall.

At the next heave, he pitched headforemost into the young preacher, driving him through the door and falling with him half down the stairs, and after bouncing about a few moments, jerking his arms and legs violently, like a supple jack, in every direction, and all the time driving his breath with all the noise possible between his set teeth, and trying to foam at the mouth and act an epileptic fit, there he lay as if dead, the young preacher, with the same sad smile, and something of shame on his face, sitting on the stair holding his head on his shoulder, and grasping one of his hands, while his feet were extended up into the pulpit.

The third man in the pulpit, a short, aged negro, with a smiling face, and a pleasing manner, took the Bible, which was handed up to him by one of the congregation, laid it upon the desk, and, leaning over it, told the people, in a gentle, conversational tone, that the "love feast" would be held at four o'clock; gave some instructions about the tickets of admission, and severely reproved those, who were in the habit of coming late, and insisted upon being let in after the doors were locked. He then announced that the doxology would be sung, which accordingly followed, another woman going into hysterics at the close. The prostrate man rose, and released the young preacher, who pronounced the Apostles' blessing, and the congregation slowly passed out, chatting and saluting one another politely as they went, and bearing not the slightest mark of the previous excitement.

I came to Mr. R.'s plantation by a steamboat, late at night. As the boat approached the shore, near his house, her big bell having been rung some ten minutes previously, a negro came out with a lantern to meet her. The boat's bow was run boldly against the bank; I leaped ashore, the clerk threw out a newspaper and a package, saying to the negro, "That's for your master, and that's for so-and-so, tell your master, and ask him to give it to him." The boat bounded off at once, by her own elasticity, the starboard wheel was backed for a turn or two, and the next minute the great edifice was driving up the stream again—not a rope having been lifted, nor any other movement having been made on board, except by the pilot and engineer.

"Do you belong to Mr. R.?" I asked the negro. "Yes, sir; is you going to our house, master?" "Yes." "I'll show you the way, then, sir;" and he conducted me in, leaving the parcels the clerk had thrown out, where they had fallen, on the bank.

A negro woman prepared a bed for me, waited at the door till I had put out my light, and then returned to tuck in the musquito-bar tightly about the bed. This was merely from custom, as there were no musquitoes at that season. In the morning the same woman awakened me, opened the curtains, and asked me to take the money which she had found in the pockets of my clothing, while she took it out to be brushed.

Mr. R. is a Southerner by birth, but was educated at the North, where, also, and in foreign countries, he has spent a large part of his life. He is a man of more than usual precision of mind, energetic and humane; and while his negroes seemed to be better disciplined than any others I had seen, they evidently regarded him with affection, respect, and pride.

He had been ill for some weeks previous to my visit, and when he walked out with me, on the second day, it was the first time since the commencement of his illness that his field-hands had seen him.

The first negroes we met were half a dozen women, who were going up to the nursery to suckle their children—the overseer's bell having been just rung (at eleven o'clock), to call them in from work for that purpose. Mr. R. said that he allowed them two hours to be with their children while nursing at noon, and to leave work an hour earlier at night than the other field-hands. The women all stopped as we met them, and asked, with much animation:

"Oh, master! how is ou?"

"Well, I'm getting up. How are you, girls?"

"Oh, we's well, sir."

"The children all well?"

"Yes, master, all but Sukey's, sir."

"Sukey's? What, isn't that well yet?"

"No, master."

"But it's getting well, is it not?"

"Yes, master."

Soon after we met a boy, driving a cart. He pulled up as he came against us, and, taking off his hat, asked, "How is 'ou, master?"

"I'm getting well, you see. If I don't get about, and look after you, I'm afraid we shan't have much of a crop. I don't know what you niggers will do for Christmas money."

"Ha!—look heah, massa!—you jus' go right straight on de ways you's goin'; see suthin' make you laugh, ha! ha! (meaning the work that had been done while he was ill, and the good promise of a crop).

The plantation contained about nine hundred acres of tillage land, and a large tract of "swamp," or woodland, was attached to it. The tillage land was inclosed all in one field by a strong cypress post and rail fence, and was drained by two canals, five feet deep, running about twenty feet apart, and parallel—the earth from both being thrown together, so as to make a high, dry road between them, straight through the middle of the plantation.

Fronting upon the river, and but six or eight rods from the public road, which everywhere runs close along the shore inside the levee, was the mansion of the proprietor: an old Creole house, the lower story of brick and the second of wood, with a broad gallery, shaded by the extended roof, running all around it; the roof steep, and shedding water on four sides, with ornaments of turned wood where lines met, and broken by several small dormer windows. The gallery was supported by round brick columns, and arches. The parlours, library, and sleeping rooms of the white family were all on the second floor. Between the house and the street was a yard, planted formally with orange-trees and other evergreens. A little on one side of the house stood a large two-story, square dove-cot, which is a universal appendage of a sugar-planter's house. In the rear of the house was another large yard, in which, irregularly placed, were houses for the family servants, a kitchen, stable, carriage-house, smoke-house, etc. Behind this rear-yard there was a vegetable garden, of an acre or more, in the charge of a negro gardener; a line of fig-trees were planted along the fence, but all the ground inclosed was intended to be cropped with vegetables for the family, and for the supply of "the people." I was pleased to notice, however, that the negro-gardener had, of his own accord, planted some violets and other flowering plants. From a corner of the court a road ran to the sugar-works and the negro settlement, which were five or six hundred yards from the house.

The negro houses were exactly like those I have described on the Georgia Rice Plantation, except that they were provided with broad galleries in front. They were as neat and well-made externally as the cottages usually provided by large manufacturing companies in New England, to be rented to their workmen. The clothing furnished the negroes, and the rations of bacon and meal, were the same as on other good plantations. During the grinding season extra rations of flour were served, and hot coffee was kept constantly in the sugar-house, and the hands on duty were allowed to drink it almost *ad libitum*. They were also allowed to drink freely of the hot *sirop*, of which they were extremely fond. A generous allowance of *sirop*, or molasses, was also given out to them, with their other rations, every week during the winter and early summer. In extremely hot weather it was thought to be unfavourable to health, and was discontinued. Rations of tobacco were also served. At Christmas, a sum of money, equal to one dollar for each hogshead of sugar made on the plantation, was divided among the negroes. The last year this had amounted to over two dollars a head. It was usually given to the heads of families. If any had been particularly careless or lazy, it was remembered at this Christmas dole. Of course, the effect of this arrangement, small as was the amount received by each person, was to give the labourers a direct interest in the economical direction of their labour: the advantage of it was said to be evident.

Mr. R. had purchased the plantation but three years before, and had afterwards somewhat increased its area by buying out several poor people, who had owned small farms adjoining. He had greatly extended and improved the drainage, and had nearly doubled the force of negroes employed upon it, adding to the number that he purchased with the land, nearly as many more whom he had inherited, and whom he transferred to it from an old cotton plantation that he had formerly lived upon.

He had considerably more than doubled the stock of mules and oxen; had built entirely new cabins for all the negroes, and new sugar-works and stables. His whole capital, he said, when he first bought the plantation, would not have paid half the price of it and of the cost of stocking it as he had done. Most men when they buy a plantation, he informed me, go very heavily in debt; frequently the purchase is made three quarters on credit.

"Buying a plantation," were his words, "whether a sugar or cotton plantation, in this country, is usually essentially a gambling operation. The capital invested in a sugar plantation of the size of mine ought not to be less than $150,000. The purchaser pays down what he can, and usually gives security for the payment of the balance in six annual instalments, with interest (10 per cent. per annum) from the date of the purchase. Success in sugar, as well as cotton planting, is dependent on so many circumstances, that it is as much trusting to luck as betting on a throw of dice. If his first crop proves a bad one, he must borrow money of the Jews in

New Orleans to pay his first note; they will sell him this on the best terms they can—often at not less than 25 per cent. per annum. If three or four bad crops follow one another, he is ruined. But this is seldom the case, and he lives on, one year gaining a little on his debts, but almost as often enlarging them. Three or four years ago there was hardly a planter in Louisiana or Mississippi who was not in very embarrassed circumstances, nearly every one having his crops pledged to his creditors long before they were secured. The good prices and good crops of the last few years have set them all on their legs again; and this year all the jewellers' shops, and stores of rich furniture and dry goods, in New Orleans, were cleared out by the middle of the season, and everybody feels strong and cheerful. I have myself been particularly fortunate; I have made three good crops in succession. Last year I made six hundred and fifty hogsheads of sugar, and twelve hundred barrels of molasses. The molasses alone brought me a sum sufficient to pay all my plantation expenses; and the sugar yields me a clear profit of twenty-five per cent. on my whole investment. If I make another crop this year as good as that, I shall be able to discount my outstanding notes, and shall be clear of debt at the end of four years, instead of six, which was all I had hoped for."

On another plantation, which I have since visited, which had a slave population of over two hundred—counted as one hundred field-hands—the sugar works cost $40,000, and seven hundred barrels of sugar were made last year. On this plantation there is a steam-pump, which drains the rear of the plantation over a levee, when the back-water from the swamp would otherwise prevent perfect drainage.

Mr. R. modestly credited his extraordinary success to "luck;" but I was satisfied, upon examining his improvements, and considering the reasons, which he readily gave for every operation which he showed, or described to me, that intelligence, study, and enterprise had seldom better claims to reward. Adjoining his plantation there was another of nearly twice the size, on which an equal number of negroes and only half the number of cattle were employed; and the proprietor, I was told, had had rather *bad luck*: he had, in fact, made but little more than half as much sugar as Mr. R. I inquired of the latter if there was any advantage in his soil over that of his neighbour's. "I think not," he replied; "my best cane was made on a piece of land adjoining his, which, before I bought it, was thought unfit for cultivation. The great advantage I had over him last year, mainly arose from my having secured a more complete drainage of all my land."

The soil of the greater part of the plantation was a fine, dark, sandy loam; some of it, at the greatest distance from the river, was lighter in colour, and more clayey; and in one part, where there was a very slight depression of the surface over about fifty acres, there was a dark, stiffish soil. It was this to which Mr. R. alluded as having produced his best cane. It had been considered too low, wet, tenacious, and unfertile to be worthy of cultivation by the former owner, and was covered with bushes and weeds when he took it. The improvement had been effected entirely by draining and fall-ploughing. In fall-ploughing, as a remedy for tenacity of soil, this gentleman's experience had given him great faith. At various points, on my tour, I found most conflicting opinions upon this point, many (among them the President of a State Agricultural Society) having invariably observed pernicious effects result from it.

The sugar-cane is a perennial-rooted plant, and the stalk does not attain its full size, under favourable circumstances, in less growing time than twelve months; and seed does not usually form upon it until the thirteenth or fourteenth month.

This function (termed *arrowing*) it only performs in a very hot and steadily hot climate, somewhat rarely even in the West Indies. The plant is, at all stages, extremely susceptible to cold, a moderate frost not only suspending its growth, but disorganizing it so that the chemical qualities of its sap are changed, and it is rendered valueless for sugar making.

As frosts of considerable severity are common in all parts of Louisiana, during three months of the year, of course the sugar-cane is there never permitted to attain its full growth. To so much greater perfection does it arrive in the West Indies, that the cane produced on one acre will yield from 3,000 to 6,000 lbs. of sugar, while in Louisiana 1,000 is considered the average obtained. "I could make sugar in the climate of Cuba," said a Louisiana planter to me, "for half the price that, under the most favourable circumstances, it must cost here." In addition to the natural uncongeniality of the climate, the ground on which it grows in Louisiana, being lower than the surface of the river, is much of the time made cold by the infiltration of moisture. It is, therefore, only by reason of the extreme fertility of this alluvial deposit, assisted by a careful method of cultivation, that the cane is forced to a state of maturity which enables it to yield an amount of sugar which, with the assistance of a governmental protection against foreign competition, will be remunerative to the planter.

I must confess that there seems to me room for grave doubt if the capital, labour, and especially the human life, which have been and which continue to be spent in converting the swamps of Louisiana into sugar plantations, and in defending them against the annual assaults of the river, and the fever and the cholera, could not have been better employed somewhere else. It is claimed as a great advantage of Slavery, as well as of Protection, that what has been done for this purpose never would have been done without it. If it would not, the obvious reason is, that the wages, or prospect of profit would not have been sufficient to induce free men to undergo the inconveniences and the danger incident to the enterprise. There is now great wealth in Louisiana; but I question if greater wealth would not have been obtained by the same expenditure of human labour, and happiness, and life, in very many other directions.

Planting commences immediately after the sugar-manufacturing season is concluded—usually in January. New or fallow land is prepared by ploughing the whole surface: on this plantation the plough used was made in Kentucky, and was of a very good model, ploughing seven to nine inches deep, with a single pair of mules. The ground being then harrowed, drills are opened with a double mould-board plough, seven feet apart. Cuttings of cane for seed are to be planted in them. These are reserved from the crop in the autumn, when some of the best cane on the plantation is selected for this purpose, while still standing.* This is cut off at the roots, and laid up in heaps or stacks, in such a manner that the leaves and tops protect the stalks from frost. The heaps are called mattresses; they are two or three feet high, and as many yards across. At the planting season they are opened, and the cane comes out moist and green, and sweet, with the buds or eyes, which protrude at the joints, swelling. The immature top parts of the stalk are cut off, and they are loaded into carts, and carried to the ground prepared for planting. The carts used are large, with high side-boards, and are drawn by three mules—one large one being in the shafts, and two lighter ones abreast, before

* It is only on the best plantations that the seed-cane is selected with this care. On another plantation that I visited during the planting season I noticed that the best part of the stalk had been cut off for grinding, and only the less valuable part saved for seed; and this, I apprehend, is the general practice. The best cuttings probably produce the most vigorous plants.

her. The drivers are boys, who use the whip a great deal, and drive rapidly.

In the field I found the labourers working in three divisions —the first, consisting of light hands, brought the cane by arms-full from the cart, and laid it by the side of the furrows; the second planted it, and the third covered it. Planting is done by laying the cuttings at the bottom of the furrow, in such a way that there shall be three always together, with the eyes of each a little removed from those of the others— that is, all "breaking joints." They are thinly covered with earth, drawn over them with hoes. The other tools were so well selected on this plantation, that I expressed surprise at the clumsiness of the hoes, particularly as the soil was light, and entirely free from stones. "Such hoes as you use at the North would not last a negro a day," said the planter.

Cane will grow for several years from the roots of the old plants, and, when it is allowed to do so, a very considerable part of the expense is avoided; but the vigour of the plant is less when growing from this source than when starting from cuttings, and the crop, when thus obtained, is annually less and less productive, until, after a number of years, depending upon the rigour of the seasons, fresh shoots cease to spring from the stubble. This sprouting of cane from the stools of the last crop is termed "ratooning." In the West India plantations the cane is frequently allowed to ratoon for eight successive crops. In Louisiana it is usual to plant once in three years, trusting to the ratooning for two crops only, and this was the practice on Mr. R.'s plantation. The cost of sugar growing would be very greatly increased if the crop needed planting every year; for all the cane grown upon an acre will not furnish seed for more than four acres—consequently one-twelfth of the whole of each crop has to be reserved for the planting of the following crop, even when two-thirds of this is to be of ratoon cane.

Planting is finished in a favourable season—early in March. Tillage is commenced immediately afterwards, by ploughing *from* the rows of young cane, and subsequently continued very much after the usual plans of tillage for potatoes, when planted in drills, with us. By or before the first of July, the crop is all well earthed up, the rows of cane growing from the crest of a rounded bed, seven feet wide, with deep water-furrows between each. The cane is at this time five or six feet high; and that growing from each bed forms arches with that of the next, so as to completely shade the ground. The furrows between the beds are carefully cleaned out; so that in the most drenching torrents of rain, the water is rapidly carried off into the drains, and thence to the swamp; and the crop then requires no further labour upon it until frost is apprehended, or the season for grinding arrives.

The nearly three months' interval, commencing at the intensest heat of summer, corresponds in the allotment of labour to the period of winter in Northern agriculture, because the winter itself, on the sugar-plantations, is the planting-season. The negroes are employed in cutting and carting wood for boiling the cane-juice, in making necessary repairs or additions to the sugar-house, and otherwise preparing for the grinding-season.

The grinding-season is the harvest of the sugar-planter; it commences in October, and continues for two or three months, during which time, the greatest possible activity and the utmost labour of which the hands are capable, are required to secure the product of the previous labour of the year. Mr. R. assured me that during the last grinding-season nearly every man, woman, and child on his plantation, including the overseer and himself, were on duty fully eighteen hours a day.

From the moment grinding first commences, until the end of the season, it is never discontinued: the fires under the boiler never go out, and the negroes only rest for six hours in the twenty-four, by relays—three-quarters of them being constantly at work.

Notwithstanding the severity of the labour required of them at this time, Mr. R. said that his negroes were as glad as he was himself to have the time for grinding arrive, and they worked with greater cheerfulness than at any other season. How can those persons who are always so ready to maintain that the slaves work less than free labourers in free countries, and that for that reason they are to be envied by them, account for this? That at Mr. R.'s plantation it was the case that the slaves enjoyed most that season of the year when the hardest labour was required of them, I have, in addition to Mr. R.'s own evidence, good reason to believe, which I shall presently report. And the reason of it evidently is, that they are then better paid; they have better and more varied food and stimulants than usual, but especially they have a degree of freedom, and of social pleasure, and a variety of occupation which brings a recreation of the mind, and to a certain degree gives them strength for, and pleasure in, their labour. Men of sense have discovered that when they desire to get extraordinary exertions from their slaves, it is better to offer them rewards than to whip them; to encourage them, rather than to drive them.

If the season has been favourable, so that the cane is strong, and well matured, it will endure a smart early frost without injury, particularly if the ground is well drained; but as rapidly as possible, after the season has arrived at which frosts are to be expected, the whole crop is cut, and put in mattresses, from which it is taken to the grinding-mill as fast as it can be made to use it.

The business of manufacturing sugar is everywhere carried on in connection with the planting of the cane. .The shortness of the season during which the cane can be used is the reason assigned for this: the proprietors would not be willing to trust to custom-mills to manufacture their produce with the necessary rapidity. If cane should be cultivated in connection with other crops—that is, on small farms, instead of great "sugar only" plantations—neighbourhood custom-mills would probably be employed. The profit of a sugar-plantation is now large, much in proportion to its size (if it be proportionately stocked); because only a very large supply of cane will warrant the proprietor in providing the most economical manufacturing apparatus. In 1849 there were 1,474 sugar estates in Louisiana, producing 236,547 hhds. of sugar; but it is thought that half of this quantity was produced on less than 200 estates—that is, that one-eighth of the plantations produced one-half the sugar. The sugar-works on some of the large estates cost over $100,000, and many of them manufacture over 1,000,000 lbs. per annum. The profits of these, under our present tariff, in a favourable season, are immense.

The apparatus used upon the better class of plantations is very admirable, and improvements are yearly being made, which indicate high scientific. acquirements, and much mechanical ingenuity on the part of the inventors. The whole process of sugar manufacturing, although chemical analysis proves that a large amount of saccharine is still wasted, has been within a few years greatly improved, principally by reason of the experiments and discoveries of the French chemists, whose labours have been directed by the purpose to lessen the cost of beet-sugar. Apparatus for various processes in the manufacture, which they have invented or recommended, has been improved, and brought into practical operation on a large scale on some of the Louisiana plantations, the owners of which are among the most intelligent, enterprising, and wealthy men of business in the United States. Forty-three plantations in the State are now furnished with apparatus constructed in accordance with the best scientific knowledge on the subject; and 914 are driven by steam-engines—leaving but 560 to be worked by horse-power. Mr. R.'s sugar-house, for making brown sugar, was furnished with the best kind of apparatus, at a cost of $20,000. Preparations were making for the addition of works for the manufacture of white loaf sugar, which would cost $20,000 more. I have visited one plantation on which the sugar-works are said to have cost over $100,000.

At one corner of Mr. R.'s plantation, there was a hamlet consisting of about a dozen small houses or huts, built of wood or clay, in the old French peasant style. The residents owned small farms, on which they raised a little corn and rice; but Mr. R. described them as lazy vagabonds, doing but little work, and spending much time in shooting, fishing, and play. He wanted much to buy all their land, and get them to move away. He had already bought out some of them, and had made arrangements by which he hoped soon to get hold of the land of some of the rest. He was willing to pay two or three times as much as the property was actually worth, to get them to move off. As fast as he got possession, he destroyed their houses and gardens, removed their fences and trees, and brought all their land into his cane-plantation.

Some of them were mechanics. One was a very good mason, and he employed him in building his sugar-works and refinery; but he would be glad to get rid of them all, and depend entirely on slave mechanics—of these he had several already, and he could buy more when he needed them.

Why did he so dislike to have these poor people living near him, I asked? Because, he straightway answered, they demoralized his negroes. Seeing them living in apparent comfort, without much property and without steady labour, the slaves could not help thinking that it was unnecessary for men to work so hard as they themselves were obliged to, and that if they were free they would not work. Besides, the intercourse of these people with the negroes was not favourable to good discipline. They would get the negroes to do them little services, and would pay with luxuries which he did not wish his slaves to have. It was better that they never saw anybody off their own plantation; they should, if possible, have no intercourse with any other white men than their owner or overseer; especially, it was desirable that they should not see white men who did not command their respect, and whom they did not always feel to be superior to themselves, and able to command them.

The nuisance of petty traders dealing with the negroes, and encouraging them to pilfer, which I found everywhere a great annoyance to planters, seems to be greater on the banks of the Mississippi than elsewhere. The traders generally come on boats, which they moor at night on the shore, adjoining the negro-quarters, and float away whenever they have obtained any booty, with very small chance of detection. One day, during my visit at Mr. R.'s, a neighbour called to apprise him that one of these trading-boats was in the vicinity, that he might take precautions to prevent his negroes dealing with it. "The law," he observed, with much feeling, "is entirely inadequate to protect us against these rascals; it rather protects them than us. They easily evade detection in breaking it; and we can never get them punished, except we go beyond or against the law ourselves." To show me how vexatious the evil was, he mentioned that a large brass cock and some pipe had been lately stolen from his sugar-works, and that he had ascertained that one of his negroes had taken it and sold it on board one of these boats for seventy-five cents, and had immediately spent the money, chiefly for whisky, on the same boat. It had cost him thirty dollars to replace it. Mr. R. said that he had lately caught one of his own negroes going towards one of the "chicken thieves" (so the traders' boats are locally called) with a piece of machinery, unscrewed from his sugar-works, which had cost him eighty dollars, but which would, very likely, have been sold for a drink. If the negro had succeeded in reaching the boat, as he would, if a watch had not been kept, he could never have recovered it. There would have been no witnesses to the sale; the stolen goods would have been hid on board until the boat reached New Orleans; or, if an officer came to search the boat, they would have been dropped into the river, before he got on board.

This neighbour of Mr. R.'s had been educated in France. Conversing on the inconveniences of Slavery, he acknowledged that it was not only an uneconomical system, but a morally wrong one; "but," he said, "it was not instituted by us—we are not responsible for it. It is unfortunately fixed upon us; we could not do away with it if we wished; our duty is only to make the best of a bad thing; to lessen its evils as much as we can, so far as we have to do with it individually."

Mr. R. himself also acknowledged Slavery to be a very great evil, morally and economically. It was a curse upon the South; he had no doubt at all about it: nothing would be more desirable than its removal, if it were possible to be accomplished. But he did not think it could be abolished without instituting greater evils than those sought to be remedied. Its influence on the character of the whites was what was most deplorable. He was sorry to think that his children would have to be subject to it. He thought that eventually, if he were able to afford it, he should free his slaves and send them to Africa.

When I left Mr. R.'s, I was driven about twenty miles in a buggy, by one of his house servants. He was inclined to be talkative and communicative; and as he expressed great affection and respect for his owner, I felt at liberty to question him on some points upon which I had always previously avoided conversing with slaves. He spoke rapidly, garrulously; and it was only necessary for me to give a direction to his thoughts, by my inquiries. I was careful to avoid leading questions, and not to show such an interest as would lead him to reply guardedly. I charged my memory as much as possible with his very words, when this was of consequence, and made the following record of the conversation within half an hour after I left him.

He first said that he supposed that I would see that he was not a "Creole nigger;" he came from Virginia. He reckoned the Virginia negroes were better looking than those who were raised here; there were no black people anywhere in the world who were so "well made" as those who were born in Virginia. He asked if I lived in New Orleans; and where? I told him that I lived at the North. He asked:

" Da's a great many brack folks dah, massa?"

" No; very few."

" Da's a great many in Virginny; more'n da is heah?"

" But I came from beyond Virginia—from New York."

He had heard there were a great many black folk in New York. I said there were a good many in the city; but few in the country. Did I live in the country? What people did I have for servants? Thought, if I hired all my labour, it must be very dear. He inquired further about negroes there. I told him they were all free, and described their general condition; told him what led them to congregate in cities, and what the effect was. He said the negroes, both slave and free, who lived in New Orleans, were better off than those who lived in the country. Why? Because they make more money, and it is "gayer" there, and there is more "society." He then drew a contrast between Virginia, as he recollected it, and Louisiana. There is but one road in this country. In Virginia, there are roads running in every direction, and often crossing each other. You could see so much more "society," and there was so much more "variety" than here. He would not like now to go back to Virginia to live, because he had got used to this country, and had all his acquaintances here, and knew the ways of the people. He could speak French. He would like to go to New Orleans, though; would rather live in New Orleans than any other place in the world.

After a silence of some minutes, he said, abruptly—

"If I was free, I would go to Virginia, and see my old mudder." He had left her when he was thirteen years old. He reckoned he was now thirty-three. "I don't well know, dough, exactly, how old I is; but, I rec'lect, de day I was taken away, my ole mudder she tell me I was tirteen year old." He did not like to come away at all; he "felt dreadful bad;" but, now he was used to it, he liked living here. He came across the Blue Ridge, and he recollected that, when he first saw it, he thought it was a dark piece of sky, and he wondered what it would be like when they came close to it. He was brought, with a great many other negroes, in waggons, to Louisville; and then they were put on board a steamboat, and brought down here. He was sold, and put on this plantation, and had been on it ever since. He had been twice sold, along with it. Folks didn't very often sell their servants away here, as they did in Virginia. They were selling their servants, in Virginia, all the time; but, here, they did not very often sell them, except they run away. When a man would run away, and they could not do anything with him, they always sold him off. The people were almost all French. " Were there any French in New York ?" he asked. I told him there were ; but not as many as in Louisiana. " I s'pose dah is more of French people in Lusiana, dan dah is anywhar else in all de world—a'nt dah, massa ?"

" Except in France."

" Wa's dat, sar ?"

" France is the country where all the Frenchmen came from, in the first place."

" Wa's dat France, massa ?"

" France is a country across the ocean, the big water, beyond Virginia, where all the Frenchmen first came from ; just as the black people all came first from Africa, you know."

" I've heered, massa, dat dey sell one anoder dah, in de fus place. Does you know, sar, was dat so ?" This was said very gravely.

I explained the savage custom of making slaves of prisoners of war, and described the constant wars of the native Africans. I told him that they were better off here than they would be to be the slaves of cruel savages, in Africa. He turned, and looking me anxiously in the face, like a child, asked :

" *Is* de brack folks better off to be here, massa ?"

I answered that I thought so ; and described the heathenish barbarism of the people of Africa. I made exception of Liberia, knowing that his master thought of some time sending him there, and described it as a place that was settled by negroes who went back there from this country. He said he had heard of it, and that they had sent a great many free negroes from New Orleans there.

After a moment's pause, he inquired—very gravely, again:
"*Why is it*, massa, when de brack people is free, dey wants to send 'em away out of dis country?"

The question took me aback. After bungling a little—for I did not like to tell him the white people were afraid to have them stay here—I said that it was thought to be a better place for them there. He replied, he should think, that, when they had got used to this country, it was much better that they should be allowed to stay here. He would not like to go out of this country. He wouldn't like even to go to Virginia now, though Virginia was such a pleasant country; he had been here so long, seemed like this was the best place for him to live. To avoid discussion of the point, I asked what he would do, if he were free?

"If I was free, massa; *if I was free* (with great animation), I would——well, sar, de fus thing I would do, if I was free, I would go to work for a year, and get some money for myself,—den—den—den, massa, dis is what I do—I buy me, fus place, a little house, and little lot land, and den—no; den—den—I would go to old Virginny, and see my old mudder. Yes, sar, I would like to do dat fus thing; den, when I com back, de fus thing I'd do, I'd get me a wife; den, I'd take her to my house, and I would live with her dar; and I would raise things in my garden, and take 'em to New Orleans, and sell 'em dar, in de market. Dat's de way I would live, if I was free."

He said, in answer to further inquiries, that there were many free negroes all about this region. Some were very rich. He pointed out to me three plantations, within twenty miles, owned by coloured men. These bought black folks, he said, and had servants of their own. They were very bad masters, very hard and cruel—hadn't any feeling. "You might think master, dat dey would be good to dar own nation;

but dey is not. I will tell you de truth, massa; I know I'se got to answer; and it's a fact, dey is very bad masters, sar. I'd rather be a servant to any man in de world, dan to a brack man. If I was sold to a brack man, I'd drown myself. I would dat—I'd drown myself! dough I shouldn't like to do dat nudder; but I wouldn't be sold to a coloured master for anyting."

If he had got to be sold, he would like best to have an American master buy him. The French people did not clothe their servants well; though now they did much better than when he first came to Louisiana. The French masters were very severe, and " dey whip dar niggers most to deff—dey whip de flesh off of 'em."

Nor did they feed them as well as the Americans. " Why, sometimes, massa, dey only gives 'em dry corn—don't give out no meat at all." I told him this could not be so, for the law required that every master should serve out meat to his negroes. " Oh, but some on 'em don't mind Law, if he does say so, massa. Law never here; don't know anything about him. *Very often*, dey only gives 'em dry corn—I knows dat; I sees de niggers. Didn't you see de niggers on our plantation, sar? Well, you nebber see such a good-looking lot of niggers as ours on any of de French plantations, did you, massa? Why, dey all looks fat, and dey's all got good clothes, and dey look as if dey all had plenty to eat, and hadn't got no work to do, ha! ha! ha! Don't dey? But dey does work, dough. Dey does a heap o' work. But dey don't work so hard as dey does on some ob de French plantations. Oh, dey does work *too* hard on dem, sometimes."

"You work hard in the grinding season, don't you?"

"O, yes; den we works hard; we has to work hard den: harder dan any oder time of year. But, I tell 'ou, massa, I likes to hab de grinding season come; yes, I does—rader dan any oder time of year, dough we work so hard den. I wish it was grinding season all de year roun'—only Sundays."

" Why ?"

" Because—oh, because it's merry and lively. All de brack people like it when we begin to grind."

" You have to keep grinding Sundays ?"

" Yes, can't stop, when we begin to grind, till we get tru."

" You don't often work Sundays, except then ?"

" No, massa! nebber works Sundays, except when der crap's weedy, and we want to get tru 'fore rain comes; den, wen we work a Sunday, massa gives us some oder day for holiday—Monday, if we get tru."

He said that, on the French plantations, they oftener work Sundays than on the American. They used to work almost always on Sundays, on the French plantations, when he was first brought to Louisiana; but they did not so much now.

We were passing a hamlet of cottages, occupied by Acadians, or what the planters call *habitans*, poor white French Creoles. The negroes had always been represented to me to despise the habitans, and to look upon them as their own inferiors; but William spoke of them respectfully; and, when I tempted him to sneer at their indolence and vagabond habits, refused to do so, but insisted very strenuously that they were " very good people," orderly and industrious. He assured me that I was mistaken in supposing that the Creoles, who did not own slaves, did not live comfortably, or that they did not work as hard as they ought for their living. There were no better sort of people than they were, he thought.

He again recurred to the fortunate condition of the negroes on his master's plantation. He thought it was the best plantation in the State, and he did not believe there was a better lot of negroes in the State; some few of them, whom his master had brought from his former plantation, were old; but altogether, they were "as right good a lot of niggers" as could be found anywhere. They could do all the work that was necessary to be done on the plantation. On some old plantations they had not nearly as many negroes as they needed to make the crop, and they "drove 'em awful hard;" but it wasn't so on his master's: they could do all the work, and do it well, and it was the best worked plantation, and made the most sugar to the hand of any plantation he knew of. All the niggers had enough to eat, and were well clothed; their quarters were good, and they got a good many presents. He was going on enthusiastically, when I asked:

"Well, now, wouldn't you rather live on such a plantation than to be free, William?"

"Oh! no, sir, I'd rather be free! Oh, yes, sir, I'd like it better to be free; I would dat, master."

"Why would you?"

"Why, you see, master, if I was free—if I was *free*, I'd have all my time to myself. I'd rather work for myself. Yes. I'd like dat oetter."

"But then, you know, you'd have to take care of yourself, and you'd get poor."

"No, sir, I would not get poor, I would get rich; for you see, master, then I'd work all the time for myself."

"Suppose all the black people on your plantation, or all the black people in the country were made free at once, what do you think would become of them?—what would they do, do you think? You don't suppose there would be much sugar raised, do you?"

"Why, yes, master, I do. Why not, sir? What would de brack people do? Wouldn't dey hab to work for dar libben? and de wite people own all de land—war dey goin' to work? Dey hire demself right out again, and work all de same as before. And den, wen dey work for demself, dey work harder dan dey do now to get more wages—a heap harder. I tink so, sir. I would do so, sir. I would work for hire. I don't own any land; I hab to work right away again for massa, to get some money."

Perceiving from the readiness of these answers that the subject had been a familiar one with him, I immediately asked: "The black people talk among themselves about this, do they; and they think so generally?"

"Oh! yes, sir; dey talk so; dat's wat dey tink."

"Then they talk about being free a good deal, do they?"

"Yes, sir. Dey—dat is, dey say dey wish it was so; dat's all dey talk, master—dat's all, sir."

His caution was evidently excited, and I inquired no further. We were passing a large old plantation, the cabins of the negroes upon which were wretched hovels—small, without windows, and dilapidated. A large gang of negroes were at work by the road-side, planting cane. Two white men were sitting on horseback, looking at them, and a negro-driver was walking among them, with a whip in his hand.

William said that this was an old Creole plantation, and the negroes on it were worked very hard. There was three times as much land in it as in his master's, and only about the same number of negroes to work it. I observed, however, that a good deal of land had been left uncultivated the previous year. The slaves appeared to be working hard; they were shabbily clothed, and had a cowed expression, looking on the ground, not even glancing at us, as we passed, and were perfectly silent.

"Dem's all Creole niggers," said William: "ain't no Virginny niggers dah. I reckon you didn't see no such looking niggers as dem on our plantation, did you, master?"

After answering some inquiries about the levee, close inside of which the road continually ran, he asked me about the levee at New York; and when informed that we had not any levee, asked me with a good deal of surprise, how we kept the water out? I explained to him that the land was higher than the water, and was not liable, as it was in Louisiana, to be overflowed. I could not make him understand this. He seemed never to have considered that it was not the natural order of things that land should be lower than water, or that men should be able to live on land, except by excluding water artificially. At length, he said:—

"I s'pose dis heah State is de lowest State dar is in de world. Dar ain't no odder State dat is low so as dis is. I s'pose it is five thousand five hundred feet lower dan any odder State."

"What?"

"I s'pose, master, dat dis heah State is five thousand five hundred feet lower down dan any odder, ain't it, sir?"

"I don't understand you."

"I say dis heah is de lowest ob de States, master. I s'pose it's *five thousand five hundred feet* lower dan any odder; lower *down*, ain't it, master?"

"Yes, it's very low."

This is a good illustration of the child-like quality common in the negroes, and which in him was particularly noticeable, notwithstanding the shrewdness of some of his observations. Such an apparent mingling of simplicity and cunning, ingenuousness and slyness, detracted much from the weight of his opinions and purposes in regard to freedom. I could not but have a strong doubt if he would keep to his word, if the opportunity were allowed him to try his ability to take care of himself.

CHAPTER IX.

FROM LOUISIANA THROUGH TEXAS.

THE largest part of the cotton crop of the United States is now produced in the Mississippi valley, including the lands contiguous to its great Southern tributary streams, the Red River and others. The proportion of the whole crop which is produced in this region is constantly and very rapidly increasing. This increase is chiefly gained by the forming of new plantations and the transfer of slave-labour westward. The common planter of this region lives very differently to those whose plantations I have hitherto described. What a very different person he is, and what a very different thing his plantation is from the class usually visited by travellers in the South, I learned by an extended experience. I presume myself to have been ordinarily well-informed when I started from home, but up to this point in my first journey had no correct idea of the condition and character of the common cotton-planters. I use the word common in reference to the whole region: there are some small districts in which the common planter is a rich man—really rich. But over the whole district there are comparatively few of these, and in this and the next chapter, I shall show what the many are—as I found them. I shall draw for this purpose upon a record of experience extending through nearly twelve months, but obtained in different journeys and in two different years.

My first observation of the common cotton-planters was

had on the steamboat, between Montgomery and Mobile, and has already been described. My second experience among them was on a steamboat bound up Red River.

On a certain Saturday morning, when I had determined upon the trip, I found that two boats, the Swamp Fox and the St. Charles, were advertised to leave the same evening, for the Red River. I went to the levee, and, finding the Saint Charles to be the better of the two, I asked her clerk if I could engage a state-room. There was just one state-room berth left unengaged; I was requested to place my name against its number on the passenger-book; and did so, understanding that it was thus secured for me.

Having taken leave of my friends, I had my luggage brought down, and went on board at half-past three—the boat being advertised to sail at four. Four o'clock passed, and freight was still being taken on—a fire had been made in the furnace, and the boat's big bell was rung. I noticed that the Swamp Fox was also firing up, and that her bell rang whenever ours did—though she was not advertised to sail till five. At length, when five o'clock came, the clerk told me he thought, perhaps, they would not be able to get off at all that night—there was so much freight still to come on board. Six o'clock arrived, and he felt certain that, if they did get off that night, it would not be till very late. At half-past six, he said the captain had not come on board yet, and he was quite sure they would not be able to get off that night. I prepared to return to the hotel, and asked if they would leave in the morning. He thought not. He was confident they would not. He was positive they could not leave now, before Monday—Monday noon. Monday at twelve o'clock— I might rely upon it.

Monday morning, *The Picayune* stated, editorially, that the floating palace, the St. Charles, would leave for Shreveport, at five o'clock, and if anybody wanted to make a quick and luxurious trip up Red River, with a jolly good soul, Captain Lickup was in command. It also stated, in another paragraph, that, if any of its friends had any business up Red River, Captain Pitchup was a whole-souled veteran in that trade, and was going up with that remarkably low draft-favourite, the Swamp Fox, to leave at four o'clock that evening. Both boats were also announced, in the advertising columns, to leave at four o'clock.

As the clerk had said noon, however, I thought there might have been a misprint in the newspaper announcements, and so went on board the St. Charles again before twelve. The clerk informed me that the newspaper was right—they had finally concluded not to sail till four o'clock. Before four, I returned again, and the boat again fired up, and rang her bell. So did the Swamp Fox. Neither, however, was quite ready to leave at four o'clock. Not quite ready at five. Even at six - not yet quite ready. At seven, the fires having burned out in the furnace, and the stevedores having gone away, leaving a quantity of freight yet on the dock, without advising this time with the clerk, I had my baggage re-transferred to the hotel.

A similar performance was repeated on Tuesday.

On Wednesday, I found the berth I had engaged occupied by a very strong man, who was not very polite, when I informed him that I believed there was some mistake—that the berth he was using had been engaged to me. I went to the clerk, who said that he was sorry, but that, as I had not stayed on board at night, and had not paid for the berth, he had not been sure that I should go, and he had, therefore, given it to the gentleman who now had it in possession, and whom, he thought, it would not be best to try to reason out of it. He was very busy, he observed, because the boat was going to start at four o'clock; if I would now pay him the price of passage, he would do the best he could for me. When he had time to examine, he could probably put me in some other state-room, perhaps quite as good a one as that I had lost. Meanwhile he kindly offered me the temporary use of his private state-room. I inquired if it was quite certain that the boat would get off at four; for I had been asked to dine with a friend, at three o'clock. There was not the smallest doubt of it—at four they would leave. They were all ready, at that moment, and only waited till four, because the agent had advertised that they would—merely a technical point of honour.

But, by some error of calculation, I suppose, she didn't go at four. Nor at five. Nor at six.

At seven o'clock, the Swamp Fox and the St. Charles were both discharging dense smoke from their chimneys, blowing steam, and ringing bells. It was obvious that each was making every exertion to get off before the other. The captains of both boats stood at the break of the hurricane deck, apparently waiting in great impatience for the mails to come on board.

The St. Charles was crowded with passengers, and her decks were piled high with freight. Bumboatmen, about the bows, were offering shells, and oranges, and bananas; and newsboys, and peddlers, and tract distributors, were squeezing about with their wares among the passengers. I had confidence in their instinct; there had been no such numbers of them the previous evenings, and I made up my mind, although past seven o'clock, that the St. Charles would not let her fires go down again.

Among the peddlers there were two of "cheap literature," and among their yellow covers, each had two or three copies of the cheap edition (pamphlet) of "Uncle Tom's Cabin." They did not cry it out as they did the other books they had, but held it forth among others, so its title could be seen. One of them told me he carried it because gentlemen often inquired for it, and he sold a good many; at least three copies were sold to passengers on the boat. Another young man, who looked like a beneficiary of the Education Society, endeavouring to pass a college vacation in a useful and profitable manner, was peddling a Bible Defence of Slavery, which he made eloquent appeals, in the manner of a pastoral visit, to us, each personally, to purchase. He said it was prepared by a clergyman of Kentucky, and every slaveholder ought to possess it. When he came to me, I told him that I owned no slaves, and therefore had no occasion for it. He answered that the world was before me, and I perhaps yet might own many of them. I replied so decidedly that I should not, that he appeared to be satisfied that my conscience would not need the book, and turned back again to a man sitting beside me, who had before refused to look at it. He now urged again that he should do so, and forced it into his hands, open at the title-page, on which was a vignette, representing a circle of coloured gentlemen and ladies, sitting around a fire-place with a white person standing behind them, like a servant, reading from a book. "Here we see the African race as it is in America, under the blessed——"

"Now you go to hell! I've told you three times I didn't want your book. If you bring it here again I'll throw it overboard. I own niggers; and I calculate to own more of 'em, if I can get 'em, but I don't want any damn'd preachin' about it."

That was the last I saw of the book-peddler.

It was twenty minutes after seven when the captain observed—scanning the levee in every direction, to see if there was another cart or carriage coming towards us—"No use waiting any longer, I reckon: throw off, Mr. Heady." (The Swamp Fox did not leave, I afterwards heard, till the following Saturday.)

We backed out, winded round head up, and as we began to breast the current a dozen of the negro boat-hands, standing on the freight, piled up on the low forecastle, began to sing, waving hats and handkerchiefs, and shirts lashed to poles, towards the people who stood on the sterns of the steamboats at the levee. After losing a few lines, I copied literally into my note-book:

> "Ye see dem boat way dah ahead.
> CHORUS.—Oahoiohieu.
>
> De San Charles is arter 'em, dey mus go behine.
> CHO.—Oahoiohieu,
>
> So stir up dah, my livelies, stir her up; (pointing to the furnaces).
> CHO.—Oahoiohieu.
>
> Dey's burnin' not'n but fat and rosum.
> CHO.—Oahoiohieu.
>
> Oh, we is gwine up de Red River, oh!
> CHO.—Oahoiohieu.
>
> Oh, we mus part from you dah asho'.
> CHO.—Oahoiohieu.
>
> Give my lub to Dinah, oh!
> CHO.—Oahoiohieu.
>
> For we is gwine up de Red River.
> CHO.—Oahoiohieu.
>
> Yes, we is gwine up de Red River.
> CHO.—Oahoiohieu.
>
> Oh, we must part from you dah, oh.
> CHO.—Oahoiohieu."

The wit introduced into these songs has, I suspect, been rather over estimated

As soon as the song was ended, I went into the cabin to remind the clerk to obtain a berth for me. I found tw brilliant supper-tables reaching the whole length of the long cabin, and a file of men standing on each side of both of them, ready to take seats as soon as the signal was given.

The clerk was in his room, with two other men, and appeared to be more occupied than ever. His manner was, I thought, now rather cool, not to say rude; and he very distinctly informed me that every berth was occupied, and he didn't know where I was to sleep. He judged I was able to take care of myself; and if I was not, he was quite sure that he had too much to do to give all his time to my surveillance. I then went to the commander, and told him that I thought myself entitled to a berth. I had paid for one, and should not have taken passage in the boat, if it had not been promised me. I was not disposed to fight for it, particularly as the gentleman occupying the berth engaged to me was a deal bigger fellow than I, and also carried a bigger knife; but I thought the clerk was accountable to me for a berth, and I begged that he would inform him so. He replied that the clerk probably knew his business; he had nothing to do with it; and walked away from me. I then addressed myself to a second clerk, or sub-officer of some denomination, who more good-naturedly informed me that half the company were in the same condition as myself, and I needn't be alarmed, cots would be provided for us.

As I saw that the supper-table was likely to be crowded, I asked if there would be a second table. "Yes, they'll keep on eatin' till they all get through." I walked the deck till I saw those who had been first seated at the table coming out; then going in, I found the table still crowded, while many stood waiting to take seats as fast as any were vacated. I obtained one for myself at length, and had no sooner occupied it than two half-intoxicated and garrulous men took the adjoining stools.

It was near nine o'clock before the tables were cleared away, and immediately afterwards the waiters began to rig a framework for sleeping-cots in their place. These cots were simply canvas shelves, five feet and a half long, two wide, and less than two feet apart, perpendicularly. A waiter, whose good will I had purchased at the supper-table, gave me a hint to secure one of them for myself, as soon as they were erected, by putting my hat in it. I did so, and saw that others did the same. I chóse a cot as near as possible to the midship doors of the cabin, perceiving that there was not likely to bo the best possible air, after all the passengers were laid up for the night, in this compact manner.

Nearly as fast as the cots were ready they were occupied. To make sure that mine was not stolen from me, I also, without much undressing, laid myself away. A single blanket was the only bed-clothing provided. I had not lain long, before I was driven, by an exceedingly offensive smell, to search for a cleaner neighbourhood; but I found all the cots, fore and aft, were either occupied or engaged. I immediately returned, and that I might have a *dernier ressort*, left my shawl in that I had first obtained.

In the forward part of the cabin there was a bar, a stove, a table, and a placard of rules, forbidding smoking, gambling, and swearing in the cabin, and a close company of drinkers, smokers, card-players, and constant swearers. I went out, and stepped down to the boiler-deck. The boat had been provided with very poor wood, and the firemen were crowding it into the furnaces whenever they could find room for it, driving smaller sticks between the larger ones at the top, by a battering-ram method.

Most of the firemen were Irish born; one with whom I conversed was English. He said they were divided into three watches, each working four hours at a time, and all hands liable to be called, when wooding, or landing, or taking on freight, to assist the deck hands. They were paid now but thirty dollars a month—ordinarily forty, and sometimes sixty —and board. He was a sailor bred. This boat-life was harder than seafaring, but the pay was better, and the trips were short. The regular thing was to make two trips, and then lay up for a spree. It would be too hard upon a man, he thought, to pursue it regularly; two trips "on end" was as much as a man could stand. He must then take a "refreshment." Working this way for three weeks, and then refreshing for about one, he did not think it was unhealthy, no more so than ordinary seafaring. He concluded, by informing me that the most striking peculiarity of the business was, that it kept a man, notwithstanding wholesale periodical refreshment, very dry. He was of opinion that after the information I had obtained, if I gave him at least the price of a single drink, and some tobacco, it would be characteristic of a gentleman.

Going round behind the furnace, I found a large quantity of freight: hogsheads, barrels, cases, bales, boxes, nail-rods, rolls of leather, ploughs, cotton, bale-rope, and fire-wood, all thrown together in the most confused manner, with hot steam-pipes, and parts of the engine crossing through it. As I explored further aft, I found negroes lying asleep, in all postures, upon the freight. A single group only, of five or six, appeared to be awake, and as I drew near they commenced to sing a Methodist hymn, not loudly, as negroes generally do, but, as it seemed to me, with a good deal of tenderness and feeling; a few white people—men, women, and children—were lying here and there, among the negroes. Altogether, I learned we had two hundred of these deck passengers, black and white. A stove, by which they could fry bacon, was the only furniture provided for them by the boat. They carried with them their provisions for the voyage, and had their choice of the freight for beds.

As I came to the bows again, and was about to ascend to the cabin, two men came down, one of whom I recognized to have been my cot neighbour. "Where's a bucket?" said he. "By thunder! this fellow was so strong I could not sleep by him, so I stumped him to come down and wash his feet." "I am much obliged to you," said I; and I was, very much; the man had been lying in the cot beneath mine, to which I now returned and soon fell asleep.

I awoke about midnight. There was an unusual jar in the boat, and an evident excitement among people whom I could hear talking on deck. I rolled out of my cot, and stepped out on the gallery. The steamboat Kimball was running head-and-head with us, and so close that one might have jumped easily from our paddle-box on to her guards. A few other passengers had turned out beside myself, and most of the waiters were leaning on the rail of the gallery. Occasionally a few words of banter passed between them and the waiters of the Kimball; below, the firemen were shouting as they crowded the furnaces, and some one could be heard cheering them: "Shove her up, boys! Shove her up! Give her hell!" "She's got to hold a conversation with us before she gets by, anyhow," said one of the negroes. "Ye har that ar' whistlin'?" said a white man; "tell ye thar an't any too much water in her bilers when ye har that." I laughed silently, but was not without a slight expectant sensation, which Burke would perhaps have called sublime. At length the Kimball slowly drew ahead, crossed our bow, and the contest was given up. "De ole lady too heavy," said a waiter; "if I could pitch a few ton of dat ar freight off her bow, I'd bet de Kimball would be askin' her to show de way mighty quick."

At half-past four o'clock a hand-bell was rung in the cabin, and soon afterwards I was-informed that I must get up, that the servants might remove the cot arrangement, and clear the cabin for the breakfast-table.

Breakfast was not ready till half-past seven. The passengers, one set after another, and then the pilots, clerks, mates, and engineers, and then the free coloured people, and then the waiters, chambermaids, and passengers' body servants, having breakfasted, the tables were cleared, and the cabin swept. The tables were then again laid for dinner. Thus the greater part of the cabin was constantly occupied, and the passengers who had no state-rooms were driven to herd in the vicinity of the card-tables and the bar, the lobby (Social Hall, I believe it is called), in which most of the passengers' baggage was deposited, or to go outside. Every part of the boat, except the bleak hurricane deck, was crowded; and so large a number of equally uncomfortable and disagreeable people I think I never saw elsewhere together. We made very slow progress, landing, it seems to me, after we entered Red River, at every "bend," "bottom," "bayou," "point," and "plantation" that came in sight; often for no other object than to roll out a barrel of flour, or a keg of nails; sometimes merely to furnish newspapers to a wealthy planter, who had much cotton to send to market, and whom it was therefore desirable to please.

I was sitting one day on the forward gallery, watching a pair of ducks, that were alternately floating on the river, and flying further ahead as the steamer approached them. A man standing near me drew a long barrelled and very finely-finished pistol from his coat pocket, and, resting it against a stanchion, took aim at them. They were, I judged, full the boat's own length—not less than two hundred feet—from us, and were just raising their wings to fly, when he fired. One of them only rose; the other flapped round and round, and when within ten yards of the boat, dived. The bullet had broken its wing. So remarkable a shot excited, of course, not a little admiration and conversation. Half a dozen other men standing near at once drew pistols or revolvers from under their clothing, and several were fired at floating chips, or objects on the shore. I saw no more remarkable shooting, however; and that the duck should have been hit at such a distance, was generally considered a piece of luck. A man who had been "in the Rangers" said that all his company could put a ball into a tree, the size of a man's body, at sixty paces, at every shot, with Colt's army revolver, not taking steady aim, but firing at the jerk of the arm.

This pistol episode was almost the only entertainment in which the passengers engaged themselves, except eating, drinking, smoking, conversation, and card-playing. Gambling was constantly going on, day and night. I don't think there was an interruption to it of fifteen minutes in three days. The conversation was almost exclusively confined to the topics of steamboats, liquors, cards, black-land, red-land, bottom-land, timber-land, warrants, and locations, sugar, cotton, corn, and negroes.

After the first night, I preferred to sleep on the trunks in the social hall, rather than among the cots in the crowded cabin, and several others did the same. There were, in fact, not cots enough for all the passengers excluded from the state-rooms. I found that some, and I presume most of the passengers, by making the clerk believe that they would otherwise take the Swamp Fox, had obtained their passage at considerably less price than I had paid.

On the third day, just after the dinner-bell had rung, and most of the passengers had gone into the cabin, I was sitting alone on the gallery, reading a pamphlet, when a well-dressed middle-aged man accosted me.

"Is that the book they call Uncle Tom's Cabin, you are reading, sir?"

"No, sir."

"I did not know but it was; I see that there are two or three gentlemen on board that have got it. I suppose I might have got it in New Orleans: I wish I had. Have you ever seen it, sir?"

"Yes, sir."

"I'm told it shows up Slavery in very high colours."

"Yes, sir, it shows the evils of Slavery very strongly."

He took a chair near me, and said that, if it represented extreme cases as if they were general, it was not fair.

Perceiving that he was disposed to discuss the matter, I said that I was a Northern man, and perhaps not well able to judge; but that I thought that a certain degree of cruelty was necessary to make slave-labour generally profitable, and that not many were disposed to be more severe than they thought necessary. I believed there was little wanton cruelty. He answered, that Northern men were much mistaken in supposing that slaves were generally ill-treated. He was a merchant, but he owned a plantation, and he just wished I could see his negroes. "Why, sir," he continued, "my niggers' children all go regularly to a Sunday-school, just the same as my own, and learn verses, and catechism, and hymns. Every one of my grown-up niggers are pious, every one of them, and members of the church. I've got an old man that can pray——well, sir, I only wish I had as good a gift at praying! I wish you could just hear him pray. There are cases in which niggers are badly used; but they are not common. There are brutes everywhere. You have men, at the North, who whip their wives—and they kill them sometimes."

"Certainly, we have, sir; there are plenty of brutes at the North; but our law, you must remember, does not compel women to submit themselves to their power. A wife, cruelly treated, can escape from her husband, and can compel him to give her subsistence, and to cease from doing her harm. A woman could defend herself against her husband's cruelty, and the law would sustain her."

"It would not be safe to receive negroes' testimony against white people; they would be always plotting against their masters, if you did."

"Wives are not always plotting against their husbands."

"Husband and wife is a very different thing from master and slave."

"Your remark, that a bad man might whip his wife, suggested an analogy, sir."

"If the law was to forbid whipping altogether, the authority of the master would be at an end."

"And if you allow bad men to own slaves, and allow them to whip them, and deny the slave the privilege of resisting cruelty, do you not show that you think it is necessary to permit cruelty, in order to sustain the authority of masters, in general, over their slaves? That is, you establish cruelty as a necessity of Slavery—do you not?"

"No more than of marriage, because men may whip their wives cruelly."

"Excuse me, sir; the law does all it can, to prevent such cruelty between husband and wife; between master and slave it does not, because it cannot, without weakening the necessary authority of the master—that is, without destroying Slavery. It is, therefore, a fair argument against Slavery, to show how cruelly this necessity, of sustaining the authority of cruel and passionate men over their slaves, sometimes operates."

He asked what it was Uncle Tom "tried to make out."

I narrated the Red River episode, and asked if such things could not possibly occur.

"Yes," replied he, "but very rarely. I don't know a man, in my parish, that could do such a thing. There are two men, though, in ———, bad enough to do it, I believe; but it isn't a likely story, at all. In the first place, no coloured woman would be likely to offer any resistance, if a white man should want to seduce her."

After further conversation, he said, that a planter had been tried for injuring one of his negroes, at the court in his parish, the preceding summer. He had had a favourite, among his girls, and suspecting that she was unduly kind to one of his men, in an anger of jealousy he mutilated him. There was not sufficient testimony to convict him; "but," he said, "everybody believes he was guilty, and ought to have been punished. Nobody thinks there was any good reason for his being jealous of the boy."

I remarked that this story corroborated "Uncle Tom's Cabin;" it showed that it was all possible.

"Ah!" he answered, "but then nobody would have any respect for a man that treated his niggers cruelly."

I wondered, as I went into dinner, and glanced at the long rows of surly faces, how many men there were there whose passions would be much restrained by the fear of losing the respect of their neighbours.*

My original purpose had been to go high up Red River at this time, but the long delay in the boat's leaving New Orleans, and her slow passage, obliged me to change my plans. The

* John Randolph, of Roanoke, himself a slaveholder, once said, on the floor of Congress (touching the internal slave-trade): "What are the trophies of this infernal traffic? The handcuff, the manacles, the blood-stained cowhide. *What man is worse received in society for being a hard master? Who denies the hand of sister or daughter to such monsters?*"

following year, I returned, in company with my brother, as narrated in "The Texas Journey." Some portion of what follows is taken from that volume.

At a place called Alexandria, our progress was arrested by falls in the river which cannot be passed by boats at low stages of the water. The village is every bit a Southern one—all the houses being one story in height, and having an open verandah before them, like the English towns in the West Indies. It contains, usually, about 1,000 inhabitants, but this summer had been entirely depopulated by the yellow fever. Of 300 who remained, 120, we were told, died. Most of the runaway citizens had returned, when we passed, though the last case of fever was still in uncertain progress.

It has apparently not the best reputation for morality. At Nachitoches, the next village above on the river, a couple of men were waiting for their breakfast at the inn, when one, who looked and spoke more like a New Englander than a Southerner, said to the other, whom I presumed to be an Alexandrian—possibly Elder Slocum himself:—

"I had a high old dream, last night."

"What was it?"

"Dreamt I was in hell."

"Rough country?"

"Boggy—sulphur bogs. By and by I cum to a great pair of doors. Something kinder drew me right to 'em, and I had to open 'em, and go in. As soon as I got in, the doors slammed to, behind me, and there I see old boss devil lying asleep, on a red-hot sofy. He woke up, and rubbed his eyes, and when he see me, he says, 'Halloo! that you?' 'Yes, sir,' says I. 'Where'd you come from?' says he. 'From Alexandria, sir,' says I. 'Thought so,' says he, and he took down a big book, and wrote something in to't with a red-hot spike. 'Well, sir, what's going on now in Alexandria?' says he. 'Having a "protracted meeting" there, sir,' says I. 'Look here, my friend,' says he, 'you may stop lyin', now you've got here.' 'I aint lyin', sir,' says I. 'Oh!' says he, 'I beg your pardon; I thought it was Alexandria on Red River, you meant.' 'So it was,' says I, 'and they are having a protracted meeting there, sure as you're alive.' 'Hell they are!' says he, jumpin' right up; 'boy, bring my boots!' A little black devil fetched him a pair of hot brass boots, and he began to draw 'em on. 'Whose doin' is that?' says he. 'Elder Slocum's, sir,' says I. 'Elder Slocum's! Why in hell couldn't you have said so, before?' says he. 'Here, boy, take away these boots;' and he kicked 'em off, and laid down again."

French blood rather predominates in the population in the vicinity of Nachitoches, but there is also a considerable amount of the Spanish and Indian mongrel breed. These are often handsome people, but vagabonds, almost to a man. Scarcely any of them have any regular occupation, unless it be that of herding cattle; but they raise a little maize, and fish a little, and hunt a little, and smoke and lounge a great deal, and are very regular in their attendance on divine worship, at the cathedral.

In the public bar-room I heard a person, who I suppose would claim the appellation of a gentleman, narrating how he had overreached a political opponent, in securing the "Spanish vote" at an election, and it appeared from the conversation that it was considered entirely, and as a matter of course, purchasable by the highest bidder. A man who would purchase votes at the North, would, at least, be careful not to mention it so publicly.

We spent several days in Nachitoches, purchasing horses and completing the preparations for our vagrant life in Texas.

One mild day of our stay we made a trip of some ten or fifteen miles out and back, at the invitation of a planter, whose acquaintance we had made at the hotel. We started in good season, but were not long in losing our way and getting upon obscure roads through the woods. The planter's residence we did not find, but one day's experience is worth a note.

We rode on from ten o'clock till three, without seeing a house, except a deserted cabin, or meeting a human being. We then came upon a ferry across a small stream or "bayou," near which was a collection of cabins. We asked the old negro who tended the ferry if we could get something to eat anywhere in the neighbourhood. He replied that his master sometimes took in travellers, and we had better call and try if the mistress wouldn't let us have some dinner.

The house was a small square log cabin, with a broad open shed or piazza in front, and a chimney, made of sticks and mud, leaning against one end. A smaller detached cabin, twenty feet in the rear, was used for a kitchen. A cistern under a roof, and collecting water from three roofs, stood between. The water from the bayou was not fit to drink, nor is the water of the Red River, or of any springs in this region. The people depend entirely on cisterns for drinking water. It is very little white folks need, however—milk, whisky, and, with the better class, Bordeaux wine, being the more common beverages.

About the house was a large yard, in which were two or three China trees, and two fine Cherokee roses; half a dozen hounds; several negro babies; turkeys and chickens, and a pet sow, teaching a fine litter of pigs how to root and wallow. Three hundred yards from the house was a gin-house and stable, and in the interval between were two rows of comfortable negro cabins. Between the house and the cabins was a large post, on which was a bell to call the negroes. A rack for fastening horses stood near it. On the bell-post and on each of the rack-posts were nailed the antlers of a buck, as well as on a large oak-tree near by. On the logs of the kitchen a fresh deer-skin was drying. On the railing of the piazza lay a saddle. The house had but one door and no window, nor was there a pane of glass on the plantation.

Entering the house, we found it to contain but a single room, about twenty feet by sixteen. Of this space one quarter was occupied by a bed—a great four-poster, with the curtains open, made up in the French style, with a strong furniture-calico day-coverlid. A smaller camp bed stood beside it. These two articles of furniture nearly filled the house on one side the door. At the other end was a great log fire-place, with a fine fire. The outer door was left constantly open to admit the light. On one side the fire, next the door, was a table; a kind of dresser, with crockery, and a bureau stood on the other side, and there were two deer-skin seated chairs and one (Connecticut made) rocking chair.

A bold-faced, but otherwise good-enough-looking woman of a youngish middle age, was ironing a shirt on the table. We stated our circumstances, and asked if we could get some dinner from her. She reckoned we could, she said, if we'd wait till she was done ironing. So we waited, taking seats by the fire, and examining the literature and knick-knacks on the mantel-piece. These consisted of three Nachitoches *Chronicles*, a Patent Office Agricultural Report, "Christie's Galvanic Almanac," a Bible, "The Pirate of the Gulf," a powder-horn, the sheath of a bowie-knife, a whip-lash, and a tobacco-pipe.

Three of the hounds, a negro child, and a white child, had followed us to the door of the cabin, three chickens had entered before us, a cat and kittens were asleep in the corner of the fire-place. By the time we had finished reading the queer advertisements in French of runaway negroes in the *Chronicle* two of the hounds and the black child had retired, and a tan-coloured hound, very lean, and badly crippled in one leg, had entered and stood asking permission with his tail to come to the fire-place. The white child, a frowzy girl of ten, came toward us. I turned and asked her name. She knitted her brows, but made no verbal reply. I turned my chair towards her, and asked her to come to me. She hung her head for an instant, then turned, ran to the hound and struck him a hard blow in the chops. The hound quailed. She struck him again, and he turned half around; then she began with her feet, and kicked him out, taking herself after him.

At length the woman finished her ironing, and went to the kitchen, whence quickly returning, she placed upon the table a plate of cold, salt, fat pork; a cup of what to both eye and tongue seemed lard, but which she termed butter; a plate of very stale, dry, flaky, micaceous corn-bread; a jug of molasses, and a pitcher of milk.

"Well, now it's ready, if you'll eat it," she said, turning to us. "Best we've got. Sit up. Take some pone;" and she sat down in the rocker at one end of the table. We took seats at the other end.

"Jupiter! what's the matter with this child?" A little white child that had crawled up into the gallery, and now to my side—flushed face, and wheezing like a high-pressure steamboat.

"Got the croup, I reckon," answered the woman. "Take some 'lasses."

The child crawled into the room. With the aid of a hand it stood up and walked round to its mother.

"How long has it been going on that way?" asked we.

"Well, it's been going on some days, now, and keeps getting worse. 'Twas right bad last night, in the night. Reckoned I should lose it, one spell. Take some butter."

We were quite faint with hunger when we rode up, but didn't eat much of the corn-cake and pork. The woman and the high-pressure child sat still and watched us, and we sat still and did our best, making much of the milk.

"Have you had a physician to see that child?" asked my brother, drawing back his chair.

She had not.

"Will you come to me, my dear?"

The child came to him, he felt its pulse and patted its hot forehead, looked down its throat, and leaned his ear on its chest.

"Are you a doctor, sir?"

"Yes, madam."

"Got some fever, hasn't it?"

"Yes."

"Not nigh so much as't had last night."

"Have you done anything for it?"

"Well, thar was a gentleman here; he told me sweet ile and sugar would be good for't, and I gave it a good deal of that: made it sick, it did. I thought, perhaps, that would do it good."

"Yes. You have had something like this in your family before, haven't you? You don't seem much alarmed."

"Oh yes, sir; that ar one (pointing to the frowzy girl, whose name was Angelina) had it two or three times—onst most as bad as this. All my children have had it. Is she bad, doctor?"

"Yes. I should say this was a very serious thing."

"Have you any medicine in the house?" he asked, after the woman had returned from a journey to the kitchen. She opened a drawer of the bureau, half full of patent medicines and some common drugs. "There's a whole heap o' truck in thar. I don't know what it all is. Whatever you want just help yourself. I can't read writin'; you must pick it out."

Such as were available were taken out and given to the mother, with directions about administering them, which she promised to obey. "But the first and most important thing for you to do is to shut the door, and make up the fire, and put the child to bed, and try to keep this wind off her."

"Lord! sir, you can't keep *her* in bed—she's too wild."

"Well, you must put some more clothes on her. Wrap her up, and try to keep her warm. The very best thing you can do for her is to give her a warm bath. Have you not got a washing tub?"

"Oh! yes, sir, I can do that. She'll go to bed pretty early; she's used to going 'tween sundown and dark."

"Well, give her the warm bath, then, and if she gets worse send for a physician immediately. You must be very careful of her, madam."

We walked to the stable, and as the horses had not finished eating their corn, I lounged about the quarters, and talked with the negro.

There was not a single soul in the quarters or in sight of the house except ourselves, the woman and her children, and the old negro. The negro women must have taken their sucklings with them, if they had any, to the field where they were at work.

The old man said they had "ten or eleven field-hands, such as they was," and his master would sell sixty to seventy bags of cotton: besides which they made all the corn and pork they wanted, and something over, and raised some cattle.

We found our way back to the town only late in the evening. We had ridden most of the day over heavily-timbered, nearly flat, rich bottom land. It is of very great fertility; but, being subject to overflow, is not very attractive, in spite of its proximity to a market.

But it must be remembered that they were having the first use of a very fine alluvial soil, and were subject to floods and fevers. The yellow fever or cholera another year might kill half their negroes, or a flood of the Red River (such as occurred August, 1849, and October, 1851) destroy their whole crop, and so use up several years' profits.

A slate hung in the piazza, with the names of all the cotton-pickers, and the quantity picked the last picking day by each, thus: Gorge, 152; David, 130; Polly, 98; Hanna, 96; Little Gorge, 52, etc. The whole number of hands noted was fourteen. Probably there were over twenty slaves, big and little, on the plantation.

When our horses were ready, we paid the negro for taking care of them, and I went in and asked the woman what I might pay her.

"What!" she asked, looking in my face as if angry.

I feared she was offended by my offering money for her hospitality, and put the question again as delicately as I could. She continued her sullen gaze at me for a moment, and then answered as if the words had been bullied out of her by a Tombs lawyer—

"Dollar, I reckon."

"What!" thought I, but handed her the silver.

Riding out at the bars let down for us by the old negro, we wondered if the child would be living twenty-four hours later, and if it survived, what its moral chances were. Poor, we thought. Five miles from a neighbour; ten, probably, from a Louisiana* school; hound-pups and negroes for playmates.

---

* The State Superintendent lately recommended that two out of three of the Directors of Common Schools in Louisiana should be required to know how to read and write; and mentioned that in one parish, instead of the signature the mark of twelve different directors was affixed to a teacher's certificate.

On the Emigrant Road into Texas.—Five minutes' ride took us deep into the pines. Nachitoches, and with it all the tumult and bother of social civilization, had disappeared. Under the pines and beyond them was a new, calm, free life, upon which we entered with a glow of enthusiasm, which, however, hardly sufficed to light up a whole day of pine shadows, and many times afterwards glimmered very dull over days on days of cold corn-bread and cheerless winter prairies.

For two days, we rode through these pines over a sandy surface, having little rise and fall, watered here and there by small creeks and ponds, within reach of whose overflow, present or past, stand deciduous trees, such as, principally, oaks and cotton-woods, in a firmer and richer soil. Wherever the road crosses or approaches these spots, there is or has been, usually, a plantation.

The road could hardly be called a road. It was only a way where people had passed along before. Each man had taken such a path as suited him, turning aside to avoid, on high ground, the sand; on low ground, the mud. We chose, generally, the untrodden elastic pavement of pine leaves, at a little distance from the main track.

We overtook, several times in the course of each day, the slow emigrant trains, for which this road, though less frequented than years ago, is still a chief thoroughfare. Inexorable destiny it seems that drags or drives on, always Westward, these toilworn people. Several families were frequently moving together, coming from the same district, or chance met and joined, for company, on the long road from Alabama, Georgia, or the Carolinas. Before you come upon them you hear, ringing through the woods, the fierce cries and blows with which they urge on their jaded cattle. Then the stragglers appear, lean dogs or fainting negroes, ragged and spiritless. An old granny, hauling on, by the hand, a weak boy—

too old to ride and too young to keep up. An old man, heavily loaded, with a rifle. Then the white covers of the waggons, jerking up and down as they mount over a root or plunge into a rut, disappearing, one after another, where the road descends. Then the active and cheery prime negroes, not yet exhausted, with a joke and a suggestion about tobacco. Then the black pickininnies, staring, in a confused heap, out at the back of the waggon, more and more of their eyes to be made out among the table legs and bedding, as you get near; behind them, further in, the old people and young mothers, whose turn it is to ride. As you get by, the white mother and babies, and the tall, frequently ill-humoured master, on horseback, or walking with his gun, urging up the black driver and his oxen. As a scout ahead, is a brother, or an intelligent slave, with the best gun, on the look-out for a deer or a turkey. We passed in the day perhaps one hundred persons attached to these trains, probably an unusual number; but the immigration this year had been retarded and condensed by the fear of yellow fever, the last case of which, at Nachitoches, had indeed begun only the night before our arrival. Our chances of danger were considered small, however, as the hard frosts had already come. One of these trains was made up of three large waggons, loaded with furniture, babies, and invalids, two or three light waggons, and a gang of twenty able field-hands. They travel ten or fifteen miles a day, stopping wherever night overtakes them. The masters are plainly dressed, often in home-spun, keeping their eyes about them, noticing the soil, sometimes making a remark on the crops by the roadside; but generally dogged, surly, and silent. The women are silent too, frequently walking, to relieve the teams; and weary, haggard, mud be-draggled, forlorn, and disconsolate, yet hopeful and careful. The negroes, mud-incrusted, wrapped in old blankets or gunny-bags, suffering from cold, plod on, aimless, hopeless, thoughtless, more indifferent, apparently, than the oxen, to all about them.

We met, in course of the day, numerous cotton waggons, two or three sometimes together, drawn by three or four pairs of mules or oxen, going slowly on toward Nachitoches or Grand Ecore, each managed by its negro-driver. The load is commonly five bales (of 400 lbs. each), and the cotton comes in this tedious way, over execrable roads, distances of 100 and even 150 miles. It is usually hauled from the eastern tier of Texan counties to the Sabine; but this year there had been no rise of water in the rivers, and from all this region it must be carried to Red River. The distance from the Sabine is here about fifty miles, and the cost of this transportation about one cent a pound; the freight from Grand Ecore to New Orleans from one to one and a quarter cents. If hauled 150 miles in this way, as we were told, the profit remaining, after paying the charges of transportation and commission, all amounting to about five cents, must be exceedingly small in ordinary years.

At night we met three or four of these teams half-mired in a swamp, distant some quarter of a mile one from another, and cheering themselves in the dark with prolonged and musical " Yohoi's," sent ringing through the woods. We got through this with considerable perplexity ourselves, and were very glad to see the light of the cabin where we had been recommended to stop.

This was " Mrs. Stokers'," about half way to the Sabine. We were received cordially, every house here expecting to do inn-duty, but were allowed to strip and take care of our own horses, the people by no means expecting to do landlord's duty, but taking guests on sufferance. The house was a double log cabin—two log erections, that is, joined by one long roof, leaving an open space between. A gallery, extending across the whole front, serves for a pleasant sitting-room in summer, and for a toilet-room at all seasons. A bright fire was very welcome. Supper, consisting of pork, fresh and salt, cold corn-bread, and boiled sweet potatoes, was served in a little lean-to behind the house. After disposing of this we were shown to our room, the other cabin, where we whiled away our evening, studying, by the light of the great fire, a book of bear stories, and conversing with the young man of the family, and a third guest. The room was open to the rafters, and had been built up only as high as the top of the door upon the gallery side, leaving a huge open triangle to the roof, through which the wind rushed at us with a fierce swoop, both while we were sitting at the fire and after we retreated to bed. Owing to this we slept little, and having had a salt supper, lay very thirsty upon the deep feather bed. About four o'clock an old negro came in to light the fire. Asking him for water, we heard him breaking the ice for it outside. When we washed in the piazza the water was thick with frost, crusty, and half inclined not to be used as a fluid at all.

After a breakfast, similar in all respects to the supper, we saddled and rode on again. The horses had had a dozen ears of corn, night and morning, with an allowance of fodder (maize leaves). For this the charge was $1 25 each person. This is a fair sample of roadside stopping-places in Western Louisiana and Texas. The meals are absolutely invariable, save that fresh pork and sweet potatoes are frequently wanting. There is always, too, the black decoction of the South called coffee, than which it is often difficult to imagine any beverage more revolting. The bread is made of corn-meal, stirred with water and salt, and baked in a kettle covered with coals. The corn for breakfast is frequently unhusked at sunrise. A negro, whose business it is, shells and grinds it in a hand-mill for the cook. Should there be any of the loaf left after breakfast, it is given to the traveller, if he wish it, with a bit of pork, for a noon-"snack," with no further charge. He is conscious, though, in that case, that he is robbing the hounds, always eagerly waiting, and should none remain, none can be had without a new resort to the crib. Wheat bread, if I am not mistaken, we met with but twice, out of Austin, in our whole journey across the State.

The country was very similar to that passed over the day before, with perhaps rather more of the cultivable loam. A good part of the land had, at some time, been cleared, but much was already turned over to the "old-field pines," some of them even fifteen years or more. In fact, a larger area had been abandoned, we thought, than remained under cultivation. With the land, many cabins have, of course, also been deserted, giving the road a desolate air. If you ask, where are the people that once occupied these, the universal reply is, "Gone to Texas."

The plantations occur, perhaps, at an average distance of three or four miles. Most of the remaining inhabitants live chiefly, to appearances, by fleecing emigrants. Every shanty sells spirits, and takes in travellers. We passed through but one village, which consisted of six dwellings. The families obtained their livelihood by the following occupations: one by shoeing the horses of emigrants; one by repairing the wheels of their waggons; one by selling them groceries. The smallest cabin contained a physician. It was not larger than a good-sized medicine chest, but had the biggest sign. The others advertised "corn and fodder." The prices charged for any article sold, or service performed, were enormous; full one hundred per cent. over those of New Orleans.

We met Spaniards once or twice on the road, and the population of this district is thought to be one half of Spanish origin. They have no houses on the road, however, but live in little hamlets in the forest, or in cabins contiguous to each other, about a pond. They make no progress in acquiring capital of their own, but engage in hunting and fishing, or in herding cattle for larger proprietors of the land. For this business they seem to have an hereditary adaptation, far excelling negroes of equal experience.

The number of cattle raised here is now comparatively small, most of the old herd proprietors having moved on to pastures new in Western Texas. The cane, which is a natural growth of most good soils at the South, is killed if closely fed upon. The blue-joint grass (not the blue-grass of Kentucky) takes its place, and is also indigenous upon a poorer class of soils in this region. This is also good food for cattle, but is killed in turn if closely pastured. The ground then becomes bare or covered with shrubs, and the "range" is destroyed. The better class of soils here bear tolerable crops of cotton, but are by no means of value equal to the Red River bottoms or the new soils of any part of Texas. The country is, therefore, here in similar condition to that of the Eastern Slave States. The improvements which the inhabitants have succeeded in making in the way of clearing the forest, fencing and tilling the land, building dwellings, barns, and machinery, making roads and bridges, and introducing the institutions of civilization, not compensating in value the deterioration in the productiveness of the soil. The exhausted land reverts to wilderness.

Eastern Texas.—Shortly after noon rain began to fall from the chilly clouds that had been threatening us, and sleet and snow were soon driving in our faces. Our animals were disposed to flinch, but we were disposed to sleep in Texas, and pushed on across the Sabine. We found use for all our wraps, and when we reached the ferry-house our Mackintoshes were like a coat of mail with the stiff ice, and trees and fields were covered. In the broad river bottom we noticed many aquatic birds, and the browsing line under the dense mass of trees was almost as clean cut as that of Bushy Park. The river, at its low stage, was only three or four rods across. The old negro who ferried us over, told us he had taken many a man to the other side, before annexation, who had ridden his horse hard to get beyond the jurisdiction of the States.

If we were unfortunate in this stormy entrance into Texas, we were very fortunate in the good quarters we lighted upon. The ferry has long been known as Gaines's Ferry, but is now the property of Mr. Strather, an adjacent planter, originally from Mississippi, but a settler of long standing. His log-house had two stories, and being the first we had met having glass windows, and the second, I think, with any windows at all, takes high rank for comfort on the road. At supper we had capital mallard-ducks from the river, as well as the usual Texan diet.

We were detained by the severity of the weather during the following day, and were well entertained with huntsman's stories of snakes, game, and crack shots. Mr. S. himself is the best shot in the county. A rival, who had once a match against him for two thousand dollars, called the day before the trial, and paid five hundred dollars to withdraw. He brought out his rifle for us, and placed a bullet, at one hundred and twenty yards, plump in the spot agreed upon. His piece is an old Kentucky rifle, weighing fourteen pounds, barrel fourty-four inches in length, and throwing a ball weighing forty-four to the pound.

A guest, who came in, helped us to pass the day by exciting our anticipations of the West, and by his free and good advice. He confirmed stories we had heard of the danger to slavery in the West by the fraternizing of the blacks with the Mexicans. They helped them in all their bad habits, married them, stole a living from them, and ran them off every day to Mexico. This man had driven stages or herded cattle in every state of the Union, and had a notion that he liked the people and the state of Alabama better than any other. A man would get on faster, he thought, in Iowa, than anywhere else. He had been stage-driver in Illinois during the cold winter of 1851-2, and had driven a whole day when the mercury was at its furthest below zero, but had never suffered so much from cold as on his present trip, during a norther on a Western prairie. He was now returning from Alexandria, where he had taken a small drove of horses. He cautioned us, in travelling, always to see our horses fed with our own eyes, and to "hang around" them till they had made sure of a tolerable allowance, and never to leave anything portable within sight of a negro. A stray blanket was a sure loss.

Mr. S. has two plantations, both on upland, but one under the care of an overseer, some miles from the river. The soil he considers excellent. He averaged, last year, seven and a half bales to the hand; this year, four and a half bales. The usual crop of corn here is thirty bushels (shelled) to the acre.

Hearing him curse the neighbouring poor people for stealing hogs, we inquired if thieves were as troublesome here as in the older countries. "If there ever were any hog-thieves anywhere," said he, "it's here." In fact, no slave country, new or old, is free from this exasperating pest of poor whites. In his neighbourhood were several who ostensibly had a little patch of land to attend to, but who really, he said, derived their whole lazy subsistence from their richer neighbours' hog droves.

The negro-quarters here, scattered irregularly about the house, were of the worst description, though as good as local custom requires. They are but a rough inclosure of logs, ten feet square, without windows, covered by slabs of hewn wood four feet long. The great chinks are stopped with whatever has come to hand—a wad of cotton here, and a corn-shuck there. The suffering from cold within them in such weather as we experienced, must be great. The day before, we had seen a young black girl, of twelve or fourteen years, sitting on a pile of logs before a house we passed, in a driving sleet, having for her only garment a short chemise. It is impossible to say whether such *shiftlessness* was the fault of the master or of the girl. Probably of both, and a part of the peculiar Southern and South-western system of "get along," till it comes better weather.

The storm continuing a third day, we rode through it twenty-five miles further to San Augustine. For some distance the country remains as in Louisiana. Then the pines gradually disappear, and a heavy clay soil, stained by an oxide of iron to a uniform brick red, begins. It makes most disagreeable roads, sticking close, and giving an indelible stain to every article that touches it. This tract is known as the Red Lands of Eastern Texas.

On a plantation not far from the river, we learned they had made eight bales to the hand. Mentioning it, afterwards, to a man who knew the place, he said they had planted earlier than their neighbours, and worked night and day, and, he believed, had lied, besides. They had sent cotton both by Galveston and by Grand Ecore, and had found the cost the same, about $8 per bale of 500 lbs.

We called at a plantation offered for sale. It was described in the hand-bills as having a fine house. We found it a cabin without windows. The proprietor said he had made ten bales to the hand, and would sell with all the improvements, a new gin-house, press, etc., for $6 per acre.

The roadside, though free from the gloom of pines, did not cheer up, the number of deserted wrecks of plantations not at all diminishing. The occupied cabins were no better than before. We had entered our promised land; but the oil and honey of gladness and peace were nowhere visible. The people we met were the most sturdily inquisitive I ever saw. Nothing staggered them, and we found our account in making a clean breast of it as soon as they approached.

We rode through the shire-town, Milam, without noticing it. Its buildings, all told, are six in number.

We passed several immigrant trains in motion, in spite of the weather. Their aspect was truly pitiful. Splashed with a new coating of red mud, dripping, and staggering, beating still the bones of their long worn-out cattle, they floundered helplessly on.

San Augustine made no very charming impression as we entered, nor did we find any striking improvement on longer acquaintance. It is a town of perhaps fifty or sixty houses, and half a dozen shops. Most of the last front upon a central square acre of neglected mud. The dwellings are clap-boarded, and of a much higher class than the plantation dwellings. As to the people, a resident told us there was but one man in the town that was not in the constant habit of getting drunk, and that this gentleman relaxed his Puritanic severity during our stay in view of the fact that Christmas came but once that year.

Late on Christmas eve, we were invited to the window by our landlady, to see the pleasant local custom of The Christmas Serenade. A band of pleasant spirits started from the square, blowing tin horns, and beating tin pans, and visited in succession every house in the village, kicking in doors, and pulling down fences, until every male member of the family had appeared, with appropriate instruments, and joined the merry party. They then marched to the square, and ended the ceremony with a centupled tin row. In this touching commemoration, as strangers, we were not urged to participate.

A gentleman of the neighbourhood, addicted, as we knew, to a partiality towards a Rip Van Winkle, tavern-lounging style of living, told us he was himself regarded by many of his neighbours with an evil eye, on account of his "stuck-up" deportment, and his habit of minding too strictly his own business. He had been candidate for representative, and had, he thought, probably been defeated on this ground, as he was sure his politics were right.

Not far from the village stands an edifice, which, having three stories and sashed windows, at once attracted our attention. On inquiry, we learned a story, curiously illustrative of Texan and human life. It appeared that two universities were chartered for San Augustine, the one under the protection of the Methodists, the other of the Presbyterians. The country being feebly settled, the supply of students was short, and great was the consequent rivalry between the institutions. The neighbouring people took sides upon the subject so earnestly, that, one fine day, the president of the Presbyterian University was shot down in the street. After this, both dwindled, and seeing death by starvation staring them in the face, they made an arrangement by which both were taken under charge of the fraternity of Masons. The buildings are now used under the style of "The Masonic Institute," the one for boys, the other for girls. The boys occupy only the third story, and the two lower stories are falling to ludicrous decay—the boarding dropping off, and the windows on all sides dashed in.

The Mexican habitations of which San Augustine was once composed, have all disappeared. We could not find even a trace of them.

END OF VOL. I.

www.ingramcontent.com/pod-product-compliance
Lightning Source LLC
Chambersburg PA
CBHW030357230426
43664CB00007BB/624